THE CULTURE OF TOLERANCE

(*A Study of Indian History*)

Syed Osman Sher

Originals

(an imprint of Low Price Publications)

Delhi-110052

Distributed By
D.K. Publishers Distributors (P) Ltd.
4834/24, Ansari Road, Darya Ganj,
New Delhi-110002
Phones: 3278584, 3278368, 3261465,
e-mail: dkpd@del3.vsnl.net.in
visit us at: www.dkpd.com

First Published 2001
ISBN 81-7536-231-6

Published By
Originals
(an imprint of Low Price Publications)
A-6, Nimri Commercial Centre,
Near Ashok Vihar Phase-IV,
Delhi-110052
Phones: 7401672, 7452453
e-mail: lpp@nde.vsnl.net.in
visit us at: www.lppindia.com

Printed At:
D K Fine Art Press P Ltd.
Delhi-110052

Dedicated to my parents
Khadijatul Kubra
Syed Sadruddin Sher

Contents

1
INTRODUCTION

History is not the story of rulers and their politics alone. It encompasses all occurrences and chain of events, major or minor, in all spheres of life on a continual basis. Of the various elements which constitute, influence and shape history, tolerance is by far the most important. It is the hallmark of civilization, and a bulwark against injustice and belligerence. It opens up the possibility of cooperation among divergent peoples. Presupposing the existence of differences in a society, tolerance thwarts potential chaos and conflicts. It provides harmony and happiness. It stands for liberalism, positive feelings, open heartedness, forgiveness, feeling of togetherness, putting up with one even when he is not liked, absence of discrimination against 'the other one', settling for less than what one wants, and giving support to the rights and liberties of others. In short, tolerance is refraining from taking any action against a person or a group of people pursuing different sets of values.

According to the historian Arnold Toyanbee: 'The differentiation of life into different species has brought with it both competition among some species and cooperation among others. Which, if either, of these two antithetical relations is the paramount law of nature? In the relations of non-conscious species with each other, neither cooperation nor competition is an act of deliberate choice; but the choice is deliberate in human beings, and in us it is bound up with the human sense of the difference and antithesis between right and wrong and between good and evil'[1]. On the canvas of human togetherness, tolerance presents itself as the touchstone of right and wrong, and good and evil. But it is not easy to practice, for it requires tremendous strength of character and an enormous amount of self-control; and, not many are endowed with such qualities. Accordingly, the yardstick of how far a nation has been successful in overcoming the inherent differences of its members, and how much it has been able to conquer hatred, would measure its greatness. The detailed account of the attitude of rulers towards the subject, the behavior of the people towards fellow citizens, the treatment given by the society to new comers, and the feeling of the followers of a faith towards another's faith, all portray the presence or lack of tolerance. However, at this point it must also be kept in mind that tolerance does not mean total acceptance of all sorts of behavior: for instance, a society would not tolerate crimes, a government would not tolerate subversion, and a ruler would not tolerate rebellion. But in such cases too, undue ruthlessness to curb such trends would amount to intolerance.

Tolerance assumes special importance in the case of India. From time immemorial it has experienced a continual inflow of alien people. Like a magic land it has fired the imagination of all sorts of people: wanderers, settlers, raiders, traders, conquerors, and colonizers, entering into this country and bringing with them new ethnicity, cultures, customs, religions and languages. In this regard two opposite forces, push and pull factors, have both been operating in one direction: movement of peoples towards India. In all ages, the fertility of the land, the lush green forests, sparse population, over-flowing rivers, abundant milch cows and buffaloes, harness cattle, mineral wealth, convenient trade-routes, and legendary stock of gold and precious jewels have, on the one hand, attracted invaders from outside world and, on the other, over-population and desiccation of the adjacent regions of Asia have impelled their habitants to move towards this greener pasture. Its canvas is thus a mosaic of many resplendent colors, each radiating in its own peculiar light. Very few countries have seen such an influx of people as India has seen. Its lands and rivers, forests and deserts, hills and plains have become havens to whosoever wanted to make it their abode. And, they have invariably not only been accommodated but generally assimilated. Not much distinction was ever made on the basis of who arrived in this hospitable land earlier and who came a day later.

The presence of different peoples, with different traditions and outlooks on life, has often made the situations complex, and has posed serious challenges to the country from time to time. But the country seems to have acquitted itself well demonstrating its adroitness in the art of co-existence undergoing simultaneously competition, struggle, compromise and forgiveness. The people have learned new arts and sciences of life from each other; took many things of value from one and gave their own to the other. This openness and togetherness have proved to be great spurs to the development of civilization in India. In the context of the Indian pluralistic society, therefore, we have to see tolerance as the story of equality in diversity and co-existence of peoples of different ethnic or religious backgrounds.

According to Arnold Toyanbee again 'religion is the most important of all human experiences and activities' and 'In most periods of the history of the Indian subcontinent the Indians have felt more concern about religion than about politics and economics.'[2] Playing a dominant role in the lives of the Indians, religion assumes a special position in the context of tolerance. It was this monster that when aroused and invoked it tore the country into pieces in the twentieth century. History stands witness that in all ages religious tolerance had been an Indian tradition as a rule. Religion has not been used either by the state or by the populace as a tool of persecution. On the contrary, it has been played as an instrument for demonstrating tolerance. Comparing it with the British tradition, Percival Spear writes: "The Mughal policy of tolerance was extended and amplified by the British. But while it was more complete it was more frigid, for the Mughals, while occasionally demolishing temples, would also endow others, give grants to Hindu as well as Muslim divines, and patronize Hindu festivals. The religious neutrality of the government, as pressured by Christian groups in Britain, forbade all this and left the people with a feeling of aloofness and disdain. The tradition of aloofness from religion as a complement to the policy of tolerance is not one calculated to endear the idea of the secular state to the average Indian heart."[3]

India has been host to hordes of aliens such as the Aryans, Greeks, Scythians, Parthians, Kushans, Huns, Arabs, Turks, Afghans, and Europeans. They entered here not as ordinary migrants but as conquerors. They were impure, *mlechchhas* according to the Hindu caste system. But they could not be taken as a source of irritation for a long period of time. After living together for some time they had to be treated as one's own. In view of the existence of a number of levels of social institutions in the Hindu society and religion their assimilation became easier. If caste was a problem, it could be assigned to them too. They could be kshatriyas or even Sudras. Otherwise they could be accepted into the other heterodox creeds like Jainism and Buddhism which were caste-less. Fortunately, the earlier immigrants did not bring with them strong schools of theology and religious beliefs which could create resistance or confrontation with the indigenous religious and social orders. Therefore, as religious entities they could not withstand the seductions and overwhelming embrace of the forceful Vedic religion, and were ultimately absorbed in it. But there was also an episode, different from others. It was the case of the Muslims; here the scenario was an un-common one. Islam was a strongly established religion with a new pattern of life. Since both Hinduism and Islam were firmly entrenched religions, a compromise on religious plane was not possible. But social assimilation? It did, in fact, take place. It was not merely in superficial ways of eating and dressing, but in more fundamental fields of values and culture. Thus the Muslims, though not conquered in India from the angle of religion, were subdued to a very large extent on social and cultural fronts. They adopted many Hindu customs and even values and gave in return their own. Undoubtedly, the two communities had their religious and social differences, but over the centuries they coexisted with little friction. This amalgam of the two cultures gave birth to a new Indian race.

The fabric of society which was woven with diverse strands for one thousand years was, however, torn into shreds during the British rule which created intolerance within its fold. It is a historical fact that the imperial British have been very faithful to their old colonial policy of 'divide and rule' and then divide for ever. It is also a fact that they have generally given a kick at the time of parting to their colonies by sowing seeds of dissension—sometimes on tribal lines and at other times on religious beliefs or nationalistic aspirations—with such ferocity and perfection that once they left, the colonies were torn asunder politically, geographically and socially, and remained enmeshed in dissension for decades. Take only a few examples of today: India-Pakistan (including Kashmir); Palestine-Israel; Cyprus- Greek/Turkish; and the most glaring skeleton in their own cupboard, Northern Ireland. The latest example is that of Hong Kong. Democracy, which was a taboo for the British for one hundred and fifty years was introduced in Hong Kong helter-skelter at the time of their departure despite Chinese government's protest. It was meant obviously to leave a permanent pain in the neck of the so-called undemocratic China. But the wise Chinese did not let the Hong Kong affair turn into a headache. Anyway, the British colonial policy in India resulted in the most traumatic event of history; the break-up of this ancient country, Bharatvarsha or Hindustan, into two states, namely, India and Pakistan. It was not only the political break-up of a great country and of its many regions, it was also the splitting up of its rivers and mountains, of the old set-up of society, of the prevailing culture and traditions, of spoken languages and written literature, of hearts and minds.

1. Arnold Toyanbee, *Mankind and Mother Earth*, Ch. 1
2. Arnold Toyanbee, *Mankind and Mother Earth*, Ch. 19 & 46
3. The Mughals and the British, Ch. XXV by Percival Spear in *The Cultural History of India*, edited by A.L.Basham

2
PULL OF THE LAND

India, is named after the great river Sindh (Indus). In antiquity the country was approachable, and invariably has been reached, from the west, either from the Arabian sea or by land from the north-western mountain passes. Either way, once the country had been entered, one found oneself near the Sindh river. It was the overwhelming presence of this mighty river, flowing from north to south in somewhat westerly direction and falling in the Arabian Sea, that compelled the new-comers, the Sanskrit speaking Aryans, to call this area as 'the river' or the Sanskrit equivalent 'Sindhu'. Then it became the land of Indos (Greeks), or Indus (Romans), or Hind (Persians and Arabs) after Sindhu. It came to be called India by the West. It were the Arabs who first termed its inhabitant as 'Hindu'. But the Indus basin was not the only land component of the ancient India. The Indus basin was just a small portion of the geographical unit of the vast country. The name of a greater unit generally emanates from its core component. In 1947, when the country was politically divided into two independent nations, how paradoxical it appeared that the name-giver area went over to a new nation calling itself Pakistan, while the name itself ('India') was retained by the rest of the country.

The Indian subcontinent covers an area of more than one and a half million square miles, with the Hindu Kush and Baluchi Hills in the west and the Burmese mountains in the east. Connecting these two ends, the great Himalayan mountain range is spread all over the north like an umbrella or a high wall of rock and snow, sheltering this vast country from the arctic cold and the invading armies from the north. This cone shaped country juts its southern tip into the Indian Ocean with the eastern side facing the Bay of Bengal and the western side towards the Arabian Sea. From ancient times to modern days India could attain political unity as a single country only rarely. It happened during the Mauryans in the third century BC, the Delhi Sultanate, the Mughals and the British. Still the whole body (India-Pakistan-Bangladesh) at no pint of time came under the rule of a single sovereign completely; some parts always eluded his control. The one unity which India has possessed throughout history was granted to it by geography. Only very rarely in the world are the geographical features so combined to constitute a single natural region.

The land may be divided into three main geographical zones: horizontally, from east to west it is a mountainous region in the north, and in the middle the Sindh (Indus) river and Ganga (Ganges) river plains. The southern portion separated by Vindhya mountain range and the Narmada river is the Deccan plateau. From north to south and east to west India extends to about 2,000 miles each way. This vast and rich land is home to varied sorts of topography, climate, and geographical formation: mountains, plateaus, rivers flowing in all directions, green forests, fertile agricultural plains, perennial draught lands and desert wastes. It is the country of sweltering heat where temperature goes up to 110 to115 F. in summer and during winters it snows in the north. It has got the area of the highest rainfall in the world: Cherapunji in Assam receives an annual average of 425 inches. The country, or the sub-continent, has been the home of the world's two highest peaks, Everest, more than 29,000 feet high on the Himalayas- now in Nepal, and K2 on the Karakoram- now in Pakistan.

The history of the people of prehistoric India is difficult to reconstruct because of the dearth of skeletal remains of the early men. Flakes of stones, used as tools, which are found scattered around the Soan river valley in northern part of Pakistan, are the earliest trace of Paleolithic man's habitation. They indicate that at some point of time during the interglacial age, between 200,000 to 400,000 years ago, humans climbed directly over the Himalayas or crossed the Hindu Kush mountains to venture into India from East or Central Asia.[1] In the Deccan during the same period, the tools take a little different shape and solidity: they are real core stone implements like axes, and not merely flakes of stones. The users of these implements must have been the same people who lived in East Africa, because such implements have also been found in South Africa, and even in southern Europe.

There seems to have been a second great wave of human migration to South Asia from East Africa or southern Europe sometimes after the final receding of the glacial ice that had so long paralyzed human progress, during the Mesolithic Age, which began around 30,000 BC. Numerous microliths have been found scattered across the face of the Deccan and up into central India, and even in the Punjab. These tiny weapons, called pygmy tools, so closely resemble those found in France, England, and East Africa that it would appear they were brought to India by hunters and food-gatherers who were quite different from South Asia's Paleolithic pioneers. However, recent finds in the , Narmada River valley, which runs through central India between the Vindhya mountains, appear to indicate an evolutionary line of development from early to middle Stone Age in that region.[2]

Thus on the basis of whatever has been found, and though basically hypothetical, anthropologists have advanced various theories and explanations of racial compositions and their movements. However, the opinion about the classification and movements of the early races as given by Dr. B.S.Guha, who had been the Director of Anthropological Survey of India, is generally deemed as the most authoritative. The early races, who lived or immigrated to India, have been classified by him into six categories:

The Negroid
The Proto-Australoid
The Mongoloid
The Mediterranean
The Western Brachycephals
The Nordic [3]

The oldest remains of the racial types found in the Indian subcontinent are those of the Negroid, also called the Negrito people. Living in the neolithic, or the later part of the Stone Age, they were food-gatherers and not food-producers. They totally vanished, probably killed by the new comers. Though the Negroid people are deemed no more to be found on the soil of India, yet traces have been linked to some tribes living in South India and in the Nagas of Assam, as also in Andaman Isles. Most probably they inhabited Africa and India together in times when both were joined but parted with each other with the separation of the continents. Or they would have traveled from Africa through Arabia and Iran. In the same way the successor race group that lived together in this part of the world or had traveled over-land from Australia when it was part of the same mass of land, is that of proto-Astroloids. Some of the tribes inhabiting central and south India represent them. They were spread over a large part of India. Then came the Mongoloids, found generally in the northeastern part of India. From pre-historic times their infiltration has been rather constant, but they preferred to settle mostly on the eastern-most side near Burma. Then were the Mediterranean type who came here from the deserts of the Middle East with physical features very different from their predecessors: slim bodies and long heads. They also belonged to a different culture. More advanced in civilization, they were city dwellers, indulged in trade and spoke Dravidian language which is the source of the present day languages like Telgu and Kannada in the Deccan and Baruhi in Baluchistan. The Dravidian language has not been traced with absolute certainty beyond the limits of the Indian land mass; but there is evidence which seems to indicate that it was introduced into India in prehistoric times. And, the influx of different peoples continued this way.

Thus we find that India has been the home to a variety of peoples and races, differing from one another in physical features, language, and culture more widely than the peoples of Europe. Among them the four primary ethnographical divisions of mankind-the white Caucasian (both blonde and dark), the Mongolian (yellow), the Semitic (brown and curly), and the Ethiopian (black)-are all represented. Also, five of the great families of human speech-the Austric, the Tibeto-Chinese, the Dravidian, Semitic (Arabic and Persian, having a great impact in modifying the Indian vernaculars), and the Indo-European-are directly represented among the living languages of India, of which no fewer than two hundred and twenty are recorded in the Census Report of 1911.[4]

When the Aryans entered into the Sindh and the Ganga valleys they encountered two types of races. One, called the Nishadas, who had developed village culture and were tilling lands from Afghanistan to Bihar. In 1929, one of the first villages was discovered near the banks of the river Sindh at Amri in Sindh province. Two, the Dasyus, or Dasas, who offered resistance to the Aryans and were deemed as enemies, but were fully over-powered and subdued, and thus the very word 'Dasa' changed its meaning to 'slave'. Because of their dark skin and stumpy nose, the fair-skinned and long-nosed Aryans ridiculed the local people. Amazingly, however, the Aryans found themselves in this new land in the midst of a civilized people, more sophisticated, technologically advanced and wealthy than they themselves were.

1. *A New History of India*, (Fifth Edition), Stanley Wolpert, Ch. One
2. H. D. Sankalia, ,"*Pre- and Proto- History in Indian and Pakistan; New Discoveries and Fresh Interpretations*", Journal Of Indian History (April 1967, p. 103), quoted in *A New History of India*, Fifth Edition, by Stanley Wolpert, Ch One
3. *The History and Culture of the Indian People*, Vol. I Ch. VIII
4. E. J. Rapson, *The New Cambridge History of India*, Vol. I , Chapter II

3
DAWN OF CIVILIZATION

The Indus Valley Civilization is one of the oldest civilizations in the world and a jewel-piece of India's glorious past. It has also lasted a very long period of time, spanning over about two millennia. The predecessors of this civilization were nomadic, hunters, fish catchers, food-gatherers, with a subsistence economy of later Stone age and the marginal small-village agricultural economy of the Baluchi Hills. But this civilization had a sophisticated agricultural and commercial economy capable of supporting a large surplus urban population, not only of Mohenjo-daro and Harappa, but of a number of small towns and villages scattered over a large area. When did the Indus Valley Civilization start? It is difficult to tell. Most historians, however, agree that it originated in the third millennium BC, around 3500 BC. With the existence of the Baruhi language of Dravidian origin in a pocket of the now arid highlands of Baluchistan we may infer that in the fourth millennium BC climatic conditions had begun to improve so much that it was able to support the evolution of a civilization along the Indus and Makran coast. From the dating of the artifacts of this civilization found in Iraq, it is proved that it was still in existence in India as late as 1500 BC. Also, nothing is certain as to when it terminated or when the Aryan or the Vedic civilization commenced in India and when it completely replaced the Indus civilization.

The recent discovery of this civilization in the early 1920s through archaeological finds in the northwest part of India (which now forms part of Pakistan) takes the knowledge about the country through the evidence of physical relics back to the far antiquity. The first two pre-historic sites were excavated at Mohenjo-Daro near Hyderabad in Sindh and at Harappa near Multan. They are located in the Indus River valley, 400 miles apart from each other. They depict mainly a city civilization and an urban society with a literate elite. Cities were well-planned with carefully laid out streets, developed water supply and drainage systems, and advanced arts and crafts. This civilization radiated with the skill in town planning. The streets were well aligned, sufficiently wide, and planned to meet the needs of dwelling houses and public buildings. Lanes were equipped with public wells, bathrooms and street lightings. Dwelling houses contained wells, baths, kitchen, courtyard, store rooms and drains leading to the larger and covered street drains. No definite trace of latrine is found but it is presumed it might have been built on the roof. Drain pipes from the roof to the ground indicate that bathrooms or latrines were built on the upper story. A few large buildings have also been unearthed such as the Great Granary, the Great Bath and the Collegiate Building, the last for housing some high officials or a college of priests. The large and costly facilities attest to the wealth of the Harappan civilization, which, like Sumer, may have been ruled by a priest-king who was worshipped as divinity incarnate. A small stone statue found at Mohenjo-daro, perhaps represent such a monarch. His elongated eyes, thick lips, and bearded face reflect a supernatural serenity and power. His jeweled head and arm-bands, as well as the clover-leaf design on his robe are signs of his exalted rank.

No trace has, however, been found of ornamentation in buildings. Also no signs of pompous tombs, shrines or altars, large monuments, grand temples or elaborate pieces of arts are present. Nevertheless, all indications are there that it had a well organized civic authority. Life was comfortable and economic prosperity was brought about through well-developed agriculture and commerce. Tools, pottery and dress were plain, simple and utilitarian. The absence of sharp weapons indicate that they were peace loving people. It is a mystery then that such a plain-minded and peaceful people achieved such a great height of civilization at that time.

Despite the fact that Mohenjo-Daro and Harappa are located 400 miles apart from each other in the Indus river valley they show homogeneity. Not only this, in about a hundred sites so far uncovered over an area of almost a thousand miles from north to south, the signs of existence of homogeneous villages and townships have been found, with the Indus as the axis of communication. Even then it cannot be said that this civilization was localized in the Indus valley. The Indus civilization has certainly been much wider in its extent than was previously supposed. The uniformity of evidences is so overwhelming that Sir Mortimer Wheeler had to term it as "something like an imperial status.... the vastest political experiment before the Roman Empire'.[1] Beyond the limits of Mohenjo-Daro and Harappa, artifacts of similar civilizations have been found, through subsequent excavations, not only at various other places in Sindh, Punjab, North Western Frontier Province and Baluchistan but as far as Gazipur, Benaras, Buxar and Patna districts in the eastern part of India. In the west, they have been found as far as in Eshnunna, Kish and Ur in Mesopotamia, in the strata of the debris of Sumero-Akkadian civilization. [2]

1. See *India: A Concise History,* Ch. Two, Francis Watson
2. Arnold Toyanbee, *Mankind and Mother Earth*

4
ARYAN HORDES

The Indus Valley Civilization is believed to have met its doom at the hands of the Aryans, an Indo-European pastoral people; 'their onslaught was like a hurricane: a people who had never known a city.'[1] These semi-nomadic barbarians, living in Eurasian steppe, the region between the Caspian and the Black seas, were forced to leave their homeland around 2,000 BC due to some natural disaster like draught, pestilence, plague or a series of Mongol invasions from Central Asia. Moving in all directions with their herds of cattle and domesticated horses they spread over a greater part of Europe in the west and Turkey, Iran and India in the south-east. This mass dispersion of people is uniquely responsible for affecting the course of world history; it set in motion a vast process of cultural cross-fertilization right from West Europe to India.

Though extremely proud of their exalted extraction, the Aryans, whose self-given name meant 'noble' or 'free-born', did not carry with them a particularly impressive culture except for their spoken language and the poetic accomplishment of their sages, as enshrined in the Vedas. They did not know the art of writing. But they were using a spoken language that has been described as primary Sanskrit or Proto-Sanskrit. Unlike the Indus people who were enjoying a thriving civilization, these semi-nomadic steppe-dwellers had, by 2,500 BC, evolved only a rudimentary culture based on domesticated horse, and horse-driven chariot. They lived in tribal villages and in houses made of bamboo or wood. They did not have the sophistication of baked bricks, elaborate baths or sewer system, nor did they know how to decorate their houses. There was no place for statues, glazed earthen wares, or seals in their life. Adept in martial art and skilled in stock breeding, they knew little about trade.

Their wealth was their cattle and no sanctity was attached to the cow. But the cows were highly valued and came to be treated as currency and were paid to brahmans for performing religious services.

The Aryans freely partook of beef and wine. The men were incorrigible gamblers. The god Savitar had a word of warning and compassion for the ruined: "Let the dice alone, tend thy farm. Rejoice in thy gods and be content. Here, gamester, are thy cattle and here thy wife."[2] The coming of the Aryans into India has, therefore, been considered by some as a 'backward step' in terms of civilization since the Northern India had to re-experience the process of evolving urban cultures from agrarian and nomadic systems.[3]

Nothing can be said with certainty about the antecedents of the Aryans. We have no archaeological evidence either, because they did not build stone or brick buildings. But we are able to piece together some pictures from their religious book, the Vedas (Books of Knowledge). The religious literature and beliefs of the Aryans were committed to memory by the priests for more than a thousand years; then written down in four Vedas: a collection of hymns and charms that were recited in liturgies. It is believed that the Rig Veda was not written before 600 BC, although the Vedic hymns were actually composed as early as 1500 BC. The oldest of the Vedas is the Rig Veda, the earliest of the surviving Indo-European literature. It is not a historical record but a book of hymns, and is addressed to the glorification of their gods asking for their bounty and thanking for their blessings. Though full of beauty for its invocations to the creative spirit of the natural world, the Rig Veda contains no historical references or details of cultural activities. But it is at the same time positive in the pride of conquest and in the concept of racial and religious superiority. Our information thus remains hazy and sketchy derived from the allegorical references in this book. The Rig Veda, however, tells of the land where it was composed. It was the land of seven rivers, or *Sapta Sindhya*, comprising Indus, Ravi, Jhelum, Beas, Chenab, Sutlej and Sarasvati; the last is now dried up and is probably only a minor stream in the Rajasthan desert. Rig Veda does not give any indication exactly when or whence they came. However, it has now been established that Sanskrit, the Language of the Aryan "Vedas" belonged to the same family as several European languages like Greek, Latin, Celtic, and German, which suggests that they had common ancestry with those European people.

Another important source of information about the Aryan's times and beliefs is the tablets found during the 1909 excavations at the Hittite site of Boghaz-koi near modern Ankara in Turkey. They tell us of a treaty concluded between the Hittite King Subiliuma and his Mitanni neighbor to the east, King Mattiwaza, who reigned in 1400 BC. The treaty, which is considered as the first document referring to the Aryans, invoked as divine witnesses four gods, Indara, Uruvna, Mitira, and the Nasatiya, whose Sanskrit names in the Rig Veda were spelled virtually the same (Indra, Varuna, Mitra, and Naksatras).[4] This indicates that the people of Asia Minor also belonged to the Aryan race who worshipped the same gods as the Aryans of India did.

While descending on India, the Aryans stormed and conquered fortified cities and defeated the Indus people, and made this country their permanent home. The vanquished were more civilized and technologically advanced; the victors though were primitive and tribal peoples, yet were toughened by their nomadic life passed among blistering sun and heavy snow and sleet. In this adventure they were helped enormously by their superior strategy, trained horses, swift-drawn chariots, hafted bronze axes and bows and arrows. These chariots were also used by them in conquering other parts in western Asia, and they were deemed so valuable that in order to keep them in good condition they were usually transported on bullock carts during their long trek. As a prime factor of the Aryan's victory, the Rig Veda contains many verses in praise of their prized possession, the horse, which was a frightening novelty for the Indus people. The following Rig Vedic Hymns is quoted by A. L. Basham in his book, *The Wonder That Was India*:

Rushing to glory, to the capture of the herds,
swooping down as a hungry falcon,
eager to be first, he darts amid the ranks of the chariots,
happy as a bridegroom making a garland,
spurning the dust and champing at the bit.

And the victorious steed and faithful,
his body obedient [to his rider] in battle,
speeding on through the melee,
stirs up the dust to fall on his brows.

And at his deep neigh, like the thunder of heaven,
the foemen tremble in fear,
for he fights against thousands, and none can resist him,
so terrible is his charge. [5]

About a quarter of the hymns of Rig Veda are addressed to the god Indra, not simply as the provider of rain but as the great storm-warrior and wielder of thunderbolt, strong, fair-complexioned and bursting with energy and brute force. It is believed that the old habitants had built a big dam across the Indus for flood control and irrigation. The dam was proving itself a great barrier for the invaders. The Rigveda is all praise to the god Indra as the releaser of waters and destroyer of the *vritra*, (meaning 'demon' or ' barrier', and may refer also to dam or fortification). This battle between Indra and Vritra denotes both historical and cosmogonic significance.

One of the epithets of Indra is 'Destroyer of Citadels' who once assisted an Aryan chief by tearing to pieces 'like old clothes the defending forces of a place called Hariyuppa'—or Harappa. It, therefore, appears that after great effort and much difficulty the Aryans succeeded in destroying the dam, or the fortification, and then ascribed their success to their reigning god. It is also attested from the finds of Mohanjo-daro that it too was inundated. Its ruins covered with silt, caches of hastily hoarded jewelry, messy houses, and at one place the huddle of skeletons of about thirty persons which seems as they were unable to escape in time, all indicate that a deluge of a very great magnitude was the cause of destruction. The cause of this deluge may be the mother nature itself because merely the destruction of a dam is unlikely to obliterate a civilization. But, to quote Mortimer Wheeler, 'On circumstantial evidence Indra stands accused.'[6] In this way the Aryans may not be deemed as the only terminator of the Indus civilization. Mohenjo-Daro in particular provides evidence of trouble and decay over several centuries before the first Aryan immigrations through the Hindu Kush. Anyway, other causes of the obliteration of this civilization will continue to remain intriguing.

The Aryan irruption was enormously destructive. The natives, with no weapons or horses of their own were unable to offer any resistance. The small farming communities who resisted their onward march of expansion were destroyed and their ancient culture severely mauled. Their settlements, called *pur*, surrounded by palisades and walls, were razed to the ground. Many of the primitive habitants like the Gonds and other tribes were driven into the forest recesses of the hills eastward of the Deccan plateau and into other regions difficult of access.

Despite their strategic superiority, it was not possible for the Aryans to spread over the Indian plains all at once. Their journey of conquest was slow but steady. It was not easy because of the harsh geographical terrain on the one hand and the resistance faced from the indigenous people on the other. Another obstacle in their advance proved to be their own internal weakness. The Aryans were not a disciplined army, nor they were under the command of one great conqueror. Composed of numerous tribes they lacked internal unity and involved themselves frequently in internecine warfare. From the earliest times raiders or settlers who reached the Indus river-system had to face the Thar desert and the Aravalli hills while trying to proceed further in the east. They had to end up into a narrow neck of entry in the low ridge by the Jamuna river near Delhi before entering into the vast alluvial plain of the Ganga, or thence to the Deccan plateau. The river Ganga was barely known to the Aryans by the end of the Rig Vedic era. It took them many centuries to enter into that region. But from then on, the Ganga-Jamuna plain, thousands of square miles of flat and fertile country, once heavily forested, became the main home of the Aryans, who called it Aryavarta. It was the Hindustan of later history. Abandoning their traditional pastoral life they took to agriculture, settling down in small walled villages.

The Vedas also do not look further south than the Vindhya hills. It is through the epic Ramayana, the exploits of a virtuous and deified prince Ramachandra, lovingly called Rama, that we learn how very late, probably sometime in the second millennium BC, the Aryans penetrated in the south. By that that time they had fully established themselves in the northern plains. In the Indian setting of Trojan war, when Rama's beautiful wife Sita, daughter of Janaka, the king of Videha, was abducted by Ravana and carried to Lanka, the Aryan prince sought the help of the monkeys of the forest, whose leader was called Hanuman. Rama defeated Ravana and recovered Sita. With the mingling of the religion and politics, this mythical drama describes the conflict of Aryans and non-Aryans, this time in the setting of southern India, and showing the Aryans once again victorious. Incidentally, some students of history have viewed this tale as a depiction of the Aryan superiority over the short-statured, dark colored Dravidians who were earlier pushed south from their Sindh and Ganga basin abodes. Despite their hatred, which they had nurtured against the conquerors, these very Dravidians, referred to as monkeys in the tale, took pity on the plight of Rama and helped him in retrieving his wife from the clutches of the ruler of Lanka.

1. *India: A Concise History,* Francis Watson
2. *A Panoramic History of the Indian People*, Ch Two, D. B. Vohra; India
3. Romila Thapar, *A History of India (volume one*), Ch. 2
4. Hermann Kulke & Dietmar Rothermund, *A History of India; A Panoramic History of the Indian People*, Ch Two, D.B.Vohra,
5. Quoted in *The Indus Saga and the Making of Pakistan*, Ch.2, Aitzaz Ahsan
6. *A Panoramic History of the Indian People*, Ch One, D. B. Vohra ; India: *A Concise History, Ch. Two*, Francis Watson

5
INSTITUTION OF APARTHEID

When the Aryans began their lives in India they were already divided into three social classes, the warriors, the priests, and the commoners (*vish*), the largest class in Aryan society. These classes were hereditary. This division had provided them a convenient tool to govern their social and economic relationships. In that primitive society this class division reflected enough of the professions. But profession was neither hereditary nor were there social taboos of any kind in this regard. Free mixing and inter-marriages were practiced. Caste consciousness had not yet developed, as is clear from the remarks such as 'a bard am I, my father is a leech and my mother grinds corn'.[1]

Now a new development had taken place. The Aryans found themselves living among a people who were initially hostile, but were later vanquished and subdued. They were captives of war who were enslaved. At the same time they were an overwhelming majority. The hostile dark-skinned non-Aryans, depicted as ubiquitous foes in the Vedic texts, were Dasas and Dasyus. This word, in due course, became synonymous to the derogatory connotation of slave or bondsman, which has stuck to it even to this day. Sanskrit vocabulary is full of pejorative terms which have been used to describe these human foes of the Aryans in the land of their occupation. They were described as dark-skinned (*Krishna-tvach*) and the colour of their skin has been typified as *dasavarna*, nose-less (*anas*), flat-faced demons, evil-tongued (*mridhravach*), evil-speaking (*Kuyavch*), of demonic character, and unseemly in their ways of life. The main difference between the Dasyus and the Vedic Aryans appears to be religious. They worshipped strange gods. The Dasyu were rite-less (*a-karman*), indifferent to the gods, meaning the Aryan gods (*a-devayu*), without devotion (*a-brahman*), not sacrificing (*a-yajvan*), lawless (*a-vrata*), following strange ordinances (*anyavrata*), reviling the gods (*deva-piyu*), etc. [2] Even in post-vedic epics and Puranas they were described as one-legged aborigines who shaded themselves with a single enormous foot. If no action was taken, it was feared, the Aryans, who were of noble extraction, would be assimilated with the Dasas and thus would lose their Aryan identity.

The other group of indigenous people, the Nishadas, mentioned in the late Samhitas and Brahmanas appears to be, not the name of any particular tribe, but the generic term for non-Aryan tribes who were not under Aryan control. Probably the Nishadas were settled aborigines. The later Smritis explain the Nishadas as the off-spring of a Brahman father and a sudra mother. The epics represent the Nishadas as having their settlements in the Vindhya and Satpura ranges, and it seems that during the post-Rigvedic period also they inhabited mountainous tracts.

The enemies had to be treated differently. For convenience sake, the subjugated element, which could not be eliminated, could be admitted into the Aryan system, but only at the lowest level. The locals were to be declared a separate people, a class of their own, a caste belonging to a lower birth, totally different from the new ruling nation. In this way the Aryan political and social ascendancy would be complete. Thus the barbarian Aryans, overpowering the more numerous and the civilized city-dwellers of the Indus valley, created a fortress of a social institution. It was the regime of apartheid based on the most obvious mark of distinction between the Aryans and the local people: the colour of skin. The equivalent word for 'covering', associated with skin covering and its varying 'colours' in their language was *varna*. So the Dasas were declared to be belonging to a different *varna,* thus keeping the dark skinned native population segregated from themselves. The first step taken in this direction was to treat the Dasas as beyond the social pale. The Dasa now belonged to a different class, to that of *Sudras*. In due course their ranks were swelled by the inevitable appearance of a mixed Aryan-Dasa element in the population as well as by other subjugated tribes. The Greeks of the 4th century BC knew one such tribe as the Oxydrakoi, from which they acquired a new name-the *Sudras*-which has clung to them ever since.[3]

Since they were the original tillers of the land they were permitted to continue in this vocation, more so because they fulfilled the basic need of the Aryans for food. The indigenous people also possessed great skills as artisans. Because of their direct contact with the elements, such as fire and water, artisan like smiths and millers were both feared and despised. The despised artisans were also, therefore, consigned to the ranks of Sudras. Thus racial discrimination against these people also led to a discrimination against the trades which they plied. The original lack of skills as a cultivator or an artisan among the Aryans was probably another important reason for the emergence of the caste system. The Sudras became the scum of Vedic society and were treated with utmost contempt. They were forced to live in outlying slums and condemned to the meanest chores. Their lives were a picture of abject misery and servility and were so totally at the mercy of their Aryan superiors that a brahman who killed one of them was considered to be no more culpable than if he had killed a dog.

The indigenous people were excluded from dvija status, hence could not participate in Vedic rituals. The once-born Sudras were defined as "servants" of the twice-born and could be 'exiled at will' or 'slain at will'. They were not permitted to hear or study the Vedic hymns, which were reserved for twice-born ears only. Later legal texts prescribed "pouring molten lead" into the ears of Sudra caught secretly listening to Vedic mantras. They were, however, allowed to worship their own gods. But there was an additional feature of ritual impurity (*asuddha*), whose fear was carried to such extremes even in that early stage that certain sacrifices such as the Agnihotra had to be conducted with vessels made by an Aryan only: 'It [the sthali, an earthen milkpot] is made by an Arya, with perpendicular sides for the communion with the gods. In this way it is united with the gods. Demonical [*asurya*], indeed, is the vessel which is made by a potter on potter's wheel. (Maittrayani Samhita, I,8,3,).[4] The text quoted above also indicates that the Aryan did not bring the potter's wheel along with them but found it there. The prejudice expressed in this text against the pottery produced on such a wheel makes it highly unlikely that initially the Aryans themselves produced the famous 'painted grey ware' which was expertly fashioned on the potter's wheel. Archaeologists now tend to regard this painted grey ware as an indicator of Aryan settlements. But this type of ceramics probably originated among the indigenous people and was only spread by the Aryans in the course of their migration towards the east.[5]

This division of society on the basis of colour was eventually to become so deep-rooted in the Aryan culture that *varna* was translated later into an ultra-rigid caste system. In fact, *Varna* was labeled as the caste system by the Portuguese in the sixteenth century. It became one of the main pillars of Hindu society and religion. It is persisting tenaciously even to this day. Initially, the division was between the Aryans and the non-Aryans, but such a tool has made it easier in later times to accept new ethnic groups arriving in India. Each new group took on the characteristics of a separate sub-caste in the larger caste structure. The position of the new sub-castes in the hierarchy was dependent on their occupations and social origins.

1. Romila Thapar: *A History of India* (Volume One), Ch. 2
2. A. D. Pusalkar, *History and Culture of the Indian People, CH. XIII: Aryan Settlement in India*
3. *A Panoramic History of the Indian People*, Ch Two, D. B. Vohra
4. Hermann Kulke and Dietmar Rothermund: *A History of India,* Ch. 1. See also W. Rau, *Topferei und Tongeschirr im Vedischen Indien* (Wiesbaden, 1972)
5. Hermann Kulke and Dietmar Rothermund: *A History of India*

Frontier Province as he was to a Hindu of his own locality. It is, therefore, clear that the differences between the Hindus and the

6
VEDIC SOCIETY AND RELIGION

Up to the middle of the first millennium BC, the races intermingled, customs and beliefs were synthesized, and a new harmony was evolved. The process of conflict, reconciliation, and assimilation was bound to effect major changes in the character of Aryan society and thought, as well as in the nature of the indigenous culture. If, indeed, priest-kings were the rulers of the Indus civilization, so it might be that Aryan rajas learned to rely more heavily upon the counsels of their own brahmans. Religious worship also followed Aryan and non-Aryan forms. Facets of both have survived in the present-day Hinduism, in some cases separate, in others subtly mingled. Most of the thousands and thousands of gods of the modern day Hinduism come from the non-Aryan stock. Many of the doctrines derived from beliefs held by the non-Aryan indigenous people were incorporated in it, which eventually became the hall-mark of Hinduism. It is the vast number of pre- and post-Aryan deities, religious ideas, and practices that have contributed to the formless form of Hinduism. Their initial beliefs and codes of worship and rituals, combined with the indigenous Dravidian beliefs, later led to the Brahmanical religion. " The oldest religion of India, which the invading Aryans found among the Nagas, and which still survives in the ethnic nooks and crannies of the great peninsula, was apparently an animistic and totemic worship of multitudinous spirits dwelling in stones and animals, in trees and streams, in mountains and stars....The earliest gods of Vedas were the forces and elements of nature herself-sky, sun, earth, fire, light, wind, water and sex...A nation, like an individual, begins with poetry, and ends with prose. And as things became persons, so qualities became objects, adjectives became nouns, epithets became deities. The life giving sun became a new sun-god, Savitar the Life-Giver; the shining sun became Vivavat, Shining God; the life-generating sun became the great god Prajapati, Lord of all living things." [1]

The tenth and final "book" of the Rig Veda (X.90), explains in the hymn, 'Sacrifice of the Cosmic Man" (*Purusha-sukta*) that the four varnas emerged from different parts of the original cosmic man's anatomy: the brahmans from the head; the kshatriyas from the torso, the vaisyas from the thighs; and the Sudras from the feet:

Into how many portions did they divide this being whom they immolated? what did his mouth become? what are his arms, his thighs, and his feet now called? His mouth became a priest [*Brahmana*]; his arm was made a soldier [*Rajanya*]; his thigh was transformed into a husbandman [*Vaisya*]; from his feet sprang the servile man [*Sudra*]. [2]

Each varna was assigned its distinguishing color; white for brahmans, red for kshatriyas, brown for vaishyas, and black for Sudras. This earliest color consciousness has since remained a significant factor in determining social attitudes and values to this day. Barring the Sudras (once-born), the three upper classes, who were deemed twice born, were issued the sacred thread, which attested to their rebirth and entitled them access to Vedic lore. The less worthy Sudras were cast beyond the pale of recognized society

The position of the warrior class or the kshatriyas, was the superior-most, as they protected the community. To this class belonged the leader of the warriors, the king. The aristocracy was thus composed of this class. After them in rank were the brahmans. In the beginning domestic religious rites were not very elaborate and could be undertaken by the head of household himself. A clan did not generally consist of a large number of people, so group ceremonies were also not frequently needed. But the Aryans gradually grew into bigger tribes. Now the brahmans, who alone had memorized the Vedic hymns, had to officiate over the sacrifices and other ceremonies. Only they were able to court the gods and solicit their help in the territorial ambitions of the Aryans. With the passage of time large kingdoms arose, and the kings then realized that they would feel more secure if they assumed the mantle of the first king of the earth, Manu. He was a junior member of the fraternity of the great gods who appointed him king of the earth, which was in an extremely chaotic condition. People had forsaken dharma. From Manu sprang two dynasties of kings— the Solar and the Lunar. It is believed that all the ruling kings in India belonged to these two dynasties, hence all were Aryans. As successors to Manu the kings had to assume divinity, and only the priestly class of brahmans could bestow divinity on them.

This class thus made a *tour de force* and established itself at the highest echelon of the caste hierarchy, leaving wealth and political power for the kshatriyas. Though the king wielded all the authority, the power behind the throne was that of the brahman. It was believed that whereas he was able to protect the king with the cosmic power of magic mantra of the Vedas, he was capable of destroying him as well. Taking a Brahman's life was, therefore, declared to be the most diabolical of crimes and the most sacrilegious of sins. His primacy, however, was not wide spread but confined largely to the Yamuna-Ganga basin. The Aryas of the northwest, having to contend constantly with meager soil and turbulent frontier, cared little either for the elaborate ceremonials or for the rigid caste distinctions. Similar was the case with the powerful republics of Lachhavis and Mallas of North Bihar, which ruled with the help of their assemblies (*sabhas or samitis*) representing all house-holders. For them too, a brahman counted little.

In the meanwhile, the vocation of trade, which was not known so far, developed along with the system of ownership of new arable lands. The class of commoners, called *vish,* was then split up. A joint class of landowners and traders sprang up who were called the Vaishyas. They occupied the third position, while the tillers of the land and the artisan class continued to be the Sudras. As Hindu society enlarged itself, each of the four castes eventually split into numerous sub-castes with a view to assimilating the 'natives', the newly conquered people, and the new waves of immigrating hordes. They were incorporated into one or the other of the four basic castes. The Rig Veda makes no mention of untouchables. For those who performed unclean jobs like tanning, carcass disposal, sweeping, garbage collecting, and looking after cremation grounds, whom even the Sudras would not like to touch, it was felt necessary to add still another lower class. Beyond the pale of the four varnas, a new class of outcastes, the untouchables, also called 'panchamas' (the fifth) was thus created later.

The more abstract Brahmanic systems of belief, founded on the Vedas, appealed to a limited few; the majority preferred more earthly forms of religion and worship. Vedic religion focused on the yajnas or sacrificial rites, big and small, simple and elaborate, individual and collective, domestic and state, seasonal and special. The ritual was intended to propitiate the gods. Priests occupied special position as no rites could be performed without them. The centrality of the sacrificial ritual was, however, questioned in the late Vedic period. Polytheistic, nature worshipping, sacrificial Aryan religion underwent a major change and gave way to the mysticism of the Upanishads.

The main query related to the search for immortality and for salvation. Such discourse encouraged innovative thinking in religious belief and philosophical speculation. Ideas of *samsara* and *karma*, which had no place in early Vedic religion, now rose and spread rapidly. The Upanishads, marked the end of the Vedic era. It is remarkable, however, that they launched no frontal attack on Vedic beliefs and practices; nor did they disown the Vedic gods or decry the sacrificial cult.

In the closing period of the Vedic Age, the Dharma-sutras did not maintain any sharp distinction between public and private, or individual or collective. The society or the state was considered as an organic whole. The society which held the individual, both king and the commoner, totally subservient to it denied the latter any right or privilege, and burdened him only with duties and responsibilities. The individual's life was thus governed by the interest of the society. This was the Divine Will. Only if he submitted himself to this Will he would get what was best for him in this world and hereafter. Like the modern collectivist theories (such as Fascism) this view raises society above individuals, and strikes at the very root of personal freedom or individuality. But there is an important difference: allegiance here is not to any party or political principle, but to Dharma conceived as an eternal and immutable Law or Order, divine in character and beyond human will.[3]

1. Will Durant, *The Story of Civilization: Our Oriental Heritage*
2. Colebrooke's version as quoted in *The Oxford History of India, Ch.2*, Vincent Smith.
3. V. M. Apte, *The History and Culture of the Indian People*, Vol. III

7
POLITICAL UNIFICATION

Another thousand years had to pass before the process of historic change began to take another shape. This time it was political unification. It came in the sixth century BC under the supremacy of a small kingdom of the east, known as Magadha, or South Bihar. The new empire reached its pinnacle under the Mauryan dynasty in the early third century BC. By that time the centre of civilization shifted from the Indus Valley thousand miles east to the region of modern Patna (then called Pataliputra) in the plains of the Ganga river.

The 'Historic Period' had dawned for the world in the tenth century BC. For India, however, there was no significant development up to the seventh century BC either in secular or in political sphere, except that 'a noble culture had already been flourishing' there. The beginning of the sixth century BC felt the first breath of life with the accession of Bimbisara on the throne of Magadha. Thereafter, there was an outburst of activities on all sides: religious, cultural, political and empire building. This area became the Hindu world's new centre of gravity. Magadha began exerting influence in northern India. For the first time centripetal forces started emerging and helping in the unification of Bharatavarsha. The dawn of history in India thus emerged simultaneously with the age of Magadhan supremacy, wherewith began 'the evolution of India'.

In the words of K.M.Munshi: This period "saw the realization of the dream of centuries, the political unification of India under a Chakravartin. When the process began, the sixteen mahajanapadas were organized either into monarchies like Magadha and Avanti or republics like the Lachchhavis and the Yaudheyas, all struggling for survival, fighting each other, absorbing weaker states. So far, there was India, the geographical unit, but as yet no India as a well-accepted unit of homogeneous life and culture.....And inspired by the vast literature and tradition which had accreted to the story of the Bharata War, men's minds were slowly being impressed with the dictum that wherever Dharma prevailed, there was Bharatavarsha.

"Magadha, now Aryanised for well nigh eight hundred years, was virile with the energy of unsophisticated power. Through a succession of powerful monarchs from 544 BC to 150 BC, it gave the land of Dharma a series of Chakravartins, who made of India a single unit...."[1]

At the beginning of the sixth century BC, there were a large number of states from Kabul valley to the banks of Godavari and to the eastern coast of India. They were both kingdoms (*janapada*) and republics (*gana*), big and small. Republican states were located east of Kosala, from the Himalayas to the river Ganga, the most famous and prosperous being the Vijjian republic, with Vaisali as its capital, identified as modern Basarh and Bakhira in Muzaffarpur District of Bihar. The Vijjian republic's most powerful and respectable clan was that of the Lachchhavis, who have played an important part in the history of Magadha stretching up to the Gupta period of the fourth century AD. These republics, one of the earliest in the world, were run on modern democratic lines. The business of state was carried out by an Assembly of people, generally elders, meeting in open air, taking decisions unanimously, and having whips and committees to whom doubtful matters were referred to for consensus. King was elected but he was as symbolic as the head of state in the present day republican set up of government. The republics were more liberal to individualistic and independent opinions than the monarchies. They even tolerated unorthodox views. It was the existence of such republics that produced the two great religious leaders of what were to become the important heterodox sects: Gautama Buddha of the Sakya tribe founded Buddhism and Vardhamana Mahavira of the Jnatrika tribe founded Jainism

Despite some differences in Buddhist and Jain texts, as well as in Puranas, and with the conspicuous absence of the mention of the state of Videha, we can safely conclude that the sixteen kingdoms, flourishing at that time, were:

1. Anga (East Bihar)
2. Magadha (South Bihar)
3. Kasi (Benaras)
4. Kosala (Oudh)
5. Vrijji or Vajji (North Bihar)
6. Malla (Gorakhpur)
7. Chedi (between Jamuna and Narmada)
8. Vatsa (Allahabad)

9. Kuru (Thaneswar , Meerut and Delhi)
10. Panchala (Bareilly, Budaun and Farrakhabad)
11. Machcha (Jaipur)
12. Surasena (Mathura)
13. Assaka (on the Godavari)
14. Avanti (Malwa)
15. Gandhara (Peshawar and Rawalpindi)
16. Kamboja (Kashmir and Kafiristan)

All states were independent and sovereign in their own territories. There was no paramount power. At that time Magadha was a narrow strip of land, north to south from river Ganga in the north to the forest of Chota Nagpur in the south, with river Son in the west and river Champa in the east. It was about a sixth in size of the most powerful kingdom of Kosala, which extended from the Himalayas to the confluence of the Jamuna and Ganga, and had held its sway on the Sakyas of Kapilavastu. 'Kapilvastu was an early victim. The Buddha lived to see its conquest by Kosala and the massacre there of the Buddha's Sakya kinsmen and fellow-countrymen. In the race to become the paramount power, the eventual victor was a dark horse. In India the victor was not the relatively large and populous state Kosala; it was Magadha.'[2] Magadha emerged as the preponderant power and as the core of the first empire of India.

In the Rigvedic and later Vedic texts we find mention of universal kings or *Chakravartins* who went all over the earth and conquered the whole earth. These conquests did not involve permanent annexation. The vanquished kings (*sthapati*), were generally left to govern their territories as vassals, paying tributes to the conquerors (*rajan*). The sixth century BC saw a new development in the Indian history, i.e., the emergence of Empire. Defeated realms were now to be annexed. Magadha, for the first time, established the tradition of a superior kind of kingship or *Samrajya*, gradually absorbing first the neighboring states, then swallowing up the rest, till at last it laid the foundation of an empire extending east to west from coast to coast, and up to Mysore in the south and to Hindu Kush in the north-west, beyond the natural frontiers of India . "The new picture as shown in the Ceylon chronicles and in the classical authors (especially those based on the statements in the Indika of Megasthenes) shows us Magadha triumphant. All the kingdoms, duchies, and clans have lost their independence. Even the great Kosalan kingdom has been absorbed. And for the first time in the history there is one paramount authority from Bengal to Afghanistan, and from the Himalayas down to the Vindhya Range."[3]

Magadha rose as a 'new star'. An empire of this extent was exceptional; though another great empire was established again by Magadha in the fourth century Hindu India, it was not so extensive. The foundation of this first Empire was laid down by Bimbisara and his son Ajatasatru while it was taken to perfection by the Nandas and the Mauryas. As a result, the Ganga valley was to remain for a very long time the seat of an empire, and the centre of Indian civilization and Hindu culture; it was 'the future Hindustan'.

Some factors contributing to the emergence of Magadha as a supreme power are: the low-lying Gangetic plain with fertile land, reputed cattle wealth, vast mineral resources, admixture of races, tolerant social behaviour and liberal religious thinking. At the time when Iron Age was surfacing, Magadha with its rich iron mines was destined to dominate other powers. "Next to its strategic position, the comparative freedom from orthodoxy and the subsequent commingling of diverse cultures in Magadha may be regarded as an important factor in its development....Perhaps the Vedic polity, along with Vedic culture, had spent its force, and it was now the turn of the sturdy peoples of the east, comparatively unaffected by the Aryan invasion, to play their part. When the Puranas lament the wholesale destruction of the Kshatriya power by the Sudra king Mahapadma Nanda, they seem instinctively to refer to the end of one epoch and the rise of another. The laxity of social restrictions imposed by the orthodox Brahmin culture and the universal aspect of Buddhism and Jainism which found a congenial home in Magadha must have considerably widened the political outlook of this region and contributed to make it the nucleus of a mighty empire".[4]

It is believed that around that time India came into contact with Medo-Persian kingdom of Cyrus (558-530 BC) when he undertook his eastern campaign of conquest. It is believed that Cyrus died of the wounds inflicted in the battle which 'the Indians were fighting on the side of Derbikes (possibly a frontier tribe) whom they supplied with elephants. According to Xenophon Cyropaedia 1.1, 4), Cyrus 'brought under his rule Bactrians and Indians.' Arrian (Indica 1, 1-3) states that the Indians between the river Sindhu and Kabul (Cophen) 'were in ancient times subject to the Assyrians, the Medes, and finally to the Persians under Cyrus to whom they paid tribute he imposed upon them.' Ed. Meyer tells us that 'Cyrus appears to have subjugated the Indian tribes of the Paropanisus (Hindu Kush) and in Kabul Valley, especially the Gandarians: Darius himself advanced as far as the Indus. Herodotus (III,94) states that India counted as the twentieth satrapy of the empire of Darius (522-486 BC).[5]

1. K.M. Munshi, *The History and Culture of the Indian People*, Vol. II (Foreword)
2. Arnold Toyanbee, *Mankind and Mother Earth*, Ch. 33
3. F. J. Rapson, ., (ed.), *The New Cambridge History of India*, Vol. I, p. 190-91
4. Radha Kumud Mookerji, *The History and Culture of the Indian People*, Vol. II, Ch. II
5. Radha Kumud Mookerji, *The History and Culture of the Indian People*, Vol. II, Ch. III; *A Panoramic History of the Indian People*, D. B. Vohra

8
PHILOSOPHIC BLOSSOMS

The established orthodoxy of the Brahmanic religion was bound to meet its nemesis. Though not subdued completely nor subjected to total metamorphosis, this religion had to, on the one hand, effect self-adjustment under the emerging aspirations of new groups in the urban centres and, on the other, to face two new religions, Buddhism and Jainism, which seriously challenged the supremacy of the brahmans and the prevailing social inequality. This period also saw various schools of free thinking and wandering ascetics, 'which resulted in remarkable richness and vigour in thought which was rarely surpassed in the centuries to come.' All these religious philosophies seriously challenged the authority of the Vedas and the supremacy of the brahmans, specially the prevailing social inequality perpetrated by the institution of caste. Their *sanghas* (Order) were open to everybody regardless of caste. They enlarged the sense of community which had so far been compartmentalized by the Vedic religion. In the ensuing competition for followers, which eventually had to come from the existing pool of followers of Vedic religion, Buddhism emerged as the more successful. It was embraced both by royalty as well trading and artisan groups and low caste Sudras. Specially, the latter found the social codes of the new religions more conducive to their profession and which gave them a sense of freedom from the contempt which Brahmanism had for them.

Vaishanvism and Saivism: Stretching over a period of five or six centuries, the earlier Brahmanism took a new turn and gave rise to Puranic Hinduism. It gained new popularity, and gradually developed as the main tenets of the modern Hindu religion. In the list of old Vedic gods such as Agni, Indra, Varuna, Rudra, Surya, Soma, Pusha, Aryama, Asvini, Sarasvati, new gods were added. Offerings were not only made to Brahmanic deities, such as Siva, Skanda and Brahma, but also to deities of folk religions like Masa (month), Samvatsara (year), Vasanta (spring), and to astronomical constellation like Pushya and Tishya.

Brahmanism started reorganizing itself as a theistic movement in its two main branches of Vaishnavism and Saivism. In the Trinity of major gods, Brahma, Vishnu and Siva, Brahma was overshadowed by the other two. It was so despite the fact that Brahma even today is acknowledged as the Creator of men and even gods, while Vishnu is deemed as the Preserver and Siva as the Destroyer. The gratitude towards Vishnu and the fear of Siva, gave rise to the Bhakti, or unbounded love of God. In the Rigveda, Vishnu was recognized as an aspect of the Sun. In the later Vedic texts he was associated more with sacrifice than with devotion and grace. It becomes apparent, therefore, that Vaishnavism did not flourish as a theistic sectarian philosophy in the early Vedic age, but much later during this period.[1] This extreme devotion under Bhakti led to the development of the concept of *avtar* (incarnation), i.e., Vishnu taking births from time to time in human form to save humanity in times of calamity. It evolved into the triple identity of Narayana-Vishnu-Vasudeva. The *Bhagavad Gita* gave a philosophy to the Pancharatra school and the *Harivamsa* became a complete religious cult woven round the most vivacious and human personality of Krishna. Both appear to be literary products of the Maurya-Sunga culture-complex. The doctrine of Vibhuti-yoga as expounded in the *Gita* (ch. X) is in tune with the prevailing spirit of an age that regarded Krishna as the paramount deity in a varied pantheon of local gods and cults.[2]

As for the cult of Siva, it may be prevalent from earlier times. It was widespread in the area of modern Bihar. In Mithila, Janaka's royal family were Saivite. Siva's bow had received traditional worship. There, in a show of princely strength Rama had broken the great bow of Siva, and had earned the hands of Sita. During the period of Mahabharata war, the king Jarasandha of Magadha was a devotee of Siva, and was the greatest challenger of the supremacy of the Pandavas and their supporter, Vasudeva Krishna. The later period saw the development of Saivite Bhakti cult. Many of the earlier cults and ascetic movements were integrated into this movement. Patanjali mentions about Siva-Bhagvatas, whose devotion centered round the loving personality of Siva, his consort Parvati, and their son Skanda. "The rise of a definite religious sect, revering Siva as the Supreme God and with a philosophy and organization of its own, cannot be traced back earlier than about the beginning of the Christian era.....The earliest historical record to mention the worship of Siva is that of Megasthenes, the Greek envoy at Pataliputra about 300 BC".[3]

Wandering Ascetics and Free Thinkers: In this period we find a mushroom of religious beliefs, arising either independently or as offshoots of the existing major philosophical schools. The growing numbers of heterodox sects and cults were a great menace to orthodox Brahmanism and its caste-based society. As a reaction to this Kautilya, who himself was a brahman, disapproved in his Arthashastra premature renunciation of the world. He advocated that the responsibility of the family care came before such asceticism. He invoked legal enforcement from the authorities so that families were not left in the lurch. He was disgusted with this phenomenon so much so that he prescribed banning of such ascetics into villages for they were likely to cause disintegration in families and rural society.[4]

Most of these groups could not be systematically defined or interpreted. The main sources of information about them are the Buddhist canonical texts like Anguttara Nikaya (4th-3rd century BC) and Mahaniddesa and Chullaniddesa (2nd-1st century BC). They mention of the existence of such sects as Ajivika, Nigrantha (Jain), Munda-Sravaka, Jatilaka, Parivrajaka, Magandika, Traidandika, Aviruddhaka, Gautamaka (Buddhist), Devadharmika, Oarivrajaka. In addition, they mention about the people who worshipped elephant, horse, cow, dog and crow.

Those hermits who renounced the world were a prominent feature of the Indian society. Not only the Greek writers have taken notice of them but even Alexander once wanted to meet one of their notables. They were so fearless of bodily pang and even death that they did not hesitate to send rebuke to a king and a conqueror like Alexander. When Alexander's representative, Onesicritus, met fifteen meditating ascetics at Taxila, he told them that the Yavana king desired to learn wisdom from them. Onesicritus received the reply that 'no one coming in the drapery of European clothes—cavalry cloak and broad-rimmed hat and top-boots, such as Macedonians wore—could learn their wisdom. To do that he must strip naked and learn to sit on the hot stones beside them.' This encounter with the famous hermit, Dandamis, is described in more detail in the account of another Greek writer as follows:

"King Alexander, accordingly, when he heard of all this, was desirous of learning the doctrines of the sect, and so he sent for this Dandamis, as being their teacher and president....

"Onesicritus was therefore dispatched to fetch him, and when he found the great sage he said: 'Hail to thee, thou teacher of the Bragmanes. The son of mighty god Zeus, King Alexander, who is the sovereign lord of all men, asks you to go to him, and if you comply, he will reward you with great and splendid gifts, but if you refuse will cut off your head.'

"Dandamis, with a complacent smile, heard him to the end, but did not so much as lift up his head from his couch of leaves, and while still retaining his recumbent attitude returned this scornful answer: 'God, the Supreme King, is never the author of insolent wrong, but is the creator of light, of peace, of water, of the body of man, and souls. He alone is the god of my homage, who abhors slaughter and instigates no wars. But Alexander is not God, since he must taste of death; and how can such as he be the world's master, who has not yet reached the further shore of the river Tiberaboas, and has not yet seated himself on a throne of universal dominion?....Know this, however, that what Alexander offers me, and the gifts he promises, are all things to me utterly useless; but the things I prize, and find of real use and worth, are these leaves which are my house, these blooming plants which supply me dainty food, and the water which is my drink, while all other possessions and things, which are amassed with anxious care, are wont to prove ruinous to those who amass them, and cause only sorrow and vexation, with which every poor mortal is fully fraught. But as for me, I lie upon the forest leaves, and, having nothing which requires guarding, close my eyes in tranquil slumber; whereas had I gold to guard, that would banish sleep. The earth supplies me with everything, even as a mother her child with milk. I go wherever I please, and there are no cares with which I am forced to cumber myself, against my will. Should Alexander cut off my head, he cannot also destroy my soul. My head alone, now silent, will remain, but the soul will go away to its Master, leaving the body like a torn garment upon the earth, whence also it was taken. I then, becoming spirit, shall ascend to my God, who enclosed us in flesh, and left us upon the earth to prove whether, when here below, we shall live obedient to his ordinances, and who also will require of us, when we depart hence to his presence, an account of our life, since he is judge of all proud wrong-doing; for the groans of the oppressed become the punishments of the oppressors.

"Let Alexander, then, terrify with these threats those who wish for gold and for wealth, and who dread death, for against us these weapons are both alike powerless, since the Bragmanes neither love gold nor fear death. Go, then, and tell Alexander this : 'Dandamis has no need of aught that is yours, and therefore will not go to you, but if you want anything from Dandamis come you to him.'

"Alexander on receiving from Onesicritus a report of the interview, felt a stronger desire than ever to see Dandamis, who, though old and naked, was the only antagonist in whom he, the conqueror of many nations, had found more than his match"[5]

Those wondering ascetics and free thinkers maintained a tradition of unorthodox thinking, and, in general, philosophical speculation ranged from determinism to materialism. They held the belief that the worldly life of *samsara* was nothing but sorrow and misery. The ultimate goal of man should be to get rid of it. He should endeavour to find the Truth, that which alone is everlasting. To secure it, one had to be detached from family ties, and be deeply engrossed in meditation and thinking. These sophists and mystics could come from any caste. They had existed from earlier times. Gradually they formed themselves into groups. Each group distinguished itself by some external mark, like a particular colour of the robes, shaving the heads, growing beards and matted hair, or even going naked. Each held its own set of dogma and beliefs about the origin of life, end of the world and the way to salvation, and each had its own followers.

One of the most important and the earliest among them were called the Ajivikas. They were followers of a philosophy of complete predetermination—destiny controlled even the most insignificant action of human being and nothing could change this. They rejected the authority of the Vedas and the creator deity. Possibly, it was started by one Nanda Vachchha. He was succeeded by Kisa Samkichchha. This sect received a big boost under its third and most dynamic teacher Gosala Mamkhaliputta, who was a contemporary of Mahavira. He spent some years as the latter's disciple, then parted and claimed to have received enlightenment two years before Mahavira. The sect of Ajivikas is often identified as Digambra Jains. Though denounced by Jainism and Buddhism, both of them absorbed many of its tenets and practices. Probably it lingered up to seventh century AD, as we find a mention of it in *Harsha-charita*, but later was absorbed in the main body of Hinduism.

Atheistic sects like the Charvakas, preached total materialism: When the body dies both fool and wise alike cut off and perish. They do not survive after death. The Charvakas objected to the senseless ritual and ceremonial worship. These sects were regarded with scorn and were accused of immoral practices by the orthodox, specially the brahmans.

Jainism: According to Jain traditions there have lived twenty-four *Tirthankaras*, who were ford-makers over the sea of existence. Nothing is known about the earlier twenty-two Tirthankaras. The last two were Parsva and Vardhamana. Some facts about Parsva's life and teachings are available. Parsva died about 250 years before Vardhamana. Though Vardhamana's teachings are said to be based on those of Parsva's, he was the person who established Jainism as a faith. He was also called popularly as Mahavira or Mahabir. He was the scion of a noble family of Videha, and was born in c. 599 BC according to the prevailing 'Vira Nirvana Era', in Kundapura, a suburb of Vaisali in the Muzaffarpur district. His mother Trisala was the sister of Chetaka, the Lachchhavi king of Vaisali. Being a member of an aristocratic family he received his early education and training in a befitting manner. But he was given to meditation and was inclined to renounce the world. At the same time, he did not want to hurt the feelings of his parents. So when they died he left his home, his wife and daughter at the age of thirty to become a wandering ascetic, even discarding clothes. After twelve years of wandering and penance he attained enlightenment under a Sal tree in Jrambhikagrama, probably the present day Jambhigaon in Hazaribagh district. He found the truth about existence: one's *Karma* is responsible for his miseries in this life causing the endless cycle of birth and re-birth unless an escape from the existence is attained through right knowledge and by leading a life of asceticism and austerities. He attributed life even to material objects like earth and water, and proclaimed that they too deserve compassion and kindness from us. He started preaching and gathered disciples around him. He was welcomed and given patronage at the court of Magadha. Outside Bihar, he visited Sravasti and Ujjain, and most probably Sindh. Mahavira died at the age of seventy around 470 BC at Pavapuri. The dates of his birth and death are, however, a matter of controversy, and even Jain traditions are not unanimous in this regard. It is said that Mahavira and Buddha died within a few years of each other.

Not much information is available about the spread of this religion among the masses. More than in Bihar, it gained adherents in the areas of U.P., Avanti and Kalinga. Though adopted from time to time by some kings, Jainism never became an important factor in the political life of India, as was the case with Buddhism.

Buddhism: Unlike Mahavira, Buddha was the originator of the Faith. His name was Siddhartha, also called Gautama and Sakyamuni. He was the son of a Sakya chief, Suddhodana , and was born in c. 563 BC at a place called Lumbinivana, which is now within the political boundaries of Nepal. His mother, Maya, died a week after giving birth to him. He married the sister of the infamous Devadatta. He sired a son Rahula. Though he was passing a life of ease and luxury, he felt disgusted with the miseries of life. It is said that four events were catalytic in his decision to renounce worldly pleasures giving him the urge to find an escape from the cycle of birth and re-birth: they were the sights of a very old man, a cripple, a hermit and a dead-body. At the age of twenty-nine he left his palace and became an ascetic, wandering in remote areas. He became the disciple of learned sages of the time, first at Vaisali, then at Rajagriha, but found no satisfaction for his thirsty soul in search of the Truth. He started a life of extreme austerities, even denying himself the basic requirements of food and other necessities for many days. As a result, he frequently fainted. His meditations were disturbed. He was now convinced that self-mortification could not lead to salvation. He started taking food. At last he retired to the valley of Niranjana river, which joins the Phalgu river near Gaya. It was at the village of Uruvela near Gaya, sitting in meditation under a *pipal* tree, that the *Sakyamuni* received Enlightenment. He became the Buddha. The truth he found was that life is sorrow; one's *karma* is the cause of perpetual sorrow through re-birth; sorrow can be eliminated; and there is a path to escape from this sorrowful life. The path one should tread is, therefore, the Eight-fold Path or the Middle Path: right speech, right action, right means of livelihood, right exertion, right-mindedness, right meditation, right resolution and right point of view. These deeds and thoughts will`lead to *nirvana*: extinction of personality or freedom from the cycle of life and death.

He reached the Buddhahood at the age of thirty-five. To preach his doctrine Buddha first went to Sarnath. There he spent considerable amount of time. He then visited many places: Rajagriha, Nalanda, Pataliputra, Vaisali and Gaya. He also visited his home at Kapilavastu and converted his family members. He got royal patronage from the ruling monarchs of Magadha and Kosala. His last days were spent at Kusinara, the capital of the Mallas. He is said to have died in the eighth year of Ajatasatru's reign in c.486 BC.

Buddhism has played a very significant role in Indian history. Apart from Bimbisara and Ajatasatru, great kings like Asoka, Kanishka and Harsha Vardhana were converted to this religion. The tenets and teachings of this religion had thus important bearings on the political and social policies of the monarchs.

Both Buddhism and Jainism have many things in common. Springing up in Magadha almost at the same time from the kshatriya caste with such force that they, in the early period of their existence, became not only the religions of a great mass of the people but also of the kings. Many of their tenets belong to those of Hinduism. But it may fairly be said that the two movements were, in fact a revolt, against Hinduism as both rejected the authority of the Vedas, the creator deity and sacrificial rituals. Hinduism's basic tenets of polytheism and caste system were anathema to them. They challenged the superiority of the elite castes, specially of the privileged position of the brahmans as the custodian of Hindu religion and their sole right to priesthood. Both have their own canons, separate from Hinduism. They perceived life as the source of all miseries, and both prescribe a medicine for escape from it. The prescription is practical rather than philosophical. The direction is: master the mind and do not be a slave to the body. Most importantly, both are silent on the existence of mythological gods or even the Almighty God. In other words, one's own *karma* (deeds) is the final arbiter for his sorrowful cycle of birth.

Social Condition: The society was as usual divided by Chaturvrana. The legal system, based on Manu-smriti, had its prime focus on the class division as the basic foundation of the society.[6] The criminal law reflected caste disabilities and privileges. According to Manu, for Sudras 'service was his portion of life' (Manu VIII. 410,413); he is a slave (Manu VIII 413-14, 417); he could not receive sacraments nor could hear sacred texts (Manu IV, 99; X 4); 'a Sudra majority in a country (Sudra-bhumyisthan) would spell doom' (Manu III 156); if a Sudra even mentions names and castes of a djiva with insolence, 'an iron rail ten fingers long shall be thrust red-hot in his mouth'; if he insults him with gross invective, his tongue shall be cut off 'for he is of low origin'; 'with whatever limb a man of lower caste injures a man of the three higher castes, even that limb shall be cut off' (Manu VIII 279); the brahmans can compel a Sudra, whether purchased or not, to servile work, and can without hesitation appropriate his possessions (Manu VIII 413-14, 416-17); if he is arrogant to teach a Brahman his duties, ' the king shall cause hot oil to be poured into his mouth and into his ears'; Brahman shall be subjected to penance for killing a Sudra as for killing a cat, a frog, or a crow (Manu XI.132); for defaming a brahman, a kshatriya was to be fined a hundred panas, a vaishya from one hundred and fifty to two hundred, while a Sudra was to be given corporal punishment. However, a brahman will be fined only fifty, twenty-five and twelve panas for defaming a kshatriya, a vaishya and a Sudra, respectively. 'No greater crime is known on earth than slaying a brahman; a king, therefore, must not conceive in his mind the thought of killing a brahman.' A brahman's punishment was his banishment allowing him to take all his belongings with him.

Mention about the fifth caste of untouchables or Panchamas, who belonged to a specially low rank, has been made earlier. They were now given the name of Chandalas. Buddhists texts also mentions about the fifth caste, 'hina jati', who were pursuing low occupations, 'hina-sippa'. As the lowest mortals they were placed in the category of dogs and crows (Manu III 92, 239; X26); they were to eat in broken dishes, and vessels used by them were to be thrown away (Manu X 51, 52, 54). They had to wear distinct dress and outward masks, they were to live outside villages and towns, and their occupation was the disposal of unclaimed bodies and execution of criminals (Manu X 51-52, 55-56).

Slavery, as an old institution of Vedic times continued to this period. The Buddhist texts mention about the existence of various classes of slaves, viz. slaves by birth, by purchase, by capture in war, and by self-choice (mortgaging one's self for some consideration in order to meet critical needs). Manu (Viii 415) mentions about seven kind of slaves: (i) purchased, (ii) acquired in inheritance, (iii) given by others, (iv) enslaved by way of punishment, (v) captured in war, (vi) born in master's household, and (vii) accepting slavery for food. Laying down the primeval law of warriors, Manu says (vii 96) that one who singly gains a woman in battle becomes her owner.[7]

Overall, social and religious environment was peaceful. "In India, too, the struggle for existence between the governments of the states did not disrupt the society's social and cultural unity. Gaya, where the Buddha won his Enlightenment, was in Magadha; the sacred dear-park at Sarnath, which was the principal scene of the Buddha's subsequent preaching, was in Kasi. The park adjoined the holy city of Benaras, which was already a pilgrimage-resort, and the attraction of the park for the Buddha was presumably the possibility of finding there an audience drawn from all parts of the Indian World. Neither Gaya nor Sarnath was in the Buddha's home state; and, though the Buddha spent much of his time in the well-frequented park at Sarnath, he and his disciples were itinerant, except during the season of the monsoon rains, when travelling was difficult. The political frontiers were barriers for armies and were obstacles for spies, but they did not impede the movements of religious preachers and ascetics."[8]

1. *The History and Culture of the Indian People*, Vol. II, Ch. XIX
2. *Bihar Through the Ages*
3. *The History and Culture of the Indian People*, Vol. II, Ch. XIX
4. *A Comprehensive History of India*, Edited by N. A. Nilakanta Sastri, Ch. III
5. McCrindle, *Megasthenes*, pp. 124-126, quoted in *History and Culture of Indian People*, Vol. II, Chapter XXI, by Radha Kumud Mookerji and R. C. Majumdar
6. *The History and Culture of the Indian People*, Vol. II, Ch. XVIII, Law and Legal Institutions by Beni Prasad and R. C. Majumdar, & Ch. XXI, Social Condition by Radha Kumud Mookerji and R. C. Majumdar; *A Comprehensive History of India*, Ed. K. A. Nilakanta Sastri, Ch. XV
7. *A Comprehensive History of India*, Ed. K. A. Nilakanta Sastri, Ch. XV
8. Arnold Toyanbee, *Mankind and Mother Earth*, Ch. 33

9
INITIATION OF EMPIRES

Even before the Mahabharata War, Magadha had already risen to great prominence under Jarasandha of the Brihadratha dynasty. Under his suzerainty, Karna, one of the principal heroes of the Mahabharata, ruled Anga for some time. Jarasandha's son-in-law Kamsa, the Yadava king of Mathura, had also accepted Jarasandha's suzerainty. Kamsa, was, however, tyrannical to his people. Vasudeva Krishna became so enraged over the ill-treatment of his subjects that he killed Kamsa. Jarasandha, raging with anger at this extreme step against his son-in-law, led a number of campaigns against Krishna and his allies, and defeated them many times. Jarasandha made their lives such a hell that the Yadavas of Mathura decided to leave the territory, *en masse*, as they were afraid of a total annihilation. Krishna led them to the west coast and settled them down at Dvaraka.

The Puranas provides the following list of twenty-two kings of the Brihadratha dynasty in the post-Mahabharata period: 1. Somadhi, 2.Srutasravas, 3.Ayutayus 4.Niramitra, 5.Sukshatra 6.Brhatkarman, 7.Senajit, 8.Srutanjaya, 9.Vibhu, 10.Suchi, 11.Kshema, 12.Suvrata, 13.Dharmanetra or Sunetra, 14.Nirvrti, 15.Trinetra or Susrama, 16.Drdhasena, 17.Sumati or Mahinetra, 18.Sucala, 19.Sunetra, 20.Satyajit, 21.Visvajit, and 22.Ripunjaya. The Brihadratha dynasty lasted for more than a thousand years till the sixth century BC.

According to some Buddhist accounts, Bimbisara occupied the throne of Magadha immediately after Ripunjaya, sixty years before the death of the Buddha. Bimbisara was only fifteen then. According to the Cantonese tradition,[1] which is deemed more reliable in regard to the death of the Buddha, *Parinirvana* happened in 486 BC. The reign of Bimbisara has been given a period of 52 years; thus he is said to have ruled from c.546 BC to c.493 BC. Some historians believe that his father must be a minister or chief of the army, who staged a coup and placed his son Bimbisara on the throne. According to some sources, his father's name was Bhattiya or Mahapadma, although these names are never mentioned in *Mahavamsa*. Though popularly known as Bimbisara, he was also called Srenika. Asvaghosha, in his *Buddhacharita*, mentions that he was a scion of Haryanka-kula. He and his son Ajatasatru 'were the first known Indian kings to conceive of a large kingdom and the policy of expansion'

Bimbisara was both energetic and innovative. He immediately started on the career of expansion. It is believed that Bimbisara's father was earlier defeated by the king of Anga, called Brahmadatta. As such, his first campaign was against Brahmadatta, and in this venture he achieved total success. He annexed the kingdom of Anga, and appointed his son Ajatasatru as the governor. This was Magadha's first step towards empire building. Kasi had already been annexed by virtue of his marriage. He demonstrated skillful diplomacy by maintaining friendly relations with the kings of Gandhara and Avanti who were at daggers drawn with each other. He received the Ambassador of Gandhara in his court; while he sent his personal physician, Jivika, to Avanti to treat Pradyota's jaundice.

A vast area and probably eighty thousand villages were now under Bimbisara's domain. He was 'the first of these Chakravartins', who laid the foundation of the greatness of Magadha. Under Bimbisara, Magadha became a prosperous kingdom, ascending to an all-India rank. His benign administration and noble polices promoted learning and religious teachings. History's two great teachers and enlightened men, Gautama Buddha and Vardhamana Mahavira, found such a conducive environment for the propagation of their doctrines in his reign, that they could bequeath to the world two great religions.

Both the Buddhist and Jain scriptures claim that Bimbisara was a follower of their religion. Buddhist sources say that Bimbisara had first met the Buddha at his old capital, Grivraja, seven years before his Enlightenment. Impressed by the force of his personality, Bimbisara offered Gautama Buddha a high position with enormous wealth attached to it. But the great teacher politely declined. After attaining the Buddhahood he again met the king along with a large number of his disciples and learned scholars, including renowned brahman ascetics, the Kassapas, and their Jatila adherents at the new capital, Rajagriha. They all proclaimed the Buddha as their 'Lord'. Bimbisara treated Buddha with utmost respect. He feasted the group at his palace and even served the meals personally. At this moment he accepted Buddhism and made offerings to the holy man, including a piece of land (Venuvana, the Bamboo garden), where huts could be built to accommodate people of the Buddhist Order. His wife Khema embraced the Buddhist religion, and she became so devoted and knowledgeable that she gave instructions in Buddhist laws to the king. Bimbisara also placed his personal physician, Jivika, in attendance of the Buddha and his sangha. On one occasion when the Buddha had no money to pay to the ferryman, who had carried him across the Ganga river, the king was so moved that in honour of the Great Master he passed orders for a general remission of fares for all ascetics. The Uttaradhyayana Sutra mentions that Bimbisara, "the lion of Kings", visited the other "lion of homeless ascetics" (*anagara-siham*), Mahavira, with his wives, servants and relations, and became a staunch believer in Jainism. Another source, Hemachandra, tells about the time when the country was under a blight of cold; at that critical period the king accompanied by his wife Chellana went to worship Mahavira. Chellana is believed to have accepted Jainism.

Under Bimbisara, Magadha became a prosperous kingdom. His benign administration and noble policies caused the flourishing of learning and religious teachings. After a reign of 52 years, Bimbisara lost his life at the hands of his son Ajatasatru. It was eight years before the Buddha's death. The Buddhist sources say that Ajatasatru was instigated by Devadatta, the Buddha's cousin, to occupy the throne by killing his father, although it is believed that Bimbisara had already declared Ajatasatru as the heir to the throne. Later, Ajatasatru felt extreme remorse and confessed his guilt to the Buddha: '*May the Lord accept my transgression as transgression that I may be restrained in future. Sin overcame me, Lord, weak and foolish that I am, in that for the sake of sovereignty I put to death my father, that righteous man, that righteous king*'. Jain texts, however, say that in the last days of Bimbisara, Ajatasatru put his father in prison and occupied the throne. But when he heard that the devoted queen Chellana, who served him in the prison, even sucked the wound of a thumb of his father in order to relieve him of the intense pain, Ajatasatru was very much moved. Saying, '*A sorry return have I made to my father*', he rushed to break his father's fetters. Bimbisara, thinking that his son was going to kill him, ate poison and took his own life.

Ajatasatru had a strong and forceful personality. In order to enlarge his kingdom he resorted to Machiavellian tactics of the later days. He is nevertheless regarded as the founder of 'one of the greatest empires in the Indian history'. After annexing Kosala, Ajatasatru's main task for the expansion and consolidation of his empire was to contend with the Vijjian republics of the Lachchhavis in the north of Magadha. But they were so strong that they could not be overcome by force. At this moment Ajatasatru had to seek the advice of 'the great teacher'. He sent his trusted minister Vassakara to the Buddha for advice in regard to their fight with the Lachchhavis The Buddha confirmed that as long as the Lachchhavis were united and loyal to their leaders they could not be defeated. Ajatasatru took the hint, and came to the conclusion that he could defeat the enemy only through cunning.

As the first line of strategy, Ajatasatru built a fort on the southern bank of the river Ganga, at the village Patali. It was not convenient to direct the military operations from the capital Rajagriha which was far away in the south. The fort was constructed under the supervision of his ministers, Vassakara and Sunidha. This area developed into the future capital city of Pataliputra. Ajatasatru then thought of the ways to break the internal unity of the Republicans. Thus the second strategy he adopted was to fake the dismissal of Vassakara. To make it more real he humiliated Vassakara in public. Vassakara was made to escape to Vaisali, where freedom of speech was granted to the general public as a matter of state policy. Taking advantage of this freedom Vassakara poisoned the relations of the leaders with each other. After residing in Vaisali for three years he sowed enough seeds of dissension. When the atmosphere became favourable, Vassakara signaled Ajatasatru to launch an attack with full force. However, Chetaka, chief of the Lachchhavis, was not alone in this difficult moment; he was backed by his republican confederates as well as other kings that included his sons-in-law. It was a very protracted war, probably spanning over a period of sixteen years, from c.484 BC to c.468 BC. It was such an important event of the time that even the Buddha could not keep himself detached from it. He advised the Lachchhavis to stick to various moral principles, though impracticable in a war situation, in order to achieve victory. To the Lachchhavis, the Buddha is said to have given the following advice, repeated to Ananda, one of his zealous assistants: *So long, Ananda, as the Vijjians meet together in concord, and rise in concord, and carry out their undertakings in concord—so long as they enact nothing not already established, abrogate nothing that has been already enacted, and act in accordance with the ancient institutions of the Vijjians as established in former days—so long as they honour and esteem and revere and support the Vijjian elders, and deem it a point of duty to hearken to their words—so long as no women or girls belonging to their clans are detained among them by force or abduction—so long as they honour and esteem and revere and support the Vijjian shrines in town or country, and allow not the proper offerings and rites, as formerly given and performed, to fall into desuetude—so long as the rightful protection, defence, and support shall be fully provided for the Arahats among them, so that Arahats from a distance may enter the realm, and the Arahats therein may live at ease—so long may the Vijjians be expected not to decline, but to prosper.*[2] The Buddha probably thought it appropriate that like a religious chakravartin, as he was, there should also be a political chakravartin, and that could only be the ruling monarch of Magadha. In the end, Ajatasatru achieved complete success not only in destroying the powers of the Republic of Vaisali, but also the republican system itself.

Like his father, Ajatasatru is also claimed by both the Buddhists and the Jains as their follower. Jain texts claim that Ajatasatru visited Mahavira many times along with his queens, and once even declared his faith and allegiance to Mahavira. As for Buddhism, his relations with the Buddha were earlier strained under the influence of the Buddha's scheming cousin Devadatta. It is said that Devadatta had once asked Ajatasatru: *Give an order, O king, to our men that I may deprive Samana Gautama of life.* Ajatasatru then ordered his men: *Whatsoever the worthy Devadatta tells you, that do.* The Buddha's reaction to this was: *Monks, the king of Magadha, Ajatasatru, is a friend to, an intimate of, mixed with, whatever is evil.*[3] Later, wanting to get rid of the feeling of guilt for the murder of his father and to get peace of mind Ajatasatru approached the learned sages of the time, including Mahavira. But in the end he got solace from Gautama Buddha. The result was that he started venerating the Buddha so much that when he died, Ajatasatru rushed to Kusinara to obtain the relics of the Buddha's body, having sent a messenger in advance with the message: "The Lord was a Kshatriya; I too am a Kshatriya; I am worthy of a share of the relics of the Lord. I will erect a stupa over the relics of the Lord and make a feast". Having received the major portion of the Buddha's relics, Ajatasatru enshrined it in a stupa at Rajagriha. He built *Dhatu-chaityas* all around the capital. He also associated himself with the first General Council of Buddhism, held at Rajagriha, by providing all facilities for the conduct of business and for serving the delegates with the four requisites of clothing, food, dwelling places and drugs.

Ajatasatru died in c. 462 BC after reigning for thirty-two years. After the rules of a few successors of Ajatasatru, the hereditary monarchy was supplanted by an elected monarchy. Sisunaga was a viceroy at Varanasi at the end of Nagadasaka's reign. He was elected king by the assembly of chiefs and nobles. No definite information is available about his origin. *Mahavamsatika* mentions that he was the son of a Lachchhavi prince and the chief courtesan of Vaisali. Because of the constant hostility of the Pradoyta of Avanti, he took his capital back to Rajagriha. But ultimately he destroyed this menace and absorbed Avanti in his kingdom, as also the kingdoms of Vatsa and Kosala. The whole of North India thus came under the fold of the Magadhan Empire.

Sisunaga ruled for 18 years according to *Dipavamsa*, and for forty years according to the Puranas. He was succeeded by his son Kalashoka or Kakavarna, who made his abode back in the old capital, Pataliputra. The most important event of his time was the holding of the second Grand Council of Buddhism. He was killed by someone who thrust a dagger into his throat. According to the Greek writer Curtius, a barber who became the paramour of the queen, treacherously murdered the king, became the regent of the ten princes, then murdered them, and 'begot the present king'. The account of Curtius is based on information collected within less than half a century of the actual event, hence seems more reliable; it is also corroborated by the Jain tradition. The joint rule of the ten kings is said to have lasted for ten years. The ninth and tenth kings of this dynasty are mentioned as Nandivardhana and Mahanandin or Panchamaka, sons of Kalashoka.

The Puranic texts mention that 'the son of king Mahanandin by a Sudra women' was the founder of the new Nanda dynasty. Whether the founder of the Nanda dynasty was the son of a Sudra women or whether he was the son of a barber, there appears little doubt that he was of a low origin. But, he was also a person of great abilities. The name of the first king of this dynasty is not definitively known; he was called Mahapadma Nanda or Ugrasena. Mahapadma may be an epithet, signifying the lord of an infinite host or of immense wealth. Greek historians refer to the king of India at the time of Alexander's invasion as Agrammes, which may be the Greek substitute for the word Augrasainya, i.e., son of Ugrasena. [4]

The Nanda dynasty is famous by the name of the Nine Nandas. In other words, the dynasty was composed of nine rulers in all.

the time of Alexander's invasion as Agrammes, which may be the Greek substitute for the word Augrasainya, i.e., son of Ugrasena. [4]

The Nanda dynasty is famous by the name of the Nine Nandas. In other words, the dynasty was composed of nine rulers in all. Sometimes it is reported that the nine comprised a father and his eight sons, while other accounts say that there were nine brothers. Nothing is sure if the father ruled once and after him his eight sons ruled together in a group or one after another. The Nine Nandas are named in the Buddhist text, *Mahabodhivamsa,* as Ugrasena, Panduka, Pandugati, Bhutapala, Rashtrapala, Govishanaka, Dashasiddhaka, Kaivarta and Dhana. Of these nine, some details are available only about the first and the last kings.

The founder of the dynasty, Mahapadma Nanda was a great conqueror. He annihilated almost all the kshatriya kingdoms of north and even south India and merged them into his own empire, and earned the title of the second *Parasurama* or *Bhargava*. Thus he rang the death knell of such kingdoms as Aikshvakus, Panchalas, Kasis, Haihayas, Kalingas, Ashmakas, Kurus, Maithilas, Surasenas, and Vitihotras. Evidence of his rules is found in Ayodhya, Kalinga, Bombay, Mysore, Hyderabad and Karnataka. By his conquests he also earned the title of *Eka-chatra*, the whole sovereign. Thus for the first time, the Indus basin, the Jamuna-Ganga basin and also the Deccan were united with each other politically. Mahapadma can rightly be called the first great historical emperor of Northern India. He also ended the age-long tradition of the political supremacy of the kashatriyas.[5]

1. A record was kept in Cantonese by putting a dot every year after the death of the Buddha till AD 489. At that time the number of dots was 975: (486 BC+AD 489). It may be kept in mind, however, that if the Chinese were putting dots each year according to the lunar calendar, the lunar year being shorter, 975 dots were a lot more. In that case, *parinirvana* must have happened about 30 years earlier than AD 486. However, nothing is definite about it and many theories and dates have been advanced in this regard.

2. *Bihar Through the Ages*, Appendix

3. *The History and Culture of the Indian People*, Vol. II. Ch. II

4. *Bihar Through the Ages*, Ch. V; *The History and Culture of the Indian People*, Vol. II.

5. *The History and Culture of the Indian People*, Vol. II. Ch. II

10
ALEXANDER VISITS INDIA

With the rise of the Achaemanid power in Persia (Iran), India was once again subject to assaults from outside through the north-west. Cyrus (c.558-530 BC) had annexed Gandhara to the Persian Empire as a satrapy. His successor, Darius, extended his sway further across the Indus. The most important impact of this relationship was the introduction of a written language in India. The Gandhāran capital of Taxila subsequently gained the reputation as an intellectual centre.

At the end of the third quarter of the fourth century BC Alexander the Macedonian was set to achieve a lofty ideal. He embarked on a campaign of conquests of *ekumene or Oikoumene*, meaning, 'the inhabited part of the world', thus aiming at world domination. " But Alexander was not seeking to annex new territories. What he wanted was to incorporate all men in his *ekumene*. So long as any segments of the human race remained outside his monarchy, his task would remain incomplete. The only way to ensure that they would all be included was to reach the ocean which, according to Herodotus, circled the world".[1] He "planned a mighty world empire, seeing it not simply as Macedonian conquest of the world, but as a melting together of racial traditions".[2]

By first seeking that ocean to the north and finding it futile he thought it advisable to seek it by marching eastward. He crushed his opponents in Greece and the Balkans and invaded Asia Minor in 334 BC. Then he entered Syria and defeated the army of Persia at Issus. Proceeding down the coast of Tyre and cutting off the bases of the Persian fleet he seized Egypt. He then directed his attack on the mainland of Persia and defeated the Persian emperor Darius III putting his capital Persepolis on fire. The emperor being killed, Alexander declared himself the successor of Darius and embarked on recovering his kingdom.

Overrunning all the lands between Alexandria and Kabul river, Alexander proceeded towards India in 327 BC. Gandhara and the Punjab had been Persian satrapies for two hundred years. He sent messages in advance to all the kings west of the river Sindhu to discuss terms of their surrender. The rulers of Takshasila, Ambhi, and of a frontier hill-state, Sashigupta, returned assurances of allegiance to Alexander and of military assistance in his campaigns. To Alexander's invitation, Porus, the king of the region between the rivers Jhelum and Chenab, sent the reply that he would, of course, meet Alexander but with arms in his hands and ire in his eyes. Alexander then proceeded to subjugate the defiant ones. Facing resistance at every step by small principalities, and defeating them promptly, he set foot on the friendly soil of Takshasila (Taxila) in 326 BC. The territory beyond Takshasila was the kingdom of Porus who had refused to bow before the authority of Alexander. Crossing Jhelum, Alexander faced the army of Porus. Porus gave a tough fight, but in the end he was defeated. Even after his defeat he maintained his dignity, and when asked by Alexander how he should be treated, Porus replied, 'Like a king'. Alexander, showing magnanimity, reinstated Porus as the king. Porus was only required to regard himself as a member of the world realm under Alexander. Alexander thus brought the Indo-Persian connection to an end.

Undaunted, Alexander now saw the triumphant route wide open before him which could lead him to the sources of the sun. Fully confident that no man, no obstacle, would be powerful enough to bar his way, he marched further ahead. In these victories, he was helped by Porus with elephants and 6,000 soldiers.[3] In marching further eastward, he could fulfill his dream of crowning himself as the king of the inhabited world. Crossing Ravi, and defeating various small principalities and republican peoples, Alexander reached Beas (Hyphasis). But beyond Beas was the kingdom of a great monarchy, that of Parsii and Gangaridae, 'a nation by repute brave, well equipped, more civilized than those through which he had passed like a flaming sword'. The Greek writers refer to the king of that monarchy, whose capital was at Pataliputra, as Agrammes, whose rule extended from the far east of India to the banks of the river Beas in the Punjab. By some Greek accounts Dhana Nanda had a very large army: 80,000 cavalry, 200,000 infantry, 8,000 four-horsed chariots, and 6,000 war-elephants. " For the rumor ran that near the head waters of the Ganges, Xandrames, an Indian prince, had blocked the way with two hundred thousand foot, twenty thousand horses, two thousand chariots, and three thousand elephants."[4] It is said that Alexander's army refused to step into that territory. Despite Alexander's repeated commands and pleadings his army did not yield. Alexander finding the army unwilling to advance beyond the Beas convoked the officers in commnad of brigades, before the disorder and despondency should be further developed among the soldiers. He addressed them:" Are you afraid there are other barbarians who may yet successfully resist you although of those we have already met some have willingly submitted, others have been captured in flight, while others have left us their deserted country to be distributed either to allies or to those who have voluntarily submitted to us." After a long time, silence was broken by one Koinos who summoned up courage and replied: "Moderation in the midst of success is, O king! The noblest of virtues, for though, at the head of so brave an army, you have nothing to dread from mortal foes, yet the visitations of the deity cannot be foreseen, and man cannot, therefore, guard against them." When Koinos concluded, those present signified their approval of what he said by laud applause, while many with streaming tears expressed more aversion to encounter further dangers.[5]

The bank of Beas was Alexander's last outpost in the east; and the occasion was the shattering of his dream of *ekumene.* "Within reach of the world's end, and not to reach it-this was the disappointment which Alexander suffered at the Hyphasis.... He supposed that the Ganges discharged its waters into the ocean which bounded the earth on the east."[6] V.A.Smith is of the opinion that if Alexander had advanced further his force 'might have been overwhelmed by the mere numbers of his adversaries', and that the rebellious troops 'may be credited with having prevented the annihilation of the Macedonian army'. "Possibly he would have pushed eastward across the deserts to the Ganges valley, but his troops refused to go further. Possibly, had they not done so, then or later he would have gone on until he vanished eastward out of history. But he was forced to turn about".[7]

Indian sources do not even mention of Alexander's arrival in India. His presence in India was a matter of least disturbance for the heartland of Indian power. No details are thus available as to what military preparations were, or ever, made by the ruler of Magadha to face Alexander the Great. He had been able to subdue only petty rajahs and chiefs of tribes of the north-west. For his retreat from the western banks of the Beas, Alexander ordered a fleet of 1000 ships to be built.

The return journey began in the southerly direction, sailing down the Jhelum and Sindhu rivers. Once again facing resistance from various tribes and republican states on the way, and then crushing them, Alexander reached Patella at the head of the Indus delta in the summer of 325 BC. From there he proceeded to Babylon, where he died in the palace of Nebuchadnezzar at the age of thirty-two in mid June, 323 BC.

1. Benoist-Mechin, Jaques, *Alexander The Great*
2. Wells, H. G., *The Outline of History*
3. Shastri, K.A. Nilakanta and Srinivasachari, G., *Advanced History of India*
4. Theodore Ayrault Dodge, *Alexander,* p. 580
5. *The Invasion of India by Alexander the Great,* Book Fourth, chs. xxv & xxvii, J.W. M'crindle
6. J.B.Bury and Russell Meiggs, *A history of Greece*, P.485
7. Wells, H. G., *The Outline of History*

11
FIRST WAR OF INDEPENDENCE

Despite the abundance of wealth and the enormous size of the army of Dhana Nanda, there was at least one undaunted and even smarter person who could challenge his authority and destroy him. And that was his own compatriot, Chandragupta Maurya. There are different accounts of his origin. Some say that he was the son of a peacock (*mayur*) tender while others say that his mother's name was Mura, thus calling himself Maurya. Other traditions say that he was a Sudra; he was a member of Mura or Maurya clan; he was from the ruling Kshatriya clan; he belonged to the Sakya clan; he was a prince of the ruling family; he was an illegitimate child of the Nanda king or he was a military chief of the Nandas having his own grievances against them. A Buddhist tradition tells the story of his origin and boyhood that he was the son of the chief of the Maurya clan, who was killed in a battle. His destitute mother then went to Pataliputra where she gave birth to her illustrious son. He was brought up in a village by a cowherd or a peacock hunter. One day a Brahman, Chanakya, also known by the names of Kautilya and Vishnugupta, who was Chandragupta Maurya's future guru and chief minister, was passing by the village that he saw the promising lad, who always preferred to play the King with his companions. Chanakya bought him with money and took him to Takshasila, where he tutored him in various arts and sciences.

Whatever Chandragupta's origin may have been, the fact is that he established such a vast empire that was never matched by any other empire in the history of Hindu India. In those early days he stretched the boundaries of his kingdom beyond the natural frontiers of India, as it is known today or was known at that time; and by virtue of his conquests his grandson Asoka had the privilege of calling in Rock Edicts II and XIII the Syrian emperor Antiochus as his immediate neighbour. It goes to his credit that he liberated India from the foreign yoke, whose North-West region including the Punjab, was for more than two hundred years under the suzerainty, first, of the Persians and, then, of the Greeks. Before departing from India, Alexander had left Greek and Indian satraps to govern his conquered territories. But Alexander's demise in 323 BC dealt a death blow to his empire. In immediate succession the satraps Nicanor of Qandhar and Philips of the upper Sindhu valley were killed. There was disruption and turmoil all over. The bitter taste of foreign occupation was too much for the people. Taking full advantage of this mess, Chandragupta Maurya plunged himself into a war of liberation: 'the earth long harassed by outlanders now turned for protection and refuge' to him. He declared himself king, gradually finished off the Greek and Indian satraps and became the ruler of Sindh and the Punjab. According to Justin, "The author of this liberation was Sandrocottos". Chandragupta Maurya was the victorious hero of India's 'First War of Independence'.

The ruler of the eastern part of Alexander's empire was Seleucus. Considering himself as Alexander's successor he advanced towards India to recover Alexander's lost possessions from Chandragupta Maurya. He was at Sindhu river in 305 BC. But it was not easy for him to wrest the lost empire back from the new king. It was not that part of India of Alexander's time which was divided into small principalities and satrapies and whom Alexander could conquer piecemeal. In the ensuing struggle, Seleucus, instead of receiving back the lost territories, had to cede, in a humiliating treaty, to Chandragupta new territories west of Indus and south of Hindu Kush, which included Qandhar, Kabul, Herat, Gandhara and a part of Baluchistan on the eastern fringe of the former Persian dominions. According to some tradition, he also gave his daughter in marriage to the new king of India. Chandragupta gave Seleucus, in return, 500 war elephants for use against his Macedonian rival, Antigonus. Thereafter, the relations between the two were to remain ever cordial, so much so that a Greek ambassador was posted at the Mauryan court. He was Megasthenes, who lived at Pataliputra between 304 and 299 BC, and whose accounts of Chandragupta's rule serve as one of the most important sources of Indian history.

Chandragupta had become the architect of an all-India empire, whose writ ran for the first time to the length and breadth of the country. Despite the vastness of his empire no detailed accounts of Chandragupta Maurya's conquests are available. Plutarch and Justin, however, mention that he overran and subdued the whole of India with a massive army of 600,000 men. The author of *Mudrarakshasa* describes Chandragupta's supremacy as over the entire region from the Himalayas to the shores of the southern ocean (*Dakshinarnava*). Tamil sources suggest that *Vamba Mauryar* (Maurya upstart) had penetrated as far south as the Podiyil Hill in the Tinnevelly district. The vast extent of his empire is confirmed by other facts too. His son Bindusara is not known to history as a great conqueror, while his grandson Asoka is said to have conquered only Kalinga, after which he denounced further conquests. But Asoka's inscriptions are found over a very wide area up to Afghanistan in the north-west and in Maharashtra and Andhra in the western and southern India. Thus, Asoka must have ruled over the territories conquered by his grandfather. A record is available that Chandragupta Maurya's governor, Pushyagupta, was posted as far away as Junagadh.

Chandragupta was the supreme head of state as well as the law giver, the judge, the chief executive and the commander-in-chief. According to Megasthenes: "The king does not sleep in day-time but remains in the court the whole day for the purpose of judging cases and other public business, and this is not interrupted even when the hour arrived for massaging his body." People enjoyed a contended life mainly due to the fertility of land, availability of water and prosperity of agriculture. The principle of equity was observed in the distribution of water through the canals. Life and property of the people were safe, and theft and other crimes were rare. Chandragupta, in disguise, occasionally undertook nightly tours of the city. Thus 'his reign came to be looked upon as the beginning of a golden age.'[1] His reign saw "India politically and administratively unified; re-establishment of *dharma* as the supreme law; the organization of life on which was founded the invulnerable culture and consciousness of Indians in succeeding ages."[2]

Chandragupta Maurya was an orthodox follower of the Vedic religion, but in his last days he embraced the Jain faith. A Tibetan account mentions that Chanakya was not happy over this decision; so he advised Chandragupta to abdicate in favour of his son, Bindusara. Anyway, in c. 300 BC, Chandragupta, along with his Jain guru Bhadrabahu, retired to Shravana Belgola in Mysore, where he subjected himself to severe penance and fasted himself to death in c 299 BC.

One interesting story is recorded about the successor king Bindusara that he once requested the king of Syria, Antiochus I Soter, to buy for him sweet wine, dried figs and a sophist. To this, the king of Syria replied: "We shall send you the figs and the wine, but in Greece the laws forbid a sophist to be sold." Bindusara reigned for about twenty-five years. No important developments appear to have taken place during his reign, but the most significant contribution of Bindusara was to bequeath to India the Greatest of Kings, his son Asoka.

1. Roberts, J.M., *History of the World*
2. Edwards, Michael, *A History of India*

12
NOBLEST KING OF HISTORY

Asoka succeeded Bindusara to the throne of India in c. 273 BC His coronation was delayed by four years probably because of the war of succession to which Asoka emerged finally triumphant after bloodshed. His mother was Subhadrangi, also called Dharma. He had several brothers and sisters. Tishya was his youngest brother. Asoka mentions dearly about his brothers, sisters and relatives, and of his private life in his various inscriptions. He had many queens. The first was Sakyakumari and the second Karuvaki. His eldest son Mahendra and eldest daughter Sanghamitra, who were sent to Lanka as Buddhist missionaries in the spirit of self-sacrifice in the service of religion, were born of his first wife. The chronicles of Sri Lanka, however, say that his first wife was Devi or Vidishamahadevi whom he married when he was governor of Vidisa, and from whom the above mentioned son and daughter were born. His other wives were Padmavati, Asandhimitta and Tissarakkhita of Kalinga. His other sons were Tivara, Kunala and Jalauka.

There is a universal recognition by historians of the world that Asoka is one of the greatest and noblest kings in history. For his acclaimed greatness it would suffice to quote here H.G.Wells. He writes in The *Outline of History*: Asoka is "one of the greatest monarchs of history, whose dominions extended from Afghanistan to what is now the province of Madras. He is the only military monarch on record who abandoned warfare after victory. He had invaded Kalinga (225 BC), a country along the east coast of Madras, perhaps with some intention of completing the conquest of the tip of the Indian peninsula. The expedition was successful, but he was disgusted by what he saw of the cruelties and horrors of war....For eight-and-twenty years Asoka worked sanely for the real needs of men. Admist the tens of thousands of names of monarchs that crowd the columns of history, their majesties and graciousnesses and serenities and royal highnesses and the like, the name of Asoka shines, and shines almost alone, a star. From the Volga to Japan his name is still honoured. China, Tibet, and even

India, though it has left his doctrine, preserve the tradition of his greatness. More living men cherish his memory to-day than have ever heard the names of Constantine or Charlemagne."[1]

By adding Kalinga to the empire as inherited from his grand-father, Asoka ruled over the greatest empire in Indian history. The conquest of Kalinga became a landmark in Indian political history; the largest empire which existed ever in olden India got its limit and was restrained from further expansion by choice; it became at the same time a turning point in the king's character that makes him the noblest of monarchs. The victory at Kalinga was simultaneously the defeat for Asoka as a traditional worldly king. He renounced further conquests and warfare, and embraced Buddhism, the hallmark of pacifism and non-violence. Not only this, he left the advice for his descendants not to conquer territories by force, and if they had to do so they should do so with least of violence and maximum of kindness.

He was so moved by the slaughter and human sufferings in that war that he ruled afterwards only for the welfare of his subjects. His style of governance became henceforth moral, ethical and humane. He started calling himself as *Devanampiya Piyadasi* and *Devanam Priya Priyadasi* or Beloved of the Gods. Asoka thus declared about the Kalinga war, the earliest event of his reign which is recorded, as follows:

150,000 people were carried captive, 100,000 were killed and many more died. Just after taking Kalinga, *Devanum Priya* began to follow *Dharma* and to give instructions in righteousness....If today a hundredth or a thousandth part of those who suffered in the Kalinga war were to be killed or taken captive, it would be very grievous to the *Devanam Priya*.

In the Major Rock Edict XIII he further says:

On conquering Kalinga, the Beloved of the Gods felt remorse, for, when an independent country is conquered, the slaughter, death and deportation of people is extremely grievous to the Beloved of the Gods, and weighs heavily on his mind. What is even more deplorable to the Beloved of the Gods, is that those who dwell there, whether brahmanas, *Sramanas,* or those of other sects, or householders who show obedience to their superiors, obedience to mother and father, obedience to their teachers and behave well and devotedly towards their friends, acquaintances, colleagues, relatives, slaves and servants—all suffer violence, murder and separation from their loved ones. Even those who are fortunate to have escaped, and whose love is undiminished, suffer from the misfortunes of their friends, acquaintances, colleagues and relatives. This participation of all men in suffering weighs heavily on the mind of the Beloved of the Gods.

'He (Asoka) did not see Dhamma as piety resulting from good deeds inspired by formal religious beliefs, but as an attitude of social responsibility.... Dhamma was aimed at building up an attitude of mind in which social responsibility, the behaviour of one person towards another, was considered of great relevance. It was a plea for the recognition of the dignity of man, and for a humanistic spirit in the activities of society.'[2]

The following inscriptions of Asoka, *inter alia*, reflect the height of nobility a king could reach for his subjects. He also lived up fully to those high standards and ideals:

* The glory and fame of a king do not rest upon the physical extent of his dominion but upon the moral progress he can help his people to achieve.

* All men are my children and just I desire for my children that they should obtain welfare and happiness both in this world and the next, the same do I desire for all men.

* In the happiness of his subjects lies the happiness of the king; in their good his own good, and not in what is pleasing to him. He must find his pleasure in the pleasure of his subjects.

* There is no higher duty than the welfare of the whole world, and what little effort I make, what is it for?—That I may be free from debt to the creatures.

* (My ideals are engraved on rocks) in order that it may endure for a long time and that my sons, grandsons, and great-grandsons may similarly follow me for the welfare of the whole world.

Asoka not only demonstrated a personal example of this humanized style of governance and exhorted his officials to govern in the same spirit but also propagated to the world the *dharma* or the Law of Piety, encompassing his ideals of compassion, mercy, charity, truth and goodness, in the style of a preacher by engraving it on rocks from Afghanistan to the southern Deccan for the posterity. Thirty-six different inscriptions have been found all over India and Afghanistan, and it would not be wrong to say that 'Indian epigraphy really starts with him'.[3] In them he sheds light on a wide range of activities ranging from his family life, administrative measures, treatment of fellow human beings and animals, and missionary activities to the assessment of his own achievements.

Asoka's missions were aimed at spreading the message of non-violence and providing relief from suffering to all living beings, as also to carry out humanitarian works in foreign lands. Arnold Toyanbee says about him: "He charged his officials to take to heart their responsibility towards the huge numbers of people under their rule, and to treat them as gently as nurses treat children (Seventh Pillar Edict; First Separate Edict). He instituted, or at any rate, revived and maintained, the practice of sending out touring inspectors (Third Major Rock Edict); he went on tour himself (Eighth Major Rock Edict; Minor Rock Edict), and he instituted a new class of officials to superintend the administration of philanthropic foundations, religious denominations, and welfare work such as the planting of trees, the digging of wells, the establishment of hospitals for animals as well as human beings (Fifth Major Rock Edict and Seventh Pillar Edict), and restrictions on the killing of animals (First, Second and Eleventh Major Rock Edicts; Fifth and Seventh Pillar Edicts; Kandahar Inscription)."[4] Trees of medicinal value were to be planted not only in his own kingdom but also in neighbouring countries and as far as in Greece and Syria. Official tours were to ensure both that the administrative measures were well implemented and that *dharma* reigned supreme. Assigning public weal the utmost importance, Asoka had made himself available for official business at all times. In Sixth Major Rock Edict he says:

> But I have now arranged it thus. At all times—whether I am eating, or am in the women's apartments, or in my inner apartments, or at the cattle-shed, or in my carriage, or in my gardens—wherever I may be, my informants should keep me in touch with public business.

Asoka laid special emphasis on toleration, both for people and their beliefs. Though Asoka had turned a Buddhist, his magnanimity did not allow him to be intolerant to other religions, specially to the religion of the masses, Hinduism. He held the belief that one's faith in his own *dharma* should induce one to respect others' *dharma* as well. He called upon members of different faiths to observe caution and restraint while speaking about religious matters. In the Twelfth Rock Edict he expresses his passion for religious tolerance and respect for the faiths of others as:

"....consideration toward slaves and servants, obedience to mother and father, generosity towards friends, acquaintances, and relatives, and towards priests and monks....

"But the Beloved of the Gods does not consider gifts of honour to be as important as the essential advancement of all sects. Its basis is the control of one's speech, so as not to extol one's own sect or disparage that of another on unsuitable occasions....On such occasions one should honour another man's sect, for by doing so one increases the influence of one's own sect and benefits that of the other man, while, by doing otherwise, one diminishes the influence of one's own sect and harms the other man's....therefore concord is to be commended so that men may hear one another's principles...."[5]

During his official tours, which were both kingly and religious, he visited brahmanas and *sramanas* alike and held discussions on *dharma* with them. He (and his grandson Dasaratha) gave cave-dwellings in the hills near Gaya to the Ajivikas ascetics. These Brabar Caves are the earliest in the great succession of India's rock-cut architectures. In the Ninth Major Rock Edict, explaining the spirit of *dharma*, he says:

".... the ceremony includes regard for slaves and servants, respect for teachers, restrained behaviour towards living beings and donations to *sramanas* and brahmanas—these and similar practices are called the ceremony of *dharma*."

Asoka's noble philosophy and practice of tolerance would have been incomplete had it not been extended to animal lives. Kindness and compassion was to be shown in all aspects of life, because it too was part of the dhamma. He discontinued royal hunts. His personal kindness to animals is enshrined in the First Major Rock Edict as:

Formerly in the kitchens of the Beloved of the Gods, the King Piyadasi, many hundreds of thousands of living animals were killed daily for meat. But now, at the time of inscription on *dharma*, only three animals are killed, two peacocks a day and the deer not invariably. Even these three animals will not be killed in future.

In the 26th year of his reign he banned the slaughter of animals which were not to be consumed as food or for any other use. Forests were not to be burned because animals would become homeless. In one of his Edicts he says:

On the roads I have had banyan trees planted, which will give shade to beasts and men. I have had mango groves planted and I have had wells dug and rest houses built every nine miles...And I have had many watering places made everywhere for the use of beasts and men. But this benefit is important, and indeed the world has enjoyed attention in many ways from former kings as well as from me. But I have done these things in order that my people might conform to *Dhamma*.[6]

Whereas so much compassion was shown to animals, capital punishment for criminals was not abolished. Also, the state policy of non-violence was to be suspended while suppressing the troubles created by primitive tribes. This shows his concern for maintaining law and order and for giving peace of mind and physical safety to his subjects.

Beside being the king, Asoka was also head of the Buddhist church. He was personally directing missionary activities. After the Third Buddhist Council, presided over by the famous priest, Moggaliputta Tisa, he sent Buddhist missionaries within the country and abroad like Nepal, Burma, Kamboja, China, Lanka, Macedonia, Syria, Cyrene, Epirus and Egypt. The objectives of these missions were not solely to preach Buddhism in a purely sectarian sense; it was to propagate *Dhamma*. His *Dhamma* was humanism, the essence of all religions: respect for life, human and animal alike, care for parents, reverence to teachers, regards for elders, relatives and friends, care for the poor and needy, proper treatment of slaves, tolerance to others' faiths, speaking truth, etc. Asoka says: "For this is my principle: to protect through *Dhamma*, to administer affairs according to *Dhamma*, to please the people with *Dhamma*, to guard the empire with *Dhamma*". "From Asokan Buddhism emerged the concept of chakravartin, the 'wheel-turning monarch', the universal lord of righteousness.

"Fundamental beliefs in this system are the twin concepts of *dharma* and *karma*. *Dharma* (Pali, *Dhamma*) the teaching, the law has religious and social as well as political implications. It is the moral standard - the 'truth and beauty' of our Western ethic. All have their duties and obligations to discharge, but the ruler has the supreme task of maintaining harmony among his subjects by upholding the *dharma* of all while providing an example through fulfilling his own *dharma*. Here is one of the significant differences between the political fundamentals of East and West. Western man insists that the prime factor is the establishment and assertion of rights; the Asian replies that a true relation between the individual and community is created by the recognition of obligations."[7]

For developing harmony and mutual respect among different faiths, sexes and even between men and animals, Asoka established the offices of Superintendent of Religious Affairs (*Dharma-mahamatras*), of Women Apartments (*Striyadhyaksha-mahamatras*), and of Ranches (*Vraja bhaumikas*). He attached great value to women being in the workforce because their gentle disposition and affectionate nature could influence the generations to come.[8]

The last of the inscriptions which are dated at the end of his reign are engraved on Seven Pillar Edicts located in Delhi. For no known reasons, Asoka did not issue any major edicts for the next ten years up to his death. Also, we find no record giving information about his last days. He evaluates his achievements in the last (seventh) pillar as:

The advancement of *dhamma* amongst men has been achieved through two means, legislation and persuasion. But of these two, legislation has been less effective, and persuasion more so. I have proclaimed through legislation for instance that certain species of animals are not to be killed and such ideas. But men have increased their adherence to *dhamma* by being persuaded not to injure living beings and not to take life.

After a pious and glorious reign of about thirty-seven years, the noble king passed away from this sorrowful world in c.236 BC. The loss of India became the gain of history. The India of today has paid its tribute to the noble king by adopting the Lion Capital of one of his stone pillars as the symbol of its Independence.

The reasons for the Mauryan empire's disintegration within a short period of about fourteen decades may be many, but Asoka's nobility, kindness and pacifism may equally account for that. It is a virtue for the king to be noble, pious and caring, but it is equally important for the ruler to be iron-handed for his subjects and awe-inspiring for the enemies. Embracing non-violence, eschewing military conquests, asking his descendants not to resort to brutality in their conquests, and disbanding the army or keeping it in the state of inactivity for the remainder of his rule of twenty-nine years might have imparted weakness to the empire. The monarch himself declares with pride: *in consequence of the practice of morality on his part, the sound of bheri (war drum) had become the sound of morality*. However, the "moral ascendancy of Indian culture over a large part of the civilized world, which Asoka was mainly instrumental in bringing about, remained for centuries as a monument to her glory and has not altogether vanished even now after the lapse of more than two thousand years"[9]

In this context, the factors of caste and religion cannot be totally discounted. Social and family institutions, more than the spirit of nationhood, had played an overwhelmingly important part in the formation of the Hindu psyche. Therefore, when the signs of cracks started showing up, the national support for such a brilliant empire was not forthcoming. Embracing of Buddhism by Asoka and directing the state machinery for the spread of *Dharma* must have caused irritation to the brahmans, who were brought down from their lofty perch. Similarly, the warrior caste must have felt left over. Asoka's ideology proved to be a thin veneer, and, therefore, his high-mindedness was short-lived. The unwilling populace got rid of his ideology at the first opportune moment. An indirect opportunity to revert to earlier pattern was provided by the incursions of Greek Bactrians who had gradually conquered Afghanistan and parts of India, namely, Sindh, Punjab, Kathiawar and the western coast. They are said to have made inroads into Ayodhya, Panchala, Mathura and even as far as to the outskirts of the capital, Pataliputra, itself. The Greek invasions, which had created a chaos in Northern India, provided an opportunity to the brahman commander-in-chief Pushyamitra to overthrow the ruling king. When the Yavanas or the Greeks had invaded Pataliputra they were either repulsed by him or they themselves made a hasty retreat; this might have happened earlier in c.189-188 BC. This event had given him considerable popularity and self-confidence. From Banabhatta's *Harshacharita* we get the details that after the victory over the Greeks, Pushyamitra returned to Pataliputra. He paraded the entire army for review by the king, who had arranged a reception and festivities in honour of the Commander-in-Chief. It proved to be an opportune moment for carrying out his ambitious design. During the festivities the king was killed by an arrow.

Pushyamitra founded the Sunga dynasty in c.187 BC. It is believed that though he was a king yet he did not assume imperial titles; he took only the title of the *senani* (commander of the forces). This dynasty lasted for a little more than hundred years, having about ten kings. Only scant information is available about some of them and not at all about others. The boundaries of the kingdom had already shrunken, probably limited to Pataliputra, Vidisa, Ayodhya, Bhilsa and Narmada area and some parts of the Punjab. During his reign Vidarbha (Berar) was conquered and the Greeks were humiliated. It happened when the royal caravan led by Pushyamitra's grandson Vasumitra, taking the sacrificial horse to Pataliputra, was checked by the Yavanas (Greeks) at the south bank of the Sindhu river. The Greeks were then defeated. Pushyamitra is said to have twice performed the horse sacrifice demonstrating his double victory over the Greeks. Anyway, he finally drove away the Greeks beyond Sindh and rid his country of this menace. Pushyamitra's horse sacrifice signifies the end of the Buddhist rulers' ban on animal killings and the revival of brahman ascendancy. According to the Buddhist sources, he persecuted the Buddhists and destroyed their monasteries and temples. However, D. D. Kosambi is of the opinion that the Sunga's profession of Brahmanism had no effect on Buddhism, which is evident from the augmented Sunga structure at Sanchi.[10] According to the Puranas Pushyamitra ruled for thirty-six years. The Sunga dynasty met its end around 75 BC. The rule of the Sungas ended in Magadha but they probably continued to hold on in Central India. After them the Kanvayana dynasty was established. The jurisdiction of the Kanvas was now limited to Magadha as the Punjab was taken over by the Greeks. The Kanvas were later replaced by the Mitras.

1. H.G.Wells, *The Outline of History*, Ch. XXIV
2. Romila Thapar, *A History of India* ,volume one, Ch 4
3. UNESCO, *History of Mankind*, *The Ancient World*
4. Toyanbee, Arnold, *Mankind and Mother Earth*
5. Rock Edict XII, trans. R. Thapar, *Asoka and the Decline of the Mauryas*, p.255
6. Rock Edict VII, trans. R. Thapar, *Asoka and the Decline of the Mauryas*, p.265
7. Tinker, Hugh, *South Asia: A Short History*
8. *Bihar Trough the Ages*
9. Mookerji, Radha Kumud, *The History and Culture of the Indian People*, Vol. II, Ch V
10. *Ancient India: A History of its Culture and Civilization*, D.D. Kosambi

13
LIFE UNDER THE MAURYAS

During the rule of the Mauryas and their successors, intellectualism achieved a high degree of excellence. Under the patronage of the monarchs, discussions on literature, philosophy and science (*Shastrakara Pariksha*) were held at the capital Pataliputra in which celebrated intellectuals of the time participated. We find the mention in Patanjali's works of the assembly of learned men called, Chandragupta Maurya Sabha and the Pushyamitra Sunga Sabha, corroborated by Megasthenes that the Brahmanas were employed by kings specially for the Great Synod where, at the beginning of the new year, all the philosophers are gathered together. Any philosopher who might have committed any useful suggestion to writing, or observed any means of improving crops and cattle, or for promoting public interest, declared it publicly.[1] Mauryan monarchs also retained a patriarchal simplicity, not being encased in the structure of an imperial bureaucracy.[2] Kautilya, the architect of Mauryan administration, declared: *'In the happiness of his subjects lies his happiness, in their welfare his welfare; whatever pleases himself he shall not consider as his good but whatever pleases his subjects he shall consider as good.'....'For a king, his vrata (religious vow) is constant activity in the cause of his people (utthanam); his best religious ceremony is the work of administration (karyanusasanam); his highest charity (dakshina) is equality of treatment meted to all.'*[3] Public opinion was not to be disregarded. Kings were accessible to the public. On occasions of religious and social festivities, alms were generously distributed en-route the king's processions to the needy without discrimination.

One of the aims of the founder of the Mauryan dynasty was to restore and to put new vigour in the sacred values of Aryan culture. As a result the Brahmanas started to emerge in this period as the fountainhead of authority on religious and social aspects of life. Vedic Samhitas, Brahmanas, Upanishads, Kalpa-Sutras, and Grihya-Sutras were composed during this period.[4] The Puranas were produced, and the Ramayana and the Mahabharata were revised and written in the present form during the Mauryan period.

The Yavanas and other foreigners visited the country in such a large number that in the administration of Chandragupta Maurya a special department was created which oversaw their arrival, stay, and departure. One of Asoka's governors was a Greek. On the one hand, the foreign invading bands of Greeks and Parthians were absorbed in the Indian society, and on the other, this neo-Hinduism was carried to remote lands with proselytizing and missionary zeal even beyond the seas. Hinduism did no more lose its purity by crossing the 'black water'

Slavery was not a full-fledged institution. Slave markets did not exist in India. Megasthenes, well aware of the existing slave markets in Greece, records in that spirit : *All Indians are free and not one of them is a slave...the Indians do not even use aliens as slaves and much less a countryman of their own*. Yet slavery was seen in the form of domestic slaves, or those persons who sold themselves in order to escape hunger, or those who were unable to pay debts. However, use of free labour by the state was in practice. In this regard, Sudras, criminals and prisoners of war were forced to work for developing waste lands for agriculture, for bringing new areas for settlements, and for working in the state-owned mines.

Before the political unification and stability was brought by the Guptas in early fourth century AD, Buddhism and Jainism had received a very big boost in the changing political scenes of the next four hundred years mainly because of two reasons. First, the new comers like the Greeks, the Shakas (Scythians) Parthians, and the Kushans were to be Indianized and assimilated in the local society. Their assimilation in Hinduism was not possible because of the fact that it required them to belong to one caste or the other, but caste was determined at birth and so they were caste-less. Thus conversion to Buddhism became the most convenient tool for their assimilation. In view of the political clout and power of the foreign race, however, the brahman orthodoxy later had also to adjust their thinking. For winning them to their fold they adopted the strategy of granting them kshatriya status. Brahmanism itself witnessed change from within. By accepting the Buddha as the latest of the nine incarnations of Vishnu it tried to embrace Buddhism in its fold. At least, Buddhism ceased to be a challenging force against Brahmanism. Secondly, with the rising urbanization, trade and crafts, this period saw the growth of a prosperous merchant class and their guilds. They generously supported religious institutions. Their donations were directed towards building stupas, maintaining caves and carving religious sculptures.

This type of charitable activity was not limited, however, to the merchant community only. Even rulers were not lacking in such charitable activities. An order of a Saka ruler on cave inscriptions at Nasik records the endowment to a temple for which large sum of money was invested with a guild of weavers. The interest from this investment was to be spent on the upkeep of the temple.

"In the year 42, in the month of Vesakha, Ushavadatta son of Dinika and son-in-law of king Nahapana, the Kshaharata Kshatrapa, has bestowed this cave on the Sangha generally; he has also given a perpetual endowment, three thousand - 3,000 *kahapanas* which, for the members of the Sangha of any sect and any origin dwelling in this cave, will serve as cloth money and money for outside life; and those *kahapanas* have been invested in guilds dwelling in Govardhana - 2,000 in a weavers guild, interest one *pratika* (monthly) for the hundred and 1,000 in another weavers guild, interest 3/4 of a *padika* (monthly) for the hundred, and those kahapanas are not to be repaid, their interest only to be enjoyed. Out of them, the two thousand, 2,000 at one *pratika* per cent are the cloth money; out of them to every one of the twenty monks who keep the *vassa* (the rainy season when monks remained at the monastery) in my cave, a cloth money of twelve *kahapanas*. As to the thousand which has been invested at an interest of 3/4 of a *pratika* per cent, out of them the money for Kushana. And at the village of Chinkalapandra in the Kapura district have been given eight thousand - 8,000 - stems of coconut trees, and all this has been proclaimed and registered at the town hall, at the record office, according to custom....".[5]

1. *Bihar Through the Ages*
2. Bowle, John (ed.), *The Concise Encyclopaedia of World History*
3 *A Comprehensive History of India*, Edited by K. A. Nilakanta Sastri. (Ch. I)
4. *Bihar Through the Ages*
5. Quoted in *A History of India*, Vol One, Romila Thapar

14
YAVANAS AND KUSHANS

The word Yavana was synonymous of *mlechchha* or foreigner, and was derived from the old Persian word Yauna, or Yunan of modern days. Even Asoka's records refer them as his subjects. In his Thirteen Rock-edict it is mentioned that there were no Brahmans and Sramanas in the Yona country. The Buddhist conical work Majjhimanikaya also mentions that in the land of the Yonas there existed only two varnas of Arya and Dasa and not the four varnas as in other parts of India. Patanjali's Mahabhashya and Manu-samhita speak of the Greeks of Bactria and Afghanistan who had established themselves in India early in the second century BC. Their most famous king was Menander. Menander was born in the village of Kalasi-grama in Alasanda (Alexandria near Kabul). His capital was at Sakala, or modern Sialkot in the Punjab. It is believed that he ruled in the middle of the second century BC. The famous Buddhist text Milindapanha (Questions of Milinda) describes how Menander's intelligent queries on metaphysics and philosophy were answered to his satisfaction by the scholarly monk Nagasena in an assembly in which Menander was accompanied by 500 Yavana courtiers. Menander became not only the follower of Buddhism but an ardent patron and scholar of this religion. As such he has found a permanent place in the Buddhist tradition. He was noted for his justice. He was so popular with his subjects that upon his death, which occurred in a camp, many cities vied for his ashes. Plutarch, who flourished two centuries after Menander, writes that 'the cities of his realm contended for the honour of preserving his ashes and agreed on a division among themselves, in order that the memory of his reign should not be lost.' Beside Menander, a mention about another Indo-Greek king, named Amtalikita (Antialcidas, as known from coins)) of Taxila, is found in an epigraphic record found at Besnagar. He had sent his ambassador, Heliodorus, to the court of Rajan Kautsiputra Bhaghabhadra in his 14th regal year. Heliodorus had become a Bhagvata (a devotee of Vasudeva or Vishnu), and he erected a Garuda column in honour of Krishna Vasudeva.

From the Indian literary and epigraphic texts we find information about the Sakas (Scythians) and the Pahalvas (Parthians) who came to India in the late first century BC and settled around the Sindhu river valley. The Scythians lived in the plains of Jaxartes or Syr Darya in Turkestan. They were forced to leave their place and move first to Iran and then to India by the push of Yueh-chi (the later Kushans of India). Gradually, the Yavanas, the Sakas and the Parthians adopted the Indian ways of life, religious beliefs, and names, and were ultimately absorbed in the Indian population. They were assigned the caste of aniravasita or clean Sudra and degraded kshatriya

In the middle of the first century we find an important epoch in Indian history as the Kushans of Yueh-chi race were able to establish another great empire after the Mauryas. The Yueh-chis had displaced the Scythians but their occupation of the Saka country (Seistan) had been temporary. The son of the slain Saka king soon uprooted them from that area. The Yueh-chi tribe then moved further west and south of Oxus (Amu Darya) and settled in Bactria. A branch of this tribe, called Kushana, settled in north-western India under Kujula Kadphises. Kujula's successor, Wema Kadphises, conquered the interior of India and established his capital of at Purushapura (modern Peshawar). With their ascendancy the corridor of power was shifted from Magadha to the north western India. According to Chinese account Wema or Kadphises II was the first Kushan king to extend his rule over Tien-tchou or India proper around the beginning of the first century AD. Saivism gained considerable strength and became a real force during the Kushana period. Wema Kadphises was probably initiated into Saivism in Central Asia before he came to India. He called himself *Mahesvara,* or devotee of Siva. Kushana kings minted their coins with the images of Siva and his bull, Nandi. Wema Kadphises issued gold coins according to the Roman weight-standard. On the reverse of some of his coins is found a representation of Siva with two arms with combined trident and battle-axe in the right hand. In Kharoshti the following words are inscribed on the coins: *maharajasa rajadirajasa sarva-loga mahisvara Wima Kathphisasa tratrasa* (Wima Kathphisa the great king, the king of kings, the lord of the whole world, the Mahisvara, the Savior). It indicates that he was a devotee of Siva.

Their most famous ruler was Kanishka (AD 78-101) , who accepted Buddhism as his religion. He convened the Fourth Buddhist Council to discuss matters pertaining to Buddhist theology and doctrine. and sent Buddhist missions to central Asia and China. The

Chinese say that Kia-ni Ch'a (Kanishka) conquered Eastern India and demanded large indemnity, probably 900,000 pieces of gold, from the king of Pataliputra. Unable to collect such a huge material wealth, Kanishka agreed to content himself with the spiritual: he took away the famous intellectual of the time Ashvaghosha and the Buddha's bowl with him. Tibetan accounts confirm to the fact that the king of Yue-chi invaded Magadha and took the Buddha's bowl as the prized booty. This period also saw the flourishing of art, literature and religion. Kanishka built a very large Buddhist monastery at Peshawar. Finding the teachings of various schools of Buddhism contradictory and confusing, Kanishka convened the Grand Buddhist Council at Kundalavana Vihara in Kashmir, or, according to some other accounts, at Gandhara or Jalandhara. It was presided by Vasumitra, with Ashvaghosha as the vice-president. According to Heuan Tsang 500 Buddhist elders and scholars had been summoned from all parts of his empire to this assembly. He directed the learned delegates to have all the teachings and canons systematized and codified according to the respective schools. A select body of the learned gathering was assigned the task of collecting the variant texts and to write expository commentaries on them. In this process, the Council members displayed an extraordinary acquaintance not only with Buddhist learning of various kinds, but also with the different branches of Brahmanical learning.

There is no doubt that Kanishka was a Buddhist but he was also respectful toward other religions. This is amply demonstrated by his coins which represent diverse deities: Greek (sun-god Helios and moon-goddess Selene); Sumerian/Elamite (mother-goddess Nana, Nanio or Nana-shao—Bibi Nani of Baluchistan and Naina Devi of the Kullu valley); Persian (wnid-god Vado, fire-god Athsho or Atash, moon-god Mao, and sun-god Mihir or Mitra); and Indian (Siva and Buddha).[1] Such a diversity either reflected the religious eclecticism of the monarch or represented the prevalent religions in Kansihka's dominion. But it definitely demonstrates a liberal and tolerant attitude towards those who did not follow the king's religion. Kanishka was succeeded by Vaisihka, who was followed by Huvishka in c. AD 28. The reverse of his coins too depict deities belonging to different pantheons. On some seals he is depicted standing in a suppliant pose before Vishnu and Siva, and in others before the Sumerian goddess Nana. What a serene mingling or coexistence of religious beliefs during the Kushana period! Kadphises I, the first Kushana king, was a Buddhist; his son Kadphises II was a Saivite; Kanishka, the founder of the Kushana Empire was a devout Buddhist; and his son or successor was a Bhagavata.[2] The Kushan rule from Kanishka to Huvishka is estimated to have lasted for about 60 years from c. 80 A.D to 140 AD.

1. D.C. Sircar, , *The History and Culture of the Indian People,* Vol. II, Ch IX; *A Comprehensive History of India*, Ed. K.A.Nilakanta Sastri, Vol II, Ch. VIII
2. D.C. Sircar, , *The History and Culture of the Indian People,* Vol. II, Ch IX; *A Comprehensive History of India*, edited by K. A. Nilakanta Sastri, ChVIII

15
GOLDEN AGE

In 320 AD it was again a courageous *Samrat* from Magadha who established the second greatest empire of Hindu India. He was the namesake of the founder of the Maurya dynasty: Chandra Gupta I (320-350). A succession of brilliant Gupta monarchs gave the country peace and prosperity. This period, when Hindu civilization attained its full maturity, ranks as a major era in the history of the world's culture.[1] The monarch, as glorified by Kalidasa, the shining star of drama and literature, was an ideal king who punished only to maintain law and order, and married only for the sake of progeny. He derived material gain and pleasure only through practicing religious laws.[2] The Guptas were devout followers of the Brahmanical religion, though several inscriptions of the time attest to the Buddhist leanings of some of them. They kept up the tradition of religious tolerance of the Mauryas and the Kushans. They appointed members of other religious faiths as high officials. The Buddhists were among the advisers of all the Gupta monarchs, who ignored caste principles and xenophobic sentiment by a policy of intermarriage with pre-Aryan clan families and the introduction of Kushan, Scythian and Greek women into their houselolds.[3]

A Chinese text records that king Meghavarna of Lanka had sent a mission to the court of Samudra Gupta (c.350-380) with rich presents, seeking permission to build a monastery for the pilgrims from that country. The permission was granted and the Simhali king built a grand monastery at Bodh Gaya. The mention in the Buddhist records of appointing the Buddhist scholar Vasubandhu as a minister by a Gupta king in the fourth century is believed to be the act of Samudra Gupta.

The reign of Chandra Gupta II (380-415) saw the revival of intellectual brilliance, which earned the title for the Gupta era once again as the 'Golden Age'. Arts, science and literature flourished. His court was adorned by *Nav Ratans*, one of them was Kalidasa. Some information of his reign is found in the accounts of the Chinese traveler, Fa-hien, who lived in India from 400 to 411. He does not write about the political situation prevailing at that time, not even mentioning the name of the Emperor even once in his accounts; nevertheless, he gives a detailed account of the people and the social condition, reflecting the peace and prosperity of the time. Fa-hien describes the Government as just and beneficent. The roads were well maintained. Brigandage was rare. Taxes were high. Capital punishment was not practiced. He writes about the heartland of Chandra Gupta II's kingdom as follows: "*The people are numerous and happy; they have not to register their households, or to attend to any magistrates and their rules; only those who cultivate the royal land have to pay the gain from it. If they want to go , they go; if they want to stay, they stay. The king governs without decapitation or corporal punishments.*" When the nations of Western Europe were sinking into a state of semi-barbarism, India was witnessing a high level of tolerance, social contentment, prosperity, and intellectual activity. The reign of Chandra Gupta II was worthy of comparison with Athens' Golden Age in the times of Pericles.[4]

The next king, Kumara Gupta I (c.415-455) was a follower of the Brahmanical religion like his predecessors, but his reign specially demonstrated a spirit of religious tolerance. Inscriptions registering endowments for the holy places of Brahmanism, Buddhism and Jainism alike are found in abundance throughout his empire. Gold coins were donated to Buddhist monasteries to be invested, and the interests accruing from such investments were used as a source of revenue for the maintenance of monks and monasteries. But a more secure source of sustenance was land grants or assignment of revenue of a whole village for Brahmans and Hindu temples. Several such grants inscribed on copper plates were made during the reign of Kumara Gupta I. Five sets of copper plates, from 443 to 449 AD, were found in Bengal alone.[5] Another king, Narasimha Gupta Baladitya (c.496-515) was an ardent follower of Buddhism. He saved this religion from the menace of the Huns who were out to destroy it.

The Brahmanical religion, which had witnessed new developments during the Mauryan period continued its growth during the Guptas. In the earlier period, Buddhism and Jainism had sprung up with such force that they swept away the masses as well as the monarchs. But they proved no match to the intellectual force, foresight and maneuverings of the brahman led Vedic religion, which staged a comeback in the Gupta period. The Guptas used the title of *Pramabhgvata* and inscribed it on their coins. "The Gupta emperors upheld *Dharma* in all its aspects and, in consequence, its content was enriched and its scope enlarged. An overarching law of life, though it existed from Vedic times, it received under them the form which in the main it still retains. They drew their inspiration from it, and in so doing carried the people with them. Historical continuity and conscious unity were preserved by a faith in the Vedas as the source of all knowledge and aspiration. Within the framework of this faith, myths, traditions and rituals, language and literature, the canons of conduct, ideals and modes of life, became integrating agencies. Through the *Puranas*, which sang of sacred legends, of rivers, mountains, cities, of royal houses, and of semi-divine heroes and sages, the past remained a glorious heritage to inspire the future with fresh vigour."[6] "Finally this was the age made memorable to three hundred million Hindus by the fact that it witnessed the evolution of that form of Brahmanical religion which they follow today. It saw the final development of the two great epics, the *Ramayana* and the *Mahabharata*, and the phenomenal growth of the two religious cults, Vaishnavism and Saivism, at the cost of heterodox religious creeds like Buddhism and Jainism. The vast Puranic literature which originated, or at least took definite shape, during this period, completed the break from the Vedic Age and set on a solid foundation what is now commonly known as Hinduism, the culmination of a religious movement which had behind it the rich heritage of the diverse peoples of India."[7] For Indian Civilization, this was an era of immense significance. Never before, or since, Brahmanic orthodoxy was so much consolidated or the Hindu culture so much enriched.[8]

The new form of Brahmanical religion which developed in this age, remained as it is today by the name of Hinduism. It was firmly founded on the Puranas, which became the popular religious literature replacing the old Vedic Samhitas and Brahmanas. It elaborated new religious ideas and prescribed new rituals and practices. The old Vedic pantheon receded in the background and the ritual of sacrificial offerings to Vedic gods was replaced by ceremonial worship of Brahmanical deities. A shift from the abstract to the concrete took place in the religion. It necessitated creation of images for worshipping and practicing rituals and ceremonies. Image worship and idol carving gave rise to the necessity of erecting elaborate temples. The growth and development of temples, built with separate stone blocks, ushered in a new age of architecture. With the continued devotion and fervor attached to them, Vaishnavism and Saivism remained the most prominent aspects of Hinduism. A new pantheon of five gods, Panchayatan, consisting of Vishnu, Siva, Surya, Durga and Ganesa was evolved. Lakshmi or Sri came to be conceived as the wife of Vishnu. She was given special importance by the Gupta emperors by representing her on their coins.

The most famous institution of learning that flourished in this period was the Buddhist University of Nalanda. Kumara Gupta II (c.467-475) may be identified with Huan Tsang's Sakraditya, who laid the foundation of the Nalanda monastery. 'The intellectual greatness which characterized the Gupta Age was typified in the University of Nalanda.' Students from all parts of India as well as from far away lands, specially from Tibet, China and Korea attended this University. Apart from the Buddhist and Hindu religious literature, such subjects as Pali, Sanskrit, grammar, metaphysics, philosophy, logic, art, medicine and astronomy were taught. The University, which had the strength of about five thousands students and hundreds of teachers, maintained its teaching faculty and dormitories in two or three-story buildings. It contained a huge library which occupied three buildings. The patronage and generous endowments of the Gupta emperors to this university enabled it to flourish and to attain an international stature.

However, the lot of sudras did not improve during the Gupta period too. In point of fact, the brahman's purity got strengthened. Fa Hsien mentions that the *chandalas* (the lowest-caste sudras [handler of dead animals], butchers and scavengers) were forced to live in ghettos away from regular living quarters. If they intended to visit such places they had to announce their approach by banging wooden clapper. And, if an outcaste passed at a close range of an unaware dvija, the latter had to perform ablution or to bathe to purify himself. This was in accordance with the regulations laid down in legal codes.

Buddhism, which was deemed as the most formidable challenge to Hinduism, acquired the rituals and religious practices of its rival so much so that they seemed to be a sect of Hinduism. Jainism did not undergo any major change and remained a sect of the merchant community. The second Jain Council was held in Valabhi in the sixth century. It formulated canons of Jainism which are followed even today. As such it may also be considered as the final stage of Jainism's perfection.

The Gupta period was the age of integration and freedom from foreign domination for India. It happened in the same manner as when the Mauryas had liberated the country in the fourth century BC from the Persian and Greek domination. The Guptas drove away the Huns and made the Kushans of the North-West India their subordinates. India, which was in the state of fragmentation for more than three hundred years, was once again united. One writ issued from Pataliputra ran from the Bay of Bengal to the Arabian Sea, and even across the Hindu Kush to parts of Balkh.

1 Burns Edward McNall & Philip Lee Ralph, *World Civilization*
2 John A. Carraty & Peter Gay (ed.), *The Columbia History of the World*
3 *India: A Concise History*, Ch. Four, Francis Watson
4 Burns Edward Mcnall & Philip Lee Ralph, *World Civilization*
5 *A History of India*, Hermann Kulke & Dietmar Rothermund Ch. 2
6 *The History and Culture of the Indian People*, Vol. III Foreword by K.M.Munshi
7 R.C.Majumdar, *The History and Culture of the Indian People*, Vol. III , Preface
8 John A. Carraty & Peter Gay (ed.), *The Columbia History of the World*

16
INVASION OF THE HUNS

The Huns, a descendant of the dreaded Hsing-Nu tribe from the eastern extremity of the Eurasian steppe had erupted in a massive migration in all directions around the end of the third century. In the beginning of the fourth century they demolished the great West Chin dynasty of China. Around 375, one of their branches took a westerly route, crossed the Volga and settled down in a place which took its name from them—Hun-gary. Led by Attila, the Hun, they made an all-out assault on the West Roman empire in 451, but were defeated after entering Gaul by the allied force of Romans, Visigoths, Burgundians and Franks.

In the beginning of the fifth century, a branch of the Huns, Ephthalites or the White Huns, had occupied the Oxus Valley. They raided the Persian Empire and even reached Tehran in AD 427, but were defeated by the Sassanid emperor Bahram V. The Huns captured the entire territory between Persia and Khotan and made Bamiyan in modern Afghanistan their capital. During the closing years of the reign of Kumara Gupta I, the first wave of the Huns had attacked the kingdom in the plains of Punjab. They were an avowed enemy of Buddhism and they tore down innumerable Buddhist shrines and sculptures. They were a real menace to the empire, as the Bhitari pillar inscription refers many times to the 'ruined fortunes of the family' which were restored by Skanda Gupta (c.455-467) when he was a prince. He inflicted a crushing defeat on the Huns. They turned once again towards Persia. This time the table was turned and the Sassanid monarch, Yazdigard, suffered a crushing defeat at the hands of the Huns in AD 454. The Huns were now again threatening India by pouring down through the Hindu Kush passes. They occupied Gandhara, and the region north of the Ganga as the Bhitari Inscription refers 'to the roaring of the Ganga in connection with Skanda Gupta's war against the Hunas' and about his victory over them, although they do not mention about the dates. It means that the Huns came very near to the heartland of the Empire, and that the war was fought probably on the northern bank of the Ganga. Skanda Gupta dealt such a severe blow to them that the Huns never ventured again to look towards his kingdom during his life time. With this feat of exemplary bravery, Skanda Gupta earned for himself a place in the history as the savior of India. The significance of this achievement can only be gauged in the light of the ferocity and swiftness with which the Huns had overwhelmed Europe and Asia and brought about the downfall of the mighty Roman Empire. They had no homes, and knew of no codes of ethics, morals and moderation. Their object of life seemed to wreck devastation anywhere they went, killing and burning whatever came in their way. They 'rode their horses awake and asleep' and filled terror in the hearts of those who heard their fierce yells. Such an adversary they were, whom Skanda Gupta had humbled. With the banishment of these vicious hordes from the boundaries of India the grateful people heaved a sigh of relief. Songs in his praise were sung by all, men and women, old and young.[1]

The death of the emperor Buddha Gupta (c.475-496) opened the gates once again for the Huna's advance. During the time of his successor, and younger brother, Narasimha Gupta Baladitya (c.496-515), they proved to be a grave menace under the strong leadership of Toramana and his son Mihirakula. Toramana, who had settled in Afghanistan, swooped over the North-Western India, destroyed the Kushan power, and captured East Malwa. Now was the time to test the real power of the Guptas. In a clever move, Narasimha Gupta dashed to Valabhi and consecrated the ruler Drona Simha as the Maharaja while himself remaining Mahrajadhiraja. In this way he raised his own stature and secured the allegiance of Valabhi kingdom on the western frontier of the Hun kingdom. But all this was of no avail. Toramana could not be checked. He laid waste even the heartland of the empire, including Magadha; and overrunning it even reached Gauda. The vassal ruler of Eran in Madhya Pradesh switched his loyalty from the Gupta emperor to *'Maharajadhiraja'* Toramana. Baladitya became a vassal of Toramana and agreed to pay him tribute. Toramana nominated his son Mihirakula as his successor. Mihirakula was a tyrant and a person of violent disposition, who came to power after the death of Toramana in 515. He added Kashmir and the western half of the Ganga basin to the Hun domain. It appeared that he had made it his mission to exterminate Buddhism altogether, for it was Kashmir, which had long nursed the Buddhist tradition, that was to suffer the extremities of his vandalism and sadism.

Narasimha Gupta made peace with Mihirakula and continued to pay tribute to him, and thus resumed his authority once again in Magadha around AD 514-515. When Mihirakula started persecuting the Buddhists, Narasimha Gupta, being a follower of Buddhism, showed resentment. Hiuen Tsang tells the story how Baladitya finally triumphed over Mihrakula: "Balditya-raja, king of Magadha, profoundly honoured the law of Buddha. When he heard of the cruel persecution and atrocities of Mihirakula he strictly guarded the frontiers of his kingdom and refused to pay tribute. When Mihirakula invaded his dominions, Baladitya took refuge with his army in an island. Mihirakula left the main part of his army in charge of his younger brother, embarked on boats and landed with a part of his troops on the island. He was, however, ambushed by the troops of Baladitya in a narrow pass and was taken prisoner. Baladitya resolved to execute Mihirakula, but released him on the intercession of his mother."[2] Mihirukula promised never to set foot again on Baladitya's territory. Defeated by king Yashodharman of Malwa, Mihirakula withdrew to Kashmir, where he died in AD 542. Though the Huns were not able to make a deep impact on the Indian politics, yet they were able to leave their imprint on the society. They caused massive migration of population from Rajhasthan, Gandhara and Kashmir to the eastern parts of the country. They also generated a racial fusion when majority of them opted to stay back. They merged with the local population and eventually sprang up as new tribes of the Gurjaras of West India, the Rajputs of Rajasthan and the Jats of the Punjab and Uttar Pradesh.

Fighting the Hun menace had cost the government of Magadha heavily in terms of prestige, and also finance, which is evident from the debased gold coins of Baladitya. But, at a cost, he had saved the country and the Buddhist religion. After his success over the Huns, Baladitya built a monastery and a magnificent temple in Nalanda. He called a congregation of Buddhist priests both from inside and outside the country. Later, he declared himself a *bhikshu,* and retired to Nalanda where he died.

1. *The History and Culture of the Indian People*, Vol. III, Foreword and Ch. III
2. *The History and Culture of the Indian People*, Vol. III, Ch V

17
BUDDHISM'S LAST FLICKER

With the downfall of the Imperial Guptas around the middle of the sixth century, the empire disintegrated. The Golden Age of India vanished into history. A number of smaller states, like Maukharis, Maitrakas, and Gaudas sprang up from the embers of the Gupta empire. Around the Middle of the seventh century another powerful kingdom of the Vardhanas arose in Northern India. It gained prominence at the time of king Harsha Vardhana, who came to the throne in 606 and ruled for forty-one years from Kanauj. He united almost the whole of North India under his empire, and extended his kingdom up to Bihar and Orissa, which he conquered in 641 and 643, respectively. This feat gave northern India a spell of peace but even then Harsha's empire remained only a simulacrum of the Gupta Empire.[1] Harsha Vardhana was converted to Buddhism by Hsuan Tsang, the Master of the Law.[2] Though a staunch follower of Buddhism, much like Asoka, he did not abandon the deities of his old days, like Aditya, the Sun-god, reflecting Persian influence transmitted by the Kushans. While making land grants to brahmans Harsha styled himself "High Follower of Siva" (*parama-mahesvara*). He is famous for his charity and patronage of scholarship. Every five years he organized charity festivals at the confluence of Ganga and Yamuna in Paryag where he lavishly distributed cash and other necessities to the needy, ascetics, brahmans and Buddhists. It is reported that sometimes in the end he even gave his clothes in charity. He fed thousands of such people daily from his kitchens. There is an inscription of 632 AD concerning a land grant which Harsha gave to two brahmans at Madhuban, north of Varanasi.[3] Trying to outdo the earlier Gupta emperors in support of the University of Nalanda, Harsha granted the revenues of a hundred villages to this reputed institution of learning which was still attracting students and scholars from far and wide.

Harsha's envoy to the Chinese court was a brahman. In return, Tai Tsung, the Chinese emperor, dispatched a mission in AD 643. In the meanwhile a conspiracy against Harsha was uncovered. Five hundred brahmans were arrested but Harsha pardoned them all except the leader. But in 647, in another attempt on his life, Harsha was assassinated at the instance of a coterie of disgruntled brahmans. The same year the Chinese emperor sent another mission to Harsha's court, which arrived just after Harsha's death. The mission was attacked. Its members were forced to flee to Nepal which, at that time, was under the suzerainty of Tibet. The king of Tibet, Srong-tan Gampo sent a punitive expedition to Kanauj. The usurper was captured and carried off to China. However this became the occasion when the Indian civilization captivated Tibet. This led to the development of the script of the Tibetan language in Indian style. This script, not the Chinese characters, was then employed for translating Sanskrit texts of the Mahayana Buddhist scriptures into Tibetan, and these translations anchored Tibet to India culturally. Thenceforward, Chinese cultural influence, though never absent in Tibet, was never paramount there.[4]

During Harsha Vardhana's time, the ruler of Bengal, Nagendragupta Sasanka, a staunch Sivaite had shown intolerance towards Buddhism. According to Hiuen Tsang, while travelling in Magadha (637-638 AD) in the year of the death of Sasanka, he noted that Sasanka had cut down the Bodhi tree at Gaya and removed an image of Buddha from a neighbouring temple. Other stories of persecution of Buddhism by Sasanka were also circulating. Harsha repaired the damage, but following his death, the Nalanda monastery itself was vandalized, most probably by Hindu bands. Buddhism did not prosper after the general disorder which followed Harsha's death. In the eighth century, the Pala rulers of Bengal and Magadha restored Nalanda to its former glory. They also built a number of *viharas* in the village of Odantapuri (present city of Bihar where Nalanda is situated; these *viharas* changed the name of the village into Bihar, which in turn, gave the name to the province of Bihar). By this time Buddhism had become practically extinct in the rest of the country. The Pala Kingdom proved to be the last stronghold of Buddhism, which was given its *coup de grace* in India when Bengal was conquered by Ghori Muslim invaders in 1199 or in 1202. Here the Buddhist monasteries were singled out for destruction; yet Buddhism in India might perhaps have survived even this attack if, in India, it had not been already under assault and in decline for the past six or seven centuries.[5] Jainism's fortunes were the inverse of Buddhism's. Jainism never found its way into either East or South-East Asia. On the other hand, Jainism never became extinct in India itself, though in India it never became more than a minoritarian sect.

1. Toyanbee, Arnold, *Mankind and Mother Earth*, Ch. 46

2. Apart from Harsha Vardhana, there were other families of chiefs and kings whose members followed different religious persuasions, and who showed reverence and respect for religion of others. We find, for example, adherents of different religious sects among the Parivrajakas of the Bundelkhand and Maitrakas, governors of Valabhi, under the Imperial Guptas.

3. Buhler, G., *Madhuban Copper-plates of Harsha, Epigraphia Indica,* Vol. I, pp. 67-75. See *A History of India*, Ch. 3, Hermann Kulke & Dietmar Rothermund

4. Toyanbee, Arnold, *Mankind and Mother Earth*, Ch. 46

5. Toyanbee, Arnold, *Mankind and Mother Earth*, Ch. 58

18
BHAKTI, THE LOVE OF GOD

It was the time when a popular movement of Bhakti erupted on the Indian scene. It eventually changed the character of popular Hinduism throughout the country. This time the philosophical lead was taken not by the north but by the south. The Bhakti movement reflected popular Tamil reaction to Brahmanic Aryanization. It rejected the Brahman orthodoxy and their scholarship and ritual sacrifices in which low caste people were not allowed to participate. Disregarding the special position of the brahmanized Sanskrit, their teaching was entirely in local vernacular language. The Bhakti movement down played the caste system itself. Its followers came generally from artisan and less prosperous cultivator classes. It upgraded the status of women who were encouraged to join the gatherings. Strangely, some brahmans also joined this movement.

Bhakti had its beginning in the sixth century AD in Tamil Nadu. Its main focus was not only the love of god but a childlike devotion to him. According to them, whosoever was the god, whether Vishnu or Shiva, he was not an awe inspiring deity. He was not remotely placed from the individual but a close friend, "fragrant and beautiful", an all-forgiving god, and an embodiment of love. Despite the myriad of shortcomings in human beings he loved them. He wanted man not only to love god but also all living beings. The expression of boundless devotion and worship was made through singing of religious hymns in ecstatic adoration. Tamil poet-saints, both Saivite or Vaishnavite, wrote in Tamil, the language of the common man, about their fervent devotion to god and of their adoration and love for his spirit and form. The devotees sang with the passion of intoxicated lovers. Over a period of about three hundred years, from the 7th to the 10th century, as many as seventy-five saints resorted to this unconventional mode of preaching. These poets of Tamilnad added new vitality to Hinduism that would soon sweep north. While this process led to the Aryanization of the South, the Dravidian culture and beliefs made inroads into the North which developed into a new mixture of Hinduism. There appeared several Bhakti cults, including the extremely popular Radha-Krishna and Ram-Sita cults.

Between the eighth and eleventh century two great teachers and philosophers were born in India, who gave shape to a philosophical system which was evolved after constant debates with Buddhists and Jains in what has been termed a 'Brahmin counter-reformation'. They left a profound effect on the development of Hinduism. Those prominent seers were Sankara and Ramanuja. While debating the same question they contradicted each other but the synthesis of their thoughts was helpful in the evolution of Hinduism which is witnessed today. Sankara (c. 780-820) was a native of Kerala. Ramanuja (c. 1028-1137) came from the Tamil country. Both of them were concerned with the philosophical issues of nature of the Ultimate Reality or Truth, and its relationship with human being.

It is said that Sankara became an ascetic at the age of eight. He was writing religious commentaries at twelve. Sensing a threat to his religion from Buddhism he decided to revitalize it. He was a monist, who preached the philosophy of one absolute Reality or non-duality (*kevala-advaita*). He advocated that human being is identical with the Creator, and in this way the man's soul (*atman*) is intrinsically tied up with that cosmic spirit (*Brahmana*). This world is an illusion (*maya*), but man considers it as real; hence his soul attaches itself with this maya and entangles itself in the cycle of rebirths (*samsara*). His actions restrain him from merging in the divine reality. It is so because of his ignorance (*avidya*). The gulf between the two could be bridged by right knowledge, by subduing the five senses with the help of ascetic practices, and by devotion and worship of the Supreme God (*Ishvara*). Only then he would achieve freedom from the chain of rebirths (*moksa*). As there is one Ultimate reality, according to Shankara, there is no room for a personal god or his personal devotee. The main thrust of the Buddhist philosophy being the efforts on man's part to achieve salvation by freeing oneself from the cycle of rebirths, Sankara's teaching being on the same lines led to a weakening of Buddhism. The people no more needed to attach themselves to the Buddhist philosophy as its ideas were infused in their own religion. It gave a new lease of life to orthodox Brahmanism. Later, Sankara came to be known as Sankaracharya (Sankar, the Mentor). He founded four *maths* or abbeys in different parts of the subcontinent, which soon sprouted branches and achieved phenomenal success in winning back converts from Buddhism.

Several other schools of Vedanta later gave up Sankara's philosophy of strict monism. The most popular of them was that of Ramanuja. The head priest of the Vishnu temple of Srirangam, rejected the thesis of Sankara that the universe was an illusion, and propounded the philosophy of *vishishthadvaita*, a "qualified or modified monism." He preached that despite being a part of the Cosmic Spirit, the soul has an identity of its own, and its unity with that Spirit could not be achieved through the individual's own efforts of right knowledge and ascetic practices but by the grace of the god Vishnu himself. Irrespective of the quality of one's *karma*, only the all-loving and all-forgiving god could accept his union with a true devotee. He viewed Brahmana as the divine being; the world and humanity constituting real parts of his infinitely perfect body. Ramanuja stressed the importance of bhakti or intense devotion to god as the surest path to *muksha*.

At that time Buddhism too was facing decadence. It was losing not only its identity but the force of its idealism. While residing at the Nalanda monastery, for instance, the Chinese scholar Hsuan Tsang was provided with the services of one servant and one brahman. For his conveyance needs an elephant was placed at his disposal. All these negated the monastic life of a Buddhist monk or religious scholar. Even students had not to go out for begging of alms to sustain themselves, which is a basic requirement or teaching of Buddhism, for they were provided with food and clothing by the monastery itself. Given to ease of life, young monks were quick to renounce their monastic vows in order to get married. Again, several Hindu deities like Vishnu, Siva and Ganesha found their way into the Mahyana pantheon.

19
ENTER ISLAM

In the sixth century, a new religion by the name of Islam was born in the Arabian peninsula. Islam's philosophy was so potent and forceful that it burst explosively within a hundred years of its coming into being across the whole of Middle East, Persia, India, and North Africa, and started knocking at the doors of Europe by completely overwhelming Spain. 'Never before in world history had an idea proved so contagious'. In India, after over two thousand years of Aryan invasions Islam was to cause the most profound effect and was destined to change the course of history. The commercial relations between Arabia and the western coastal region of India had existed from time immemorial. The Arabs had acquired a monopoly of sea trade in that area and had established settlements in many ports. Thus, with the advent of Islam in India in the seventh century no new racial element was introduced, but it marked the seeding of a potent idea. Strangely, its actual germination in India did not take place from the point of earlier contact, but from somewhere else; it did not start diffusing itself at that time but some time later; and the vehicle for spread of Islam was not trade but conquest.

The prophet of Islam, Muhammad, was born in 570 in the city of Makkah. Around 613 AD, he presented the basic tenet of Islam in a very simple term: *None is worthy of worship except God, and this message of God has been brought to the mankind through a fellow human, Muhammad.* Religion is not intended simply to make people believe in the Creator, per se. To check the inherent lust and self-interest of human nature, religion aims at bringing about a harmonious social order in this world so that all could live peacefully. And this is possible only if one could shun evil deeds and do good to others. Every one is accountable to the Creator for his deeds. He will have to face God on the Day of Judgement. From the very beginning, God has sent such messages to mankind through His prophets, who were all humans, such as Adam, Noah, Abraham, Ishmael, Isaac, Jacob, David, Solomon, Moses, Christ and Muhammad. A Muslim believes that Muhammad is the last in this chain. Apart from the religions received through these prophets, people have also believed in other religions which were given to them by holy and pious men in different ages and areas. The sermon of all religions appears generally the same: *there is one supreme God who has created us all: He enjoins upon us to do good to others and to be fearful of Him for the bad deeds we may do*. For a believing Muslim he has not to wander beyond the boundary of this belief. He believes that there is only one God; He is omnipotent, omniscient, omnipresent. None shares his power. He alone bestows blessings and forgiveness.

But Islam is much more than the mere affirmation of certain beliefs. Along with its simplicity in belief, Islam seems to be pragmatic and logical too. It lays stress on the ethics of social equality; it enjoins upon its followers to take special care of the poor and the destitute; and dooms a person who spreads evil on this earth. A practicing Muslim has been asked to observe five compulsory duties: one, to believe in the credo as mentioned above; two, to offer five daily prayers facing towards the '*qibla*' at Makkah; three, to make annual payment of zakat or poor-due at the rate of two and a half percent of the accumulated wealth and property, which is in addition to whatever he wants to give voluntarily as alms and charity; four, to fast from sun-rise to sun-set for full one lunar-month of Ramadan; and five, to make pilgrimage to Makkah once in his lifetime only if he has means to do so. In its practices, Islam sanctions no elaborate rituals or ceremonies; no myths or miracles; no ghosts or spirits; no high priests or special places for worship. There is no intermediary or intercessory; man is in direct communion with God, everywhere, all the time. None will bear the burden of his sins, but he himself. Islam neither humanizes God nor deifies humans; it does not create imaginary gods nor spirits. The only reality or myth is God himself; the only magic or miracle is the nature itself; and the only high priest is the individual himself. The individual is the holy; he is the sinner. A Muslim is supposed to completely *surrender* himself before God, to *accept* His will, and be at *peace* with destiny. These are the literal and spiritual meanings of the word 'Islam'.

No philosophy has so much been admired, despised, and feared as Islam has been. 'Even when Europe recovered from the Dark Ages and established its own great civilisation, the old fear of the ever-expanding Muslim empire remained. Europe could make no impression on this powerful and dynamic culture: the crusading project of the twelfth and thirteenth centuries eventually failed and, later, the

Ottoman Turks brought Islam to the very doorstep of Europe. This fear made it impossible for Western Christians to be rational or objective about the Muslim faith. At the same time as they were weaving fearful fantasies about Jews, they were also evolving a distorted image of Islam, which reflected their own buried anxieties. Western scholars denounced Islam as a blasphemous faith and its Prophet Muhammad as the Great Pretender, who had founded a violent religion of the sword in order to conquer the world.'[1] But Islam held out on its own in India, as it succeeded elsewhere, due to its own intrinsic strength as described by H.G.Wells: "The reader will note how the great tide swept over the footsteps of Yuan Chwang, and how easily in Africa the easy conquests of the Vandals were repeated in the reverse direction. And if the reader entertains any delusions about a fine civilization, either Persian, Roman, Hellenic, or Egyptian, being submerged by this flood, the sooner he dismisses such ideas the better. Islam prevailed because it was the best social and political order the times could offer. It prevailed because everywhere it found politically apathetic peoples robbed, oppressed, bullied, uneducated and unorganized, and it found selfish and unsound governments out of touch with any people at all. It was the broadest, freshest, and cleanest political idea that had yet come into actual activity in the world, and it offered better terms than any other to the mass of mankind."[2]

The process of evolution of Islam had reached its completion during the life time of the Prophet himself. But Islam too like other religions experienced schism later as a religious philosophy. It started with a dispute over inheriting the religious and political authority after the death of the Prophet, or, in other words, the caliphate. A group of people supported the idea that Ali, the young cousin of the prophet should wear his mantle. But Ali could assume the office of the caliph only as the fourth successor. This group of people, known as Shias (Shian-e-Ali or supporters of Ali), now interpret various issues of the religion differently from the majority Sunnis.

1. Karen Armstrong, *Muhammad, A Biography of the Prophet*, Introduction.
2. H. G. Wells, *The Outline of History*, Ch. XXX

20
ARAB CONQUEST

The first Muslim force reached India as early as AD 644. Facing an inhospitable environment in Sind its commander reported to his caliph that "water is scarce, the fruits are poor, and the robbers are bold; if a few troops are sent they will be slain, if many, they will starve."[1] It was, therefore after a long pause, that in AD 711 a serious attempt was made to conquer Sind, the occasion for which was an indirect one. Or, may be it was just a pretext for annexation of Sind to Transoxiana. A passing ship laden with a precious cargo for the caliph was plundered at the mouth of Indus. When asked by the caliph to return the gifts and punish the pirates, the local chief, Raja Dahir, refused to do so. He was a Chach Brahman, whose father had overthrown the Buddhist rule. It so enraged the Umayyad governor of Iraq, Hajjaj bin Yusuf, that he sent a mighty force in 712 under a young commander Muhammad bin Qasim, who was his nephew and son-in-law, to chastise the Raja. He marched through Shiraz in Iran and Makran. As a reinforcement a ballistae was dispatched from sea to Debal, an inland commercial port near Karachi. Dahir's army was safely entrenched in the stone fortification of Debal, but the rock bombardment from the Arab ballistae forced them to come to open and fight. Raja Dahir was killed and the capital, Brahmanabad (north of Hyderabad), was conquered. According to the author of Chach-nama, as translated by Fredunbeg, the artisans, merchants and common people were spared, but all the captured soldiers were slain.

The Arabs who invaded Sind in 712 were not violently anti-Hindu. Instead of converting or slaying the infidels, *zimmi* status was soon granted in return for special tax payment. Taking cognizance of their religious books, the Hindus of Sind were also taken as the people of the Book. Muhammad bin Qasim, the Arab conqueror of Sind, wrote to his superior and received the following reply: 'The letter of my dear nephew Muhammad bin Qasim has been received and the facts understood. It appears that the chief inhabitants of Brahmanabad had petitioned to be allowed to repair the temple of Budh and pursue their religion. As they have made submission and agreed to pay taxes to the Caliph, nothing more can be properly required from them. They have been taken under our protection, and we cannot in any way stretch out our hands upon their lives and property. Permission is given them to worship their gods. Nobody must be forbidden or prevented from following his own religion. They may live in their houses in whatever manner they like...'[2] Later, however, the Umayyad Caliph Umar bin Abdu'l Aziz (717-20) embarked upon a policy of converting the Hindu princes to Islam. Dahir's son, Jaisinha, embraced Islam, but then recanted and subsequently fell fighting in the battlefield.[3]

The non-Muslims were then divided for the purpose of payment of jizya (Poll tax) into three categories according to their income, high, middle and low, who were made to pay 48, 24, and 12 *dirhams* of silver, respectively. Tribute to be paid by the surrendering chieftains was also fixed according to their resources. Since the merchants and artisans had already suffered heavy loss in the process of general looting they were placed in the lowest category for payment of state tax (*mal* or revenue) at the rate of 12 silver dirhams. Village chiefs (*dihqans*) and headmen (*ra'is*) were appointed to collect it from the townspeople and villagers, and were offered a small salary. On the petitioning by the brahmans to restore their own former position and status Muhammad bin Qasim granted their request. The brahmans then visited the outlying villages, and at their persuasion the community leaders in the countryside also submitted to the Arabs and promised to pay taxes. The brahmans were permitted to collect their customary fees from the merchants, Hindu chiefs (thakurs), and the people. Their share of government revenue at the rate of 3 per cent which they had previously received was also reinstated. But, according to *Chach-nama*, the Muslim rulers did not interfere with the old societal rules practiced by the brahmans under which harsh and discriminatory treatment was meted out to the low caste Jat tribes. They were barred from putting on decent clothes and were made to wrap themselves in rough black blankets. Even their chiefs had been forbidden to ride horses, and were generally treated as brutes.[4]

The Arabs did not take their entry into Sind as a serious attempt for expansion. In 731 they founded a town and a garrison on the river Indus named Mahfuza, and later they built their capital, Mansura. The Muslim dispersion in India had to wait another three hundred years or more. And this expansion did not take place through the

Arabian Sea or from the foothold of Sind but from the gateway of the north-west frontier following Turkish eruptions. In this intervening period the Arabs had adjusted their tribal life to the Sindhi tribal pattern and adopted local customs and manners. "In 886 the Quran was translated into Sindi on the request of a Hindu chief. Arab historians who visited the region in the tenth century noted that the urban population spoke both Arabic and Sanskrit. The cultural interchange was most productive. The Kufa leather workers trained the Makran and Sind tanners in the art of tanning leather with dates. This improved the finish of indigenous leather products and made them softer. Sind shoes now fetched a high price and were regarded as a luxury item in the caliph's territories. Sind breeds of camel were also upgraded, and the demand for them rose in neighbouring countries. On the other hand, Sanskrit works on astronomy, medicine, ethics, and administration were introduced by Sindi intellectuals to the translation bureau at the Abbasid court".[5] This was the time when the Arabs gave Brahmanism the new name of Hinduism when they called the local people, the worshippers of Vishnu and Siva, by the name of Hindus. During this time the heartland of India, however, remained unaware of the happenings in Sind and of the presence of the Muslims. The host of small kings and chiefs who had sprung up over the length and breadth of the country were engaged in fratricidal wars trying to eliminate each other and to gain supremacy over their compatriots. This situation was also prevailing even when Mahmud Ghaznavi had engaged himself in a series of raids into India in the early eleventh century.

In the south of Sindh, Malabar coast had also become host to the Arab Muslims, independent of what had happened in Sind. Being mainly traders, their adjustment with local society was easier and peaceful. Unlike the Roman traders, they settled permanently in the coastal regions of south India. They were welcomed there and given land for their trading stations as also freedom to practice their religion. The Mopilla Muslims of the present day Malabar are their descendants.

Before that, Islam's zealous armies had overrun Persia. Afraid of forcible conversion a large number of the Zoroastrians of Persia fled by sea and by the coastal route to western India. They too were welcomed without any reservation. The Chalukyas gave them shelter. The Zoroastrians settled there, took to trade and founded the community, known even today as Parsis, having arrived there from

Persia (Faruss). This religion was given by a venerable sage of Iran, Zoroaster or Zarathustra. Both his date and place are uncertain, but it seems probable that he lived in the early years of the sixth century B. C. and that his field of activity was in the Oxus-Jaxartes basin, in lands that were inhabited by a sedentary population but were exposed to attack by nomads of Eurasian steppe. Zarathustra degraded all gods of the traditional Iranian pantheon save one-'the great spirit' Ahura Mazda-to the status of devils.[6] He postulated the eternal conflict of good and evil represented by gods Ahura Mazda and Ahriman, respectively. He preached that the true god of good would overcome the false god of evil only if a man devoted himself in his life to good thoughts, words and deeds. If he did not, he will be accountable after death. This religion discarded the old Aryan/Iranian belief in nature gods.

1. *Futuhu-l Buld'an of al'Bila'duri* in H.M. Eliot and John Dowson, eds., *The History of India, As Told By Its Own Historians: The Mohammadan Period: Historians of Sind, I* (Quoted in *A New History of India*, (Fifth Edition), Chapter Eight, Stanley Wolpert).

2. Eliot and Dowson, The History of India as Told by its own Historians, Vol. I, p. 185, quoted in *A History of India*, Vol One, Ch 12,Romila Thapar; *Chach-nama* (tr. Fredunbeg) See S. A. A. Rizvi, *The Wonder That Was India*, Part II

3. S. A. A. Rizvi, *The Wonder That Was India*, Part II, Ch. I

4. *Chach-nama* (tr. Fredunbeg), See S. A. A. Rizvi, *The Wonder That Was India*, Part II, Ch. I

5. I. H. Qureshi, *The Muslim Community of the Indo-Pakistan Subcontinent*, See S. A. A. Rizvi, *The Wonder That Was India*, Part II, Ch I

6. Arnold Toyanbee, *Mankind and Mother Earth*, Ch 25 & 38

21
RAIDS OF MAHMUD GHAZNAVI

By the tenth century the caliphate of Islam had shifted from Damascus to Baghdad. Flourishing commerce and industry had brought immense riches to the Muslim Empire. Since the ninth century army of Turkish slaves (Mamluks) used to be bought in Central Asia and inducted into the army to protect and strengthen the Caliphate. During the Chinese expansion in the tenth century, the Turkish nomads were driven into Persia and Afghanistan. Considerable expansion had in the meanwhile taken place in the Islamic empire. Such a vast empire became uncontrollable from the centre. As a natural corollary, independent kingdoms started to grow up on its fringes. The rulers generally assumed the secular title of Sultan, and paid homage, in name, to the Caliph. The first such kingdom was set up by a warrior Turkish slave, named Alaptagin, in Afghanistan in 962. He established himself at Ghazni. His son Subuktagin stretched the extent of this empire from the Caspian Sea to Peshawar, which he captured in 991. It was his son Mahmud (971-1030) who led seventeen raids into India between 997 and 1026. He was attracted towards the temples of India which 'were depositories of vast quantities of wealth, in cash, golden images, and jewellery - the donations of the pious - and these made them natural targets of a non-Hindu searching for wealth in northern India. Mahmud's greed for gold was insatiable. From 1010 to 1026 the invasions of Mahmud were directed to temple towns - Mathura, Thanesar, Kanauj, and finally Somnath. The concentration of wealth at Somnath was renowned, and consequently it was inevitable that Mahmud would attack it. Added to the desire for wealth was the religious motivation, iconoclasm being a meritorious activity among the more orthodox followers of the Islamic faith. The destruction of Somnath was frenzied, and its effects were to remain for many centuries in the Hindu mind and to colour its assessment of the character of Mahmud, and on occasion of Muslim rulers in general.'[1] His chroniclers have recorded: 'The whole country of India is full of gold and jewels, and of the plants which grow there are those fit for making apparel, and aromatic plants and the sugar-cane, and the whole aspect of the country is pleasant and delightful. Now, since the inhabitants are chiefly infidels and idolaters, by the order of God and his Prophet it is right for us to conquer them.'[2]

Mahumud Ghaznavi descended every few years into Punjab plains and from there to his place of choice for looting. But his raids were not directed only against non-Muslim states. No Muslim state that came in his way was spared. Balkh, Seestan, Multan and Talamba were all Muslim states that Mahmud attacked and captured. Every raid in India, however, made Mahmud and his adventurous army richer by gold, jewels, and women. On the way to plunder they smashed temples, which were depositories of wealth, and killed all those who came in their way. His court chronicler, Utbi, exposing the Sultan's prowess with a definite exaggeration, mentions that in Kanauj alone ten thousand Hindu temples were destroyed.[3] Around AD 1000, Hindu Shahis, who themselves had links with the Turks were ruling the territory of Lamghan up to the river Chenab and from southern Kashmir to the borders of Multan, with their capital at Waihind. An ancestor of their king Jayapala, a minister in the court of a Turkish ruler of Gandhara, had displaced his master in the ninth century and founded a dynasty known after the Turkish original, Hindu Shahyia. Jayapala had marched upon Ghazni in 986-7 in retaliation for an earlier invasion by Subuktagin. Jayapala was defeated. He made peace and promised to pay a huge indemnity, but later reneged. He again marched on Ghazni, this time joined by a number of confederate rajas, but was again defeated near Peshawar. Returning to Punjab or in the captivity of Mahmud, Jayapala died in 1001. An account mentions that he had killed himself. Another obstacle to Mahmud's entry into India was Abul Fath bin Dawud, the Muslim Isma'ili ruler of Multan. Being a staunch Sunni Muslim, another cause of Mahmud's irritation was the heretical belief of the ruler of Multan. In order to wipe him out Mahmud attacked Multan in 1006. Jayapala's son, Anandapala, tried to stop him but he proved no match to Mahmud.Daud fled from Multan, where Isma'ilis were slaughtered and their mosques, as well as Hindu temples, desecrated. But under Mahmud, the Hindus continued to enjoy *zimmi* status. "He did not, however, hesitate to employ the Hindus in his multiracial Muslim army. They served under their own commander, called Salar-i Hinduyan. The anonymous history of Sistan contains complaints of the ruthless massacre of Muslims and Christians by Mahmud's pagan Indian troops."[4]

In 1025, Mahmud raided Somnath on the Saurashtra coast mainly for its temple which had a reputation for containing fabulous wealth. It is said that the inhabitants of the city did not resist the army of Mahmud marching towards the temple but watched calmly confidant that the Siva, whose iron lingum (phallus) was miraculously, suspended in the air, would not let the harm come into their way. However, after the victory the lingum, which was suspended by the mechanism of a magnet, was made to crash on the ground. On being shattered it spilled immense riches in gold and jewelry. The chroniclers wrote, obviously again with exaggeration, that on that day fifty thousand Hindus were slain and that over two million *dinars'* worth of gold and jewels were taken from the hollow *lingum* shattered by Mahmud's sword.[5] Somehow Mahmud did seem interested only in fabulous wealth and not in conquest, though shortly before his death he did annex northern Punjab in his kingdom in about 1020.

Al- Biruni, Mahmud's chronicler, provides a description of the social condition when he visited India. Land-taxes were light; the brahmans who had been the first recipient of the land-gifts paid no taxes while the main burden fell on the kshatriyas. Buddhist institutions had declined, and Jains had migrated towards the west. The laws were too mild, since 'the manners and customs of the Hindus resemble those of the Christians' in recognizing unrealistic propositions of human virtue. The customs, which honored and to some degree protected women, also imposed upon the household of the chieftains the rite of sati, with its lower-class alternative of degraded widowhood. As a Muslim, he was surprised to see in India an anthropomorphic religion, demonstrated in pilgrimages to sacred rivers and spawning a multiplicity of gods presided over by a trinity which he likened to that of the Christians.[6]

1. Romila Thapar, *A History of India*, Vol One, Ch 10
2. *India: A Concise History, Ch. Six*, Francis Watson
3. Stanley Wolpert, *A New History of India* (Fifth Edition)
4. C. E. Bosworth, *The Ghaznavids*, Edinburg, 1977, p. 110, See *The Wonder That Was India*, Part II, Ch I, S. A. A. Rizvi
5. Stanley Wolpert, *A New History of India* (Fifth Edition)
6. *India: A Concise History, Ch. Six,* Francis Watson

In 1025, Mahmud raided Somnath on the Saurashtra coast, famed for its temple which had a reputation for containing fabulous wealth. It is said that the inhabitants of the city did not resist the army of Mahmud marching towards the temple but watched calmly confident that the Siva, whose idol (lingam) was [illegible] suspended in the air, would not let the Turks harm them. [illegible] however, the deity failed [illegible], as suspended by the mechanism of magnets, was made to [illegible] the ground on being shattered and spilled the treasures of gold and jewels. The chroniclers wrote, obviously again with exaggeration, that on that day fifty thousand Hindus were slain and treasures of two million dinars' worth of gold and jewels were taken from the idol [illegible] shattered by Mahmud's sword. [illegible] Mahmud did [illegible] interested only in [illegible] wealth and not in conquest, [illegible] shortly before his death [illegible] Punjab [illegible].

As Biruni, Mahmud's [illegible], provides a description of the social condition [illegible] he visited India. Land [illegible] the brahmans who had [illegible] the first recipients of the [illegible] taxes with the main burden fell on the [illegible]. Buddhist institutions had declined [illegible] had migrated towards the west. [illegible] laws were not mild since the [illegible] customs of the Hindus [illegible] of human [illegible]. The customs, which [illegible] women [illegible] the [illegible] lower class [illegible] remain [illegible].

[illegible]

22
SULTANS OF DELHI

Mahmud Ghaznavi's raids were the precursor of subsequent invasions by the Muslims and of establishing a permanent rule in India, first shattering the indigenous Hindu powers of northern India and then moving to the south. But such invasions had still to wait another hundred and fifty years after the death of Mahmud. In the second half of the twelfth century another Turkish family of Ghur, which was also of Central Asian origin, captured Ghazni itself. Sultan Muizzuddin Muhammad (Shahabuddin) Ghuri (1173-1206) made his foray into India in 1175. Reaching Peshawar he destroyed the old Ghaznavid garrison in 1179, and seized Lahore in 1186. He defeated the Hindu confederates under the command of Prithviraj at the second battle of Tarain on 1192. After the victory the Sultan returned to Khorasan leaving the campaign and the new possessions in the hands of his trusted slave lieutenant Qutbuddin Aibek, who finally reached Delhi and occupied it in 1193.

The new generation of Muslim rulers did not hesitate to give their slaves a very high position and sometimes even daughters in marriage to them. The next dynasty of rulers of India starting from Qutbuddin Aibek was, therefore, that of the Slaves. After Mahmud Ghuri was assassinated by an Isma'ili fanatic in 1206 near Lahore, Qutbuddin Aibak assumed the role of sultan of Delhi. The Sultanate era which was thus initiated lasted for more than three hundred years with rule of five successive Turco-Afghan dynasties: Slaves, Khiljis, Tughlaqs, Syeds and Lodhis. This period saw a special phase of Hindu-Muslim relationship for a new religious and ethnic element had been introduced in India.

Qutbuddin Aibek's successor, was also a slave and his son-in-law, Shamsuddin Iltemish (Iltutmish). He reigned from 1211 to 1236, kept Chengiz Khan, by some diplomatic moves, from invading the country, and thus saved the population from destruction and mayhem. Instead of imposing and foisting his authority in the administration of the country he generally acted with tolerance. Though he was a devoutly religious person, he gave Hindus the status of *zimmis*. Hindu chiefs and rajas were left to govern their own areas as long as they paid taxes for his treasury. But he did not tolerate rebellion. When Bengal rose against him he suppressed it with a strong hand, which took him four years to have full control on it. He was succeeded by his able daughter Razia Sultan, the only Muslim woman ever to rule India. Unfortunately she fell victim to court intrigues and was soon assassinated.

Another monarch, Balban, who ruled from 1266 to 1286, was ruthless in the suppression of opposition and did not hesitate even to trample his opponents with elephants. He forsook the Islamic concept of simplicity and assumed the pompous and grandiose style of monarchy on the lines of Indian and Persian traditions. He was 'a grand monarch in the traditional Hindu mould than the first-among-equals idea of the orthodox Islam.' Borrowing a leaf from Kautilya's Arthashastra he obtained the services of spies to maintain hold on his power. He reserved the highest posts in his service first to Turks, and then to Afghans. Indian-born Muslims were assigned middle positions. When he died in 1286, the nobles crowned his grandson Qaiqabad. He proved to be an inept ruler, and also a debauch.

In 1290 Jalaluddin Khilji, a Turkish noble launched a successful coup against Qaiqabad by getting himself elected by the nobles as the king. He was an old man of seventy and seemed to have lost the energy to rule with a firm hand. It is said that once in his time about 1000 thugs were arrested in Delhi, but the king refused to order their execution. Instead he ordered them to put into a boat and transported them to far off Bengal. The Khiljis were originally Turks, who later settled in Afghanistan and moved to India during the Ghaznavid and Ghuri invasions. The Khilji Sultans took the first and important step towards Indianization of the administration by relying heavily on the support of the indigenous people. Jalaluddin Khilji's nephew and son-in-law, Alauddin Khilji, arranged the king's murder in 1296 for usurping the throne. During Alauddin's reign the Sultanate reached the height of a centralized power. "The first of the Sultans of Delhi to attain an imperial hold over north India, Ala-al-Din Khilji (1296-1315), treated defeated Hindu rulers with conciliation, and married their daughters. His principal general was a converted Hindu (Malik Kafur). He was content to leave the Hindu kingdoms of the south in a tributary relationship with Delhi."[1] Alauddin Khilji was the first Sultan to penetrate in the South, capturing Devagiri in 1307, Kakatiya in 1309 and Pandyan in 1310.

As an administrative measure and to strengthen the finances of the state, Alauddin resumed many of the tax-free jagirs from the Muslim nobles, raised land tax to 50 per cent of each crop, and strictly enforced its collection from the farmers. He also imposed new taxes on milch cattle and houses, and introduced the system of wage and price control, the result of which was low prices for basic necessities like food and clothing, which made the life of the people comfortable. With the help of his spies, he successfully enforced his administrative measures, and acquired firm grip on the reins of power. He undoubtedly proved to be a very able Sultan.

Alauddin did not accept Islamic injunctions as a tool in administrating state affairs. According to Barani, the author of Tarikh-i-Feroz Shahi, he is said to have stated the following to a religious scholar: "Although I have not studied the science or the Book, I am a Muslman of Muslman stock. To prevent rebellion in which thousands perish, I issue such orders as I conceive to be for the good of the State and for the benefit of the people. Men are heedless, disrespectful, and disobey my commands; I am then compelled to be severe to bring them into obedience, I do not know whether this is lawful or unlawful, whatever I think to be for the good of the State, or suitable for the emergency, that I decree."[2]

By the end of the thirteenth century the Mongols had accepted Islam, and they had been allowed to settle in the upper reaches of Jamuna and Ganga. But these settlers had not given up their habit of being mutinous as soldiers. When in 1299, these rebels reached the gates of Delhi, Alauddin had to deal with them at the point of exterminating them. Their leader was blinded, their children massacred, their wives given to sweepers and their surviving fighting men trampled to death by elephants.[3]

Alauddin is said to have stated: "The Hindus will never become submissive and obedient till they are reduced to poverty. I have, therefore given orders, that just sufficient shall be left to them from year to year, of corn, milk, and curds, but they shall not be allowed to accumulate hoards and property."[4] Alauddin's measures were in keeping with earlier Indian traditions. Writing in *Rajatrangini* in the twelfth century AD the Brahman Kalhana, attributes the following sentiments to King Lalitaditya of Kashmir: "Those who wish to be powerful in the land must always guard against internal dissension. Those who dwell there in the mountains difficult of access, should be punished even if they give no offence, because sheltered by their fastness, they are difficult to break up if they have once accumulated wealth. Every care should be taken that there should not be left with the villagers more food supply than required for one year's consumption, nor more oxen than wanted for the tillage of their fields. Because if they keep more wealth, they would become in a single year very formidable Damaras [chiefs] and strong enough to neglect the demands of the king."[5]

The Hindus disliked Alauddin because they viewed him as an oppressor. But Alauddin was actually impartial in his ruthlessness and in the strict enforcement of discipline. If his measures were directed against Hindu nobles, he was similarly harsh with Muslim courtiers. Barani mentions that the poor Hindus in the rural areas were explicitly exempt from some of the Sultan's stern measures. Alauddin's demand of revenue amounting to 50 per cent of the standing crop was not new. It had been asked for also by Hindu rulers before him. Further, in addition to the usual one-sixth which was supposed to be the king's share according to the ancient code of Manu, middlemen had collected a great deal of additional taxes or subjected the peasants to irregular exaction. Alauddin explicitly prohibited all such additional collections.

After the Khiljis, Ghyasuddin Tughlaq founded the new dynasty. He was the son of a Turkish slave of the court and a Hindu Jat women. The most famous king of this dynasty was Muhammad Tughlaq (1325-1351), who assumed the reins of the kingdom in 1325 after his father and a brother were killed under a collapsing pavilion. When Muhammad was killed while suppressing a rebellion in Sind his cousin Firoz (1351-1388), equally a great monarch, came to the throne by the consensus of all the chief men, Hindus and Muslims alike. He was a religious person and generally considered an orthodox Muslim. Many stories are, however, told of his iconoclasm. These appear somewhat incongruous, in view of his tremendous interest in the historical and cultural past of India. When he visited a library in Kangra he was so impressed by the work of Hindu scholars that he ordered translation of various manuscripts on the subject of Hinduism from Sanskrit into Persian and Arabic. He was so fascinated by Asoka pillars that he installed two of them in a commanding position at his new citadel at Delhi: They had been brought there with great difficulty from far away

Meerut and Topra. In his curiosity he asked some Brahmans to decipher the inscription on these pillars, but even they could not read the ancient script. "He was told that it was a magical charm and that it was associated with religious ritual. If objects of infidel worship had indeed been so abhorrent to Firuz, he would have had the pillars destroyed : instead they were placed in positions of prominence".[6] But Firoz did not hesitate to destroy temples at times when he reached the point of disgust.

He had a passion for building. He built a new city near Delhi, named Firozabad, and laid it with gardens. Firoz Shah Kotla, the multi-storied citadel of his capital, is the living monument of his passion for buildings in Delhi. He cared so much for public weal that he built about thirty colleges, forty mosques, one hundred hospitals, one hundred public baths, one hundred and fifty bridges, and two hundred satellite towns around Delhi. To boost the economy, specially the agriculture, he brought uncultivated and barren lands under cultivation by constructing about thirty reservoirs and fifty dams. He seems to have been one of the most intelligent monarchs of the Sultanate. He abolished torture as part of his administration. He himself writes in a tract about his humane intentions and his religious zeal:

"The great and merciful God made me, His servant, hope and seek for His mercy by devoting myself to prevent the unlawful killing of Musalmans and the infliction of any kind of torture upon them or upon any men.

....

"The sects of Shias, also called *Rawafiz*, had endeavoured to make proselytes....I seized them all and I convicted them of their errors and perversions. On the most zealous I inflicted capital punishment (*siyasat*), and the rest I visited with censure (*tazir*), and threats of public punishment. Their books I burnt in public and by the grace of God the influence of this sect was entirely suppressed.

....

"I ordered that the leaders of these people and the promoters of this abomination (who were holding a religious fair in a village named Mula near Delhi, which was attended even by 'some graceless Musalmans') should be put to death. I forbade the infliction of any severe punishment of the Hindus in general, but I destroyed their idol temples and instead thereof raised mosques.

....

"I encouraged my infidel subject to embrace the religion of the prophet, and I proclaimed that every one who respected the creed and became a Musalman should be exempt from jizya or poll-tax. Information of this came to the ears of the people at large, and great numbers of Hindus presented themselves, and were admitted to the honour of Islam. Thus they came forward day by day from every quarter, and, adopting the faith, were exonerated from the jizya, and were favoured with presents and honours."[7]

Brahmans, who had hitherto been exempt from paying jizya, as also other taxes, were now subject to pay this tax. They protested, and even resorted to hunger strikes. The Sultan did not relent but only reduced the rate. Muslims were not spared and were made to pay *zakat*. Firoz Shah Tughlaq established a separate section in the treasury for *zakat*.

It is reported in *Tarikh-i-Firoz Shahi* of Ziauddin Barani that on his way back from Bengal in 1361, Firoz suddenly assaulted Orissa 'extirpating Rai Gajpat (Raja Gajpati), massacring the unbelievers, demolishing their temples, hunting elephants, and getting a glimpse of their enchanting country,' He destroyed the Bhanja capital, Kiching, in northern Orissa and then took the Gajapati Bhanudeva by surprise at Cuttack. Bhanudeva fled but was reinstated on condition that he paid a regular tribute to the Sultan. 'The victorious standards now set out for the destruction of the temple of Jagannath. This was the shrine of the polytheists of this land and a sanctuary of the unbelievers of the Far East. It was the most famous of their temples.' However, no other source other than Tarikh-i-Firoz Shahi reports the destruction of the temple.[8]

Firoz was the last of the strong Sultans of Delhi. Within a decade of his death, half a dozen transient monarchs held tenuous hold on the power. While rival factions were fighting among themselves for their fortunes, the Central Asian armies of Taimur, the Burlas Turk, entered Delhi in 1398 trough Punjab. They defeated a sizeable force outside Delhi, exacted a handsome ransom, carried out indiscriminate killings, destruction and plunder in Delhi for three days and left "towers built high" with the heads and ravaged bodies. Artisans and mechanics were taken as slaves to Samarkand. Apart from the Hindus, Muslim sunnis were also not spared because Taimur was a *shia*. 'In Delhi the Ulema (established theologians) and the Sayyids (who claimed the descent from the Prophet) were untouched, but other Muslim prisoners were enslaved.'

The next dynasty of the Sayyids ruled from 1414 to 1450. After them, in the dynasty of the Lodhis, Sikandar who ruled from 1489 to 1517, has been hailed by historians of his court as one of the wisest and most far-sighted of Sultans. He was a patron of literature and arts. He gathered scholars of all shades of faiths by his side and wrote poetry himself. He encouraged the compilation of books on medicine (Ma'dan-ul-Shifa) as well as music (Lahjat-i-Sikandar Shahi). "The stimulus to learning and cultural creativity provided by Sikandar's patronage seem, moreover, to have helped several important syncretisms of Islam and Hinduism to emerge at this time, though Sikandar himself was surprisingly orthodox. Perhaps the fact that his mother was Hindu and that he had early fallen in love with a Hindu princess drove him to seek by periodic displays of temple-razing and iconoclastic fervor to prove himself more orthodox than the *pirs* and *mullas* of his realm. At any rate several new sects of mystic toleration, blending the best of both great school of religious thought, came to life before Sikandar expired."[9] Iconoclasm was used sometime as a tool for impressing the superiority of the foreign rulers on the indigenous population. It was also used in this way by one state to frighten the other. Sikandar Lodhi, himself had aimed at destroying the mosques of the ruler of Jaunpur in order to demonstrate his prowess.

1. Hugh Tinker, *South Asia: A Short History*
2. *A History of India,* Ch 4, Hermann Kulke & Dietmar Rothermund
3. *India: A Concise History*, Ch. Six, Francis Watson
4. *A History of India,* Ch 4, Hermann Kulke & Dietmar Rothermund
5. M. A. Stein, Kalhana's Rajatrangini or Chronicle of the Kings of Kashmir (reprinted Delhi, 1961, Vol.I, p.154 (IV pp. 345-8), quoted in *A History of India*, Ch 4, Hermann Kulke .& Dietmar Rothermund
6. Romila Thapar, *A History of India*, Vol. I, Ch 12; *A History of India*, Hermann Kulke & Dietmar Rothermund
7. *The Oxford History of India*, Ch. 3, Book IV, fourth edition, Vincent A. Smith
8. *Tarikh-I-Firoz Shahi* (trans H. M. Elliot and J. Dawson), *The History of India as Told by its Own Historians vol. 3*. See *A History of India*, Hermann Kulke & Dietmar Rothermund
9. *A New History of India* (Fifth Edition), Ch. Eight, Stanley Wolpert

23
SPROUTING OF A MIXED CULTURE

The Turkish sultans who had established themselves in India by way of Central Asia and Afghanistan around the twelfth century had not entered India with the religious zeal and passion as had been demonstrated by the Arabs of the seventh century who had dispersed in the Middle Eastern countries, Africa and Persia. Centuries had passed. The new rulers of India were fortune hunters. They were no more bound by the cultural traditions of the old Islamic lands. They had every intention to enjoy the pomp and pleasure of royalty and avoid confrontation as far as possible. So they were also cruel without discrimination to the challengers of their authority, as any monarch anywhere of the Medieval times had been. They did not interfere with the faith and culture and traditions of the indigenous community. Even then they were not devoid of the pressure of the theologians. Even in present times, we find that a priest, a *mulla*, or a brahman has tremendous influence over the masses. So at all times the ruling elite is unable to ignore their power and pressure. The Sultans, acting fearfully and ostensibly, also had to please and appease them at times through extending financial considerations to them and to religious charities, and at times by following their dictates, even with the 'display of anti-infidel activities such as iconoclasm'. But not all Sultans felt themselves weak to be pressurized by *ulema*. Ulema too had to be discreet not to project their discord with the Sultans, lest the internal dissension was exposed to the subject race. When Barani once complained that the Sultan was not paying due attention to the duties as ordained by God, he was exiled.

Sharia was the basic law of Islam. It had to be enforced, and its interpretation had to come from the Ulema. In the beginning the new law was to operate in towns only where a good number of Muslims were generally residing. The villages continued with the old laws. "Non-Muslims were free to maintain their own legal institutions, which naturally led to many complications. Finally it was conceded that a non-Muslim code could apply to a non-Muslim provided it did not endanger the state. The interpretation of the code was kept amorphous, and this enabled decisions to be taken on the basis of expediency rather than following the letter of the law. There was some discussion, for instance, on the question of women becoming *sati*. According to the *Sharia* suicide is illegal and becoming a *sati* was an act of suicide, but it was permitted to Hindu women."[1]

Jizya or a poll tax on non-Muslims is permitted by Sharia. Jizya served many purposes: first, it was a sort of tribute to a victorious Muslim ruler accepting his over-lordship; second, it was an admission on the part of the ruler that the protection of his non-believer subjects had become his responsibility (*zimmi*); third, it provided equality with other Muslim subjects who had to pay zakat according to the *shariah;* and fourth, *jaziah* was a source of state revenue. Despite all these, its application always depended on the whims of the Sultans. Some levied it and some abolished it. Many categories of persons were exempt from time to time. In view of the religious susceptibilities, which was given due recognition by the Muslim rulers, the brahmans were often exempt from this tax. Poor people and rural population were also generally exempt. *Jiziya* was normally levied in urban areas where trade and crafts were flourishing. 'Often the tax was used for a legitimate means of increasing the revenue and not necessarily with the intention of persecuting the non-Muslim population.'

As for the iconoclasm of the Sultans, some of them have been painted by historians as temple-breakers and idol-smashers. In actual fact, their wars were waged primarily for political domination and booty. Muslim historians and poets of the time embellished their accounts with the slaying of infidels and destroying their temples.

"These activities have been written about at length by the chroniclers, presumably to prove the devotion of their patrons to Islam. In fact there may have been more than piety involved. Firuz is also described on occasion as being an iconoclast. A campaign in Orissa was given its finale with the destruction of the Jagannatha temple at Puri.

"The chroniclers had to show that the Sultan was making life difficult for the infidels, in order to earn him the respect of the orthodox in his community. Purely religious iconoclasm may be understandable in the raids of Mahmud, though even here the treasure was probably more attractive than the religious motive. But for a reigning king to decree the destruction of temples to earn religious merit would appear foolish in the extreme."[2]

So far conversion is concerned, it did, of course, take place in the land, but not as a matter state policy. "It is generally accepted that, except for a few areas such as Kashmir, the Muslim rulers did not follow any well-defined or widespread policy of conversion by force. In certain parts of the country, like Bengal and Punjab, where post-Buddhist Hinduism had not struck deep enough roots, Islam was accepted by outcaste and low-caste communities as an escape from their social bondage, or because it brought them material benefits from the new rulers. However, it appears that a significant number accepted Islam because of the popularity of the Sufi 'saints';..."[3]

The first component of Muslim community were the merchants and travelers, the second were the Turkish invaders and military aristocracy, thinly spread over the country. A major source was accession from the Hindu ranks. A small group of Hindu upper classes became Muslims from conviction and some in hope of reward. The minister Khan Jahan in the fourteenth century was one such convert. A further group were forcibly converted in times of tumult or stress. The practice undoubtedly occurred but its extent tended to be exaggerated by bigoted and boastful chroniclers. In sum, like the foregoing categories it amounted to a small percentage. By far the largest element within the Muslim community came from voluntary conversion. Its causes and means were various but the fact is certain. There were Buddhist peasants under brahman rule who preferred the relative freedom of Islam to low caste status. There were groups of outcastes or exterior castes, as the anthropologists call them, who moved to Islam for the same reason, while in places militant clans or groups went over in a body as a political tactic. The means of these conversions varied. Some groups probably went over as a result of a communal decision. A very potent factor, however, was the preaching of Muslim sufis or devotees. The sufis appealed to the heart and went among the people in simplicity and devotion. Their emphasis in fraternalism and inner devotion appealed to the many who were dissatisfied with their own condition for any reason. It was in this way that one fourth of the Indian population became Muslim.[4]

The Sultanate era was the period of adjustment just after marriage. It marked the beginning of a time when the two cultures had started mingling and assimilating with each other. But Hinduism was so conservative that the fertilization of the Hindu culture due to the contact with new ideas was much slower than expected. The hold of the brahmans on the religion and society was very firm. They considered every new dogma or creed as a threat to their own entrenched position, and as usual they braced themselves anew to fight tooth and nail to preserve the ancient Aryan religion from *'the mlechchhas'* who were projected to despoil the holy land of Bharatvarsha and the Vedic religion. The new rulers, who had the force and power to effect change, were least concerned with politicizing religion. They did not, therefore, take a firm stand either to project the superiority of their own religion or to suppress the hold of brahmans on Hinduism.

Those who converted had worked and lived for generation with their Hindu brethren and craft-and-caste fellows. These neo-Muslims acted as the first link between the local Hindus and the Muslims of foreign extraction in evolving a new culture. They had retained many of their old customs. As a result, the cultural values and domestic ceremonies in matters of birth, death and marriage started interacting. The newly recruited local army mixing with their Turco-Afghan colleagues too had a great impact in this regard. Of course, the fusion of culture was not so smooth in Hindu and Muslim aristocracy, who maintained their separateness due to their mental make up and the pressure of their respective political and religious authorities. But wherever the ordinary folk mixed up in fields, work places and markets, they evolved common codes of rituals, ceremonies, dress, food and language.

Islam did not categorically abolish slavery. As one of the dynasties of Sultans belonged to the Slaves, so many of the newly convert slaves managed to rise to positions of very high eminence in the Sultanate. Malik Kafur became Alauddin's most trusted adviser and the second most important man in the realm. Then there was Khusru Khan, an outcast, for whom Alauddin's son Qutbuddin Mubarak had an infatuation. Mubarak who was given to debauchery and drinking, made Khusru Khan a noble but lost his life at his hands. Khusru Khan achieved the incredible feat of actually assuming the mantle of sultan in 1320. Somewhat later came Khan Jahan, a convert from the Andhra region who was nominated by Firoz Tughlaq to deputize for him in Delhi while he himself was busy campaigning in Sind.[5] Firoz accepted young boys in lieu of annual tax from *iqta* holders. The imperial *karkhanas* were generally managed by these young boys.

In due course, the Hindus too made their presence felt in the Delhi sultanate. In this regard the first and foremost area of infiltration was army. For the sultanate to expand and to be militarily strong, the local Hindus had to be inducted, to begin with, in the lower and middle ranks as soldiers. Some of them so recruited rose to occupy positions of command and one of them advanced far enough in the hierarchy to be appointed governor of Sind by Muhammad bin Tughlaq. Sultan Ghiyas-ud-din Tughlaq and Sultan Sikandar Lodi had Hindu mothers, which points to the rapidity with which the process of naturalization by matrimony had advanced.[6]

North-central India had become a stronghold of Muslim population. But this position was not available to the regional sultans, and as such they had to depend largely on human resources of the native population. They were, therefore, more inclined to tolerance towards Hinduism than a typical Delhi sultan. Bahman Shah, for instance, elevated his brahman friend Gangu to position of Chief Minister. Early in the 15th century, the Bengal sultanate had a Hindu Minister called Raja Ganesha who became so powerful that his convert son was able to occupy the Lukhnawati throne for as long as sixteen years. The Sultans of Bengal showed interest in Hinduism and arranged for the *Ramayana* to be translated by the poet Krittibas into Bengali. Around 1500 AD the Muslim governor of Chittagong similarly commissioned his court poet, Kavindra Parameshvara, to translate the Mahabharata into Bengali. The sultans of Bijapur recognised Marathi as a language in which business could be transacted. But, the one sultanate that went further than any other in persecuting and forcibly converting its Hindu subjects was Kashmir-which, as it happened, had no affiliations with Delhi, having been founded by a 14th century Muslim immigrant. His sixth descendant, Sikandar (1393-1416), was a bigot, who destroyed temples and idols, and forcibly converted the bulk of the population to Islam. Even there the Brahmans survived as a small minority. Ironically, though, it was Kashmir that produced perhaps the most outstanding champion of a syncretic culture in Sultan Zain-ul-Abedin (1420-1467); thanks to his childhood association with a Hindu step-mother and the influence of a particularly enlightened Sufi. This remarkable man not only abolished the jizya and placed a ban on cow-slaughter but repaired Hindu temples, studied the Hindu scriptures and encouraged Hindus to learn Persian. Architecture too did not escape from the impact of the two cultures. Everywhere new style of Indo-Muslim architecture sprang up. A shining example is the Jayasthamba or Pillar of Victory raised by Rana Sanga's father, Rana Khumba, late in the 15th century to commemorate his triumph over the Sultan of Malwa. This pillar is not only modelled after the Qutub Minar of Delhi but bears the word Allah nine times on the third storey and three times on the ninth.[7]

1. Romila Thapar, *A History of India*, Volume One, Ch 13
2. Romila Thapar, *A History of India*, Volume One, Ch 12
3. Ranbir Vohra, *The Making of India: A Historical Survey* Ch 2
4. Percival Spear, *A History of India*, Volume Two
5. D.B.Vohra, *A Panormic History of the Indian People*, Ch. Nine
6. D.B.Vohra, *A Panormic History of the Indian People*, Ch. Nine
7. D.B.Vohra, *A Panormic History of the Indian People*, Ch. Nine ; Percival Spear, *A History of India*, Vol. Two

24
SOCIAL LIFE: ACCOUNTS OF IBN BATUTA

At this point it would not be out of place to present some extracts from the accounts of Ibn Batuta.[1] His accounts show us how the Muslims and Hindus of India were adjusting their lives and were trying in the fourteenth century to live together peacefully. Ibn Batuta (1304-1369), born in Tangier, Morocco, was a remarkable traveller. Though not a historian, he was a keen observer of men and matters, and has presented an enthralling account of life and attitudes throughout the world, from China to Spain. 'In his itineraries he sometimes misplaces the order of towns....He gives wrong names at several points, especially when he is dealing with non-Muslim countries, where his knowledge of Arabic and Persian was of little service to him. In his historical narratives, which are generally trustworthy, similar mistakes are found.'[2] Ibn Batuta visited Delhi in the time of Sultan Muhammad Tughlaq, and later proceeded to China as the envoy of the Sultan of India via Malabar, which was an independent kingdom at that time.

"The city of Delhi is made up now of four neighbouring and contiguous towns. One of them is Delhi proper, the old city built by the infidels and captured in the year 1188. The second is called Siri, known also as the Abode of the Caliphate; this was the town given by the sultan to Ghiyath ad-Din, the grandson of the 'Abbasid Caliph Mustansir, when he came to his court. The third is called Tughlaq Abad, after its founder, Sultan Tughlaq, the father of the sultan of India to whose court we came. The reason why he built it was that one day he said to a former sultan " O master of the world, it were fitting that a city should be built here." The sultan replied to him in jest "When you are sultan, build it." It came about by the decree of God that he became sultan, so he built it and called it by his own name. The fourth is called Jahan Panah, and is set apart for the residence of the reigning sultan, Muhammad Shah. He was the founder of it, and it was his intention to unite these four towns within a single wall, but after building part of it he gave up the rest because of the expenses required for its construction.

"The cathedral mosque occupies a large area; its walls, roofs and paving are all constructed of white stones, admirably squared and firmly cemented with lead....At the eastern gate there are two enormous idols of brass prostrate on the ground and held by stones, and everyone entering or leaving the mosque treads on them. The site was formerly occupied by an idol temple, and was converted into a mosque on the conquest of the city. In the northern court is the minaret, which has no parallel in the land of Islam. It is built of red stone, unlike the rest of the edifice, ornamented with sculptures, and of great height....

"The king is of all men the fondest of making gifts and shedding blood. His gate is never without some poor man enriched or some living man executed, and stories are current amongst people of his generosity and courage and of his cruelty and violence towards criminals. For all that, he is of all men the most humble and readiest to show equity and justice. The ceremonies of religion are strictly complied with at his court, and he is severe in the matter of attendance at prayer and in punishing those who neglect it. He is one of those kings whose felicity is unimpaired and surpassing all ordinary experience, but his dominant quality is generosity....

"As a rule his audience are held in the afternoon, though he often holds them early in the day....As each person enters who has an appointed place of standing on the right or left, he makes obeisance on reaching the station of the chamberlains, and the chamberlains say *Bismillah,* regulating the loudness of their utterance by the rank of the person concerned, who then retires to his appointed place, beyond which he never passes. If it is one of the infidel Hindus who makes obeisance, the chamberlains say to him 'God guide thee'....

"....On one of his (sultan) entries into the capital I saw three or four small catapults placed on elephants throwing gold and silver coins amongst the people from the moment when he entered the city until he reached the palace....

"When a famine broke out in India and Sind, and prices became so high that a maund of wheat rose to six dinars, the sultan ordered that every person in Delhi should be given six months' provisions from the granary, at the rate of a pound and a half per person per day, small or great; freeman or slave. The doctors and qadis set about compiling registers of the population of each quarter and brought the people, each of whom received six months' provisions....

"The king of China had sent valuable gifts to the sultan, including a hundred slaves of both sexes, five hundred pieces of velvet and silk cloth, musk, jewelled garments and weapons, with a request that the sultan would permit him to rebuild the idol-temple which is near the mountains called Qarajil [Himalayan]. It is in a place known as Samhal, to which the Chinese go on pilgrimage; the Muslim army in India had captured it, laid it in ruins and sacked it. The sultan, on receiving this gift, wrote to the king saying that the request could not be granted by Islamic law, as permission to build a temple was granted only to those who paid a poll-tax; to which he added "If thou wilt pay the jizya we shall empower thee to build it. And peace be on those who follow True Guidance." He requited his present with an even richer (and entrusted Ibn Batuta as an ambassador to take it to the king of China)....

"On reaching Koel we heard that certain Hindu infidels had invested and surrounded the town of al-Jalali. Now this town lies at a distance of seven miles from Koel, so we made in that direction. Meanwhile the infidels were engaged in battle with its inhabitants and the latter were on the verge of destruction. The infidels knew nothing of our approach until we charged down upon them, though they numbered about a thousand cavalry and three thousand foot, and we killed them to the last man and took possession of their horses and their weapons. Of our party twenty-three horsemen and fifty-five foot-soldiers suffered martyrdom, among them the eunuch Kafur, the cup-bearer, into whose hands the present had been entrusted. We informed the sultan by letter of his death and halted to await his reply. During that time the infidels used to swoop down from an inaccessible hill which is in those parts and raid the environs of al-Jalali, and our party used to ride out every day with the commander of that district to assist him in driving them off....

"We left Koel, therefore, and encamped at Burj Bura [Burjpur], where there is a fine hermitage in which lives a beautiful and virtuous shaykh called Muhammad the Naked, because he wears nothing but a cloth from his navel to the ground. Thence we travelled to the river known as Ab-i Siyah ["Black Water," Kalindi} and from there reached the city of Qinwaj [Kanauj]. It is a large, well-built and strongly fortified city; prices there are cheap and sugar plentiful, and it is surrounded by a great wall. We spent three days here and during this time received the sultan's reply to the letter to me. It ran thus "If no trace is found of so-and-so [i.e. Ibn Batuta], let Wajih al-Mulk, the qadi of Dawlat Abad, go on his place." We came next to the small town of Mawri, and thence reached Marh, a large town, inhabited chiefly by infidels under Muslim control. It takes its name from Malawa, a tribe of Hindus, of very powerful build and good-looking; their women specially are exceedingly beautiful and famous for the charms of their company. From Marh we travelled to 'Alabur [Alapur], a small town inhabited like the former by infidels under Muslim control. A day's journey from there lived an infidel sultan, named Qatam, who was sultan of Jambil, and was killed after besieging Guyalyur [Gwalior]. The governor of 'Alabur was the Abyssinian Badr, a slave of the sultan's, a man whose bravery passed into proverb. He was continually making raids on the infidels alone and single handed, killing and taking captive, so that his fame spread far and wide and the infidels went in fear of him. He was tall and corpulent, and used to eat a whole sheep at a meal, and I was told that after eating he would drink about a pound and a half of ghee, following the custom of the Abyssinians in their own country. He had a son nearly as brave as himself. During a raid on a village belonging to some Hindus Badr's horse fell with him into a matamore and the villagers surrounded him and killed him.

"We journeyed thereafter to Galyur or Guyalyur [Gwalior], a large town with an impregnable fortress isolated on the summit of a loft hill. Over its gate is an elephant with its mahout carved in stone. The governor of this town was a man of upright character, and he treated me very honourably when I stayed with him on a previous occasion. One day I came before him as he was about to have an infidel cut in two. I said to him "By God I beseech you, do not do this, for I have never seen anyone put to death in my presence." He ordered the man to be put in prison so my intervention was the means of his escape. From Galyur we went to Parwan, a small town belonging to the Muslims, but situated in the land of the infidels. There are many tigers there, and one of the inhabitants told me that a certain tiger used to enter the town by night, although the gates were shut, and used to seize people. It killed quite a number of townsfolk in this way. They used to wonder how it made its way in. Here is an amazing thing; a man told me that it was not a tiger who did this but a human being, one of the magicians known as *Jogis* [Yogis], appearing in the shape of a tiger. When I heard this I refused to believe it, but a number of people said the same, so let us give at this point some account of the magicians....

"To return to our subject. We went from Parwan to Kajarra, where there is a large tank about a mile long having on its bank temples with idols, which have been made examples of [i.e. mutilated] by the Muslims. Thence we journeyed through Chandiri to the town of Dhihar [Dhar], which is the chief city of Malwa, the largest province in that district. It is twenty-four days' journey from Delhi, and along the road between them are pillars, on which is engraved the number of miles from each pillar to the next. When the traveller desires to know how many miles he has gone that day and how far it is to his halting place or to the town he is making for, he reads the inscription on the pillars and so finds out. From Dhihar we travelled to Ujayn [Ujjain], a fine and populous town, and thence to Dawlat Abad, the enormous city which rivals Delhi, the capital, in importance and in the spaciousness of its planning. It is divided into three sections; one in Dawlat Abad proper, the second is called Kataka, and the third is the citadel, which is unequalled for its strength and is called Duwaygir [Deogiri].

"At Dawlat Abad resides the great khan Qutlu Khan, the sultan's tutor, who is the governor of the town, and the sultan's representative there and in the lands of Saghar, Tiling [Telingana], and their dependent territories. This province extends for three months' march, is well-populated, and wholly under his authority and that of his lieutenants. The fortress of Duwaygir mentioned above is a rock situated in a plain; the rock has been excavated and a castle built on its summit. It is reached by a ladder made of leather, which is taken up at night. In its dungeons are imprisoned those convicted of serious crime, and in these dungeons there are huge rats, bigger than cats—in fact, cats run away from them and cannot defend themselves against them, so they can be captured only by employing ruses. I saw them there and marvelled at them. The inhabitants of Dawlat Abad belong to the tribe of Marhata [Marathas]' whose women God has endowed with special beauty, particularly in their noses and eyebrows. The infidels of this town are merchants, dealing principally in jewels, and their wealth is enormous. In Dawlat Abad there is an exceedingly fine and spacious bazaar for singers and singing-girls, containing numerous shops, each of which has a door leading to the house of its proprietor. The shop is beautified with carpets, and in the centre of it there is a sort of large cradle on which the singing-girl sits or reclines. She is adorned with all kinds of ornaments and her attendants swing her cradle. In the centre of the bazaar there is a large carpeted and decorated pavilion in which the chief musician sits every Thursday after the afternoon prayer, with his servants and slaves in front of him. The singing-girls come in relays and sing and dance before him till the sunset prayer, when they withdraw. In the same bazaar there are mosques for the prayer-services. One of the infidel rulers in India used, on passing through this bazaar, to alight at the pavilion and the singing-girls used to sing before him. One of the Muhammadan sultans used to do the same....

"Three days later we reached the land of Mulaybar [Malabar], which is the pepper country. It extends for two months' journey along the coast from Sandabur [Goa] to Kawlam [Quilon, in Travancore]. The road over the whole distance runs beneath the shade of trees, and at every half-mile, there is a wooden shed with benches on which all travellers, whether Muslims or infidels, may sit. At each shed there is a well for drinking and an infidel who is in charge of it. If the traveller is an infidel he gives him water in vessels; if he is a Muslim he pours the water into his hands, continuing to do so until he signs to him to stop. It is the custom of the infidels in the Mulaybar lands that no Muslim may enter their houses or eat from their vessels; if he does so they break the vessels or give them to the Muslims. In places where there are no Muslim inhabitants they give him food on banana leaves. At all the halting-places on this road there are houses belonging to the Muslims, at which Muslim travellers alight, and where they buy all that they need. Were it not for them no Muslim could travel by it.

"On this road, which, as we have said, extends for a two months' march, there is not a foot of ground but is cultivated. Every man has his own orchard, with his house in the middle and a wooden palisade all round it. The road runs through the orchards, and when it comes to a palisade there are wooden steps to go up by and another flight of steps down into the next orchard. No one travels on an animal in that country, and only the sultan possesses horses. The principal vehicle of the inhabitants is a palanquin carried on the shoulders of slaves or hired porters; those who do not travel on palanquins go on foot, be they who they may. Baggage and merchandise is transported by hired carriers, and a single merchant may have a hundred such or thereabouts carrying his goods. I have never seen a safer road than this, for they put to death anyone who steals a single nut, and if any fruit falls no one picks it up but the owner. Indeed we sometimes met infidels during the night on this road, and when they saw us they stood aside to let us pass. Muslims are most highly honoured amongst them, except that, as we have said, they do not eat with them nor allow them into their houses. In the Mulaybar lands there are twelve infidel sultans, some of them strong with armies numbering fifty thousand men, and others weak with armies of three thousand. Yet there is no discord whatever between them, and the strong does not desire to seize the possessions of the weak. At the boundary of the territories of each ruler there is wooden gateway, on which is engraved the name of the ruler whose territories begin at that point. This is called the "Gate of Security" of such-and such a prince. If any Muslim or infidel criminal flees from the territories of one and reaches the Gate of Security of another, his life is safe, and the prince from whom he has fled cannot seize him, even though he be a powerful prince with a great army. The rulers in these lands transmit their sovereignty to their sisters' sons, to the exclusion of their own children. I have seen this practice nowhere else except among the veiled Massufa, who will be mentioned later.

"The first town in the land of Mulaybar that we entered was the town of Abu-Sarur [Barcelore], a small place on a large inlet and abounding in coco-palms. Two days' journey brought us to Fakanur [Bacanor, now Barkur], a large town on an inlet; here there is a large quantity of sugar- canes, which are unexcelled in the rest of that country. The chief of the Muslim community at Fakanur is called Basadaw. He possesses about thirty warships, commanded by a Muslim called Lula, who is an evildoer and a pirate and a robber of merchants. When we anchored, the sultan sent his son to us to stay on board the ship as a hostage. We went on shore to visit him and he treated us with the utmost hospitality for three nights, as a mark of respect for the sultan of India and also from a desire to make some profit by trading with the personnel of our vessels. It is a custom of theirs that every ship that passes by a town must needs anchor at it and give a present to the ruler. This they call the "right of *bandar*." If anyone omits to do this, they sail out in pursuit of him, bring him into the port by force, double the tax on him, and prevent him from proceeding on his journey for as long as they wish. Three days after leaving Fakanur we reached Manjarur [Mangalore], a large town on the inlet called ad-Dumb, which is the largest inlet in the land of Mulaybar. This is the town at which most of the merchants from Fars and Yemen disembark, and pepper and ginger are exceedingly abundant there.

The sultan of Manjarur is one of the principal rulers in that land, and his name is Rama Daw. There is a colony of about four thousand Muslims there, living in a suburb alongside the town. Conflicts frequently break out between them and the townspeople, but the sultan makes peace between them on account of his need of the merchants. We refused to land until the sultan sent his son, as the previous sultan had done. When he had done so, we went on shore and were treated with great consideration.

"After staying at Manjarur for three days, we set sail for the town of Hili, which we reached two days later. It is large and well-built, situated on a big inlet which is navigable for large vessels. This is the farthest town reached by ships from China; they enter only this port, the port of Kawlam, and Calicut. The town of Hili is venerated by both Muslims and infidels on account of its cathedral mosque, and sea-farers make many votive offerings to it. This mosque contains a number of students, who receive stipends from its revenues, and it has a kitchen from which travellers and the Muslim poor are supplied with food. Thence we sailed to Jurfattan [Cannanore], Dahfattan, and Budfattan; the sultan of these towns is called Kuwayl, and is one of the most powerful sultans of Mulaybar. At Dahfuttan there is a great *ba'in* and a cathedral mosque, which were built by Kuwayl's grandfather, who was converted to Islam. Most of the inhabitants of Budfattan are Brahmans, who are venerated by the infidels and who hate the Muslims; for this reason there are no Muslims living amongst them. From Budfattan we sailed to Fandarayna [Panderani], a large and fine town with orchards and bazaars. The Muslims occupy three quarters in it each, each of which has a mosque. It is at this town that the Chinese vessels pass the winter. Thence we travelled to the city of Qalicut [Calicut], which is one of the chief ports in Mulaybar and one of the largest harbours in the world. It is visited by men from China, Sumatra, Ceylon, the Maldives, Yemen and Fars, and in it gather merchants from all quarters.

"The sultan of Calicut is an infidel, known as "the Samari." He is an aged man and shaves his beard, as some of the Greeks do. In this town too lives the famous shipowner Mithqal, who possesses vast wealth and many ships for his trade with India, China, Yemen, and Fars. When we reached the city, the principal inhabitants and merchants and the sultan's representative came out to welcome us, with drums, trumpets, bugles and standards on their ships. We entered the harbour in great pomp, the like of which I have never seen in those lands, but it was a joy to be followed by distress. We stopped in the port of Calicut, in which there were at the time thirteen Chinese vessels, and disembarked, Every one of us was lodged at in a house and we stayed there three months as the guest of the infidels, awaiting the season of the voyage to China. On the Sea of China travelling is done in Chinese ships only, so we shall describe their arrangements."

1. *Ibn Batuta—Travels In Asia And Africa, 1325-1354*, published by Routledge & Kegan Paul.
2. *Ibn Batuta—Travels In Asia And Africa, 1325-1354*, published by Routledge & Kegan Paul, (Ch. 1, Introduction)

25
DIALOGUE BETWEEN HINDUISM AND ISLAM

Though the concept of the fundamental unity of God was not totally alien to Hindu thought, yet it cannot be denied that the introduction of the monotheistic religion of Islam in India encouraged the rise of religious schools preaching this unity, and then bringing the two communities together to express their devotion to that entity. A few centuries had passed before the wave of Bhakti movement which had traveled from south had reached north. There it met with the Sufis. Both found mutuality in ideas and practices. Together, they created an atmosphere of peace and serenity. Both preached union with God and love of Him and His creatures as the ultimate approach to life. They attacked institutionalized religions and the prevailing social inequalities. The interaction of Sufi and Bhakti movements produced some great teachers who had the qualities of a sufi and a bhagat at the same time. They preached the supremacy of love and peace which was deemed more important and desirable than strict adherence to the outward form of a religion and its rituals.

The Sufis: With the establishment of Muslim rule the sufis also got a foothold in India. They were mystic saints, intoxicated with love of god, and disassociated with the worldly life of ease and pleasure. Sufism had originated in Iraq in eighth century from where they moved to Iran. It derived its name from suf, the coarse wool, in which its votaries wrapped themselves up, hence called sufis. Like the Hindus intoxicated with bhakti, these Muslim saints also yearned for union with God. Their philosophy was that of *sulh-i-kul*, i.e. peace with all or total peace. They sprang up all over the length and breadth of the country and brought their message of divine love to impoverished peasants and long-abused Sudras. Their philosophy was not approved by the orthodox Muslim ulema, who considered them as heretic in thoughts, broad-minded in religion, and too liberal in their dealings and conduct. Even the Sultans remained occasionally suspicious of the centres of Sufi teachings as the potential brewer of revolt. This led the sufis to become secretive and pass their lives in seclusion cutting themselves off from the mainstream of society. Had they not been cut of from the society, they could have been more effective in mobilizing support for a social framework of a less religious nature. As the sufis laid Islamic stress on equality far more than the ulema, it was natural that they came more into contact with the artisans and the cultivators, and thus were more effective religious leaders for the common people. They did not approve of the conduct of *ulema* whom they considered mere worldly and opportunist. They considered that the ulema's conduct of mixing religion with politics and interfering in the affairs of the state by projecting their own views smacked of misrepresentation of the democratic and egalitarian spirit of Islam, which called for *sulh-i-kul*. Sometimes the sufis, who were also called dervishes (ascetics), formed an order under a *pir* or *shaikh*, equivalent of a Hindu guru. Yugis and followers of various religious cults were used to living in seclusion in India from ancient times. The sufis thus found here a conducive environment for this way of living. They appeared no stranger here, and as such they acquired a large following, both of Muslims and Hindus. By the thirteenth century various orders of sufis had appeared in India such as the Chishtis, the Firdawsis, and the Suhrawardis.

Kabir and Nanak: Among the great sufis/bhagats, the names of Kabir and Nanak survive to this day. They took inspiration from both Islamic and Indian traditions and tried to fuse their messages of love into their own, but never intended to present an eclectic ideology. Popularity to their teachings grew not as a body of theological principles but as a message to upgrade the prevailing social conditions. The large followings they won came from the lower strata of society, mainly from amongst the artisans and the cultivators, for their messages denounced the caste system and organized religions which kept men apart by denying them social equality. Naturally, they faced the antagonism of both Hindu brahmans and Muslim ulema.

Ramananda, the greatest disciple of Ramanuja, had settled near the banks of the holy Ganga at Benaras and was preaching the doctrine of divine love. He was the votary of Rama, and popularized Rama *bhakti* during the fourteenth and fifteenth centuries. The devotees were called Ramanandi *bairagis*. His disciples established *maths* or devotional centres at many places, where foods were distributed to any body who wanted a meal. They also established *pathshalas* or teaching centres and *goshalas* (home for discarded cows).

One of Ramananda's devotee was an illiterate weaver of Uttar Pradesh, Kabir (1440-1518), believed to have been the offspring of a brahman widow. As his foster father was a weaver he was trained in the same profession, which was deemed as of low caste even by the Muslims despite their apparent adherence to the egalitarian principles of Islam. Kabir eventually became disgruntled with the teachings of Ramananda, and so he began to preach his own ideas. He was concerned with effecting change in the norms of society focused towards peace and love among different people more than with mere religious reform. He spoke of love among the human beings laying stress on the brotherhood of Hindus and Muslims. He preached that the God which is worshipped by them is one; only He is recognized by them differently. So all peoples and communities should dismantle the feeling of being different from each other. 'Neither a Hindu nor a Muslim am I!' cried Kabir, 'A mere ensemble of five elements in this body, where the spirit plays its drama of joy and suffering.' He denounced worship of images in temples, purifactory bathing, ritual fasts and pilgrimage to holy places. What led to God was the path of love. It was bhakti, an ardent quest, in which Kabir was completely involved.

His followers were both Hindus and Muslims, who joined him in large numbers and called themselves Kabir-panthis. His devotional poems inspired millions of Hindu and Muslim followers to abandon the sectarian perceptions of their own religions in place of Kabir's syncretic path of simple love of God. With his simple poetry of love, easily understood and memorized by common man, and full of similes derived from a weaver's profession, he tried to bridge the gap between the people. His movement, however, waned and faded away after his death and what now remains is the legacy of love in the shape of a few couplets in two collections. His works were translated into English in 1915 by Rabindranath Tagore.

O servant, where dost thou seek Me:
Lo, I am beside thee.
I am neither in temple nor in mosque : I am neither in Kaaba nor in Kailash
Neither am I in rites and ceremonies, nor in Yoga and renunciation.
If though art a true seeker, thou shalt at once see Me : thou shalt meet Me in a moment of time.
Kabir says, 'O Sadhu, God is breath of all breath.'

...
If God be within the mosque, then to whom does this world belong?
If Ram be within the image which you find upon your pilgrimage,
then who is there to know what happens without?
Hari is in the East; Allah is in the West. Look within your heart, for
there you will find both Karim and Ram;
All the men and women in the world are His living forms.
Kabir is the child of Allah and of Ram: He is my Guru, He is my Pir.[1]

....

'Gorakh! Gorakh!'
cries the Jogi,
'Ram! Ram!'
says the Hindu.
'Allah is One'
proclaims the Muslim.
But, O Kabir,
My Lord pervades all'

....

'The god of Hindus resides in a temple;
The god of Muslims resides in a mosque.
Who resides there
Where there are no temples
Or mosques?
O seeker, follow your own path,
Forget the mosque, forget the temple,
Be your own light.
Open your eyes and see
That Rama and Allah are One!'
(Kumar 1984:31)

....

'We've lived our whole lives at your doors,
But we never met each other.
You were inside, we were outside.
You were in temple, we were on the steps
Because you thought us Untouchable.

But those days are over.
We've begun a new life.
We have found our own temples,
Regained our lost faith.
Our gods are where we are.

All are equal here...
The faith is going to
Penetrate every corner of the world.
Now you can scream.
It's fallen! It's fallen!
Brahmin *dharma* has been overthrown.
You lit your own pyre.
What can you do now?'
(By Harish Barisode, Quoted in Hiro 1982:14)

....

'When I knew nothing, I knew
My caste was despised...
The patil had kicked my father,
Cursed my mother.
They did not even raise their heads,
But I felt this "caste" in my heart.
When I climbed the step to school, Then too I knew my caste was low.
I used to sit outside, the others inside.
My skin would suddenly shiver with little thorns,
My eyes could not hold back the tears.
Our lips must smile when they cursed....
How is caste? Where is it?
It isn't seen, so does it live inside the body?
All the questions float like smoke,
And the wick of thought is sputtering.
But when I knew nothing, then I knew
My caste was low.'
(By Waman Nibalkar in Hiro 1982:14)

....

Kabir asks derisively:
'Pandit, look in your heart for knowledge.
Tell me where untouchablity
came from, since you believe in it....
Eighty-four hundred thousand vessels
Decay into dust, while the potter
keeps slapping clay
on the wheel, and with a touch
cuts each one off.
We eat by touching, we wash
By touching, from a touch
The world was born.
So who is untouched?' asks Kabir.[2]

....

The man who is kind, who practices righteousness,
Who remains passive amidst the affairs of the world,
who considers all creatures on earth as his own self:
He attains the Immortal Being,
The True God is ever with him.[3]

......

It is needless to ask of a saint the caste to which he belongs;
For the priest, the warrior, the tradesman, and all the thirty-six castes, alike are seeking God.
It is but folly to ask what the caste of a saint may be;
The barber has sought God, the washer-woman, and the carpenter-
Even Raidas was a seeker after God.
The Rishi Swapacha was a tanner by caste.
Hindus and Muslims alike have achieved that End, where remains no mark of distinction.

....

There is nothing but water at the holy bathing places; and I know that they are useless, for I have bathed in them.
The images are all lifeless, they cannot speak; for I have cried aloud to them.
The Purana and the Quran are mere words; lifting up the curtain, I have seen.
Kabir gives utterance to the words of experience; and he knows very well that all other things are untrue.[4]

Nanak Chand (1469-1539), later called with reverence as Guru Nanak, was born in a Hindu family in a village of Punjab called Rai Bhodi di Talwandi, but reared on the democratic doctrines of Islam. He was educated with the financial help of a Muslim. He became a store-keeper in the administration of Daulat Khan Lodhi, the *shiqdar* of Sultanpur. Earlier in life he had come in contact with some Muslim sufis, who left a deep impress upon his mind. Becoming restless, he travelled far and wide and even went to Makkah, the religious and spiritual centre of Islam, in search of spiritual truth. He returned to his village and family, and then turned into a minstrel who sang the message of love combining the best elements of Hinduism and Islam. He borrowed such ideas from Islam as monotheism and brotherhood. He preached for a caste-less society and laid stress on congregational prayers as a gesture of both solidarity and equality. Guru Nanak identifies himself with the lower castes: '*Be there the lowest among the low, or even the lower, Nanak is with them. There is none who is nich* (low)'- AG, 62. God, according to him, is a formless Reality, and images are not worthy of worship. '*The gods and goddesses whom you worship and to whom you pray, what can they give? You wash them yourselves; left to themselves, they will sink in the water*'-AG, 637. '*By adoring the Truth, Nanak has found the Perfect One*'- AG, 150.[5] He asserted that communion with God could be established only through the grace of a *guru* ('divine teacher'). Nanak became the first Guru. Thus came into being the Sikh (meaning 'to learn' or 'disciple') religion, drawing its recruits mostly from hard working peasantry of Hindus and Muslims.

The True One was in the beginning, the True One was in the primal age,
The True One is now also, O Nanak; the True One also shall be.
By His order bodies are produced; His order cannot be described.
By His order souls are infused into them; by His order greatness is obtained.
By His order men are high or low; by His order they obtain pre-ordained pain or pleasure.
By His order some obtain their reward; by His order others must ever wander in transmigration.
All are subject to His order; none is exempt from it.
He who understands God's order, O Nanak, is never guilty of egoism.[6]

In 1604 a holy book was compiled. That book is now known as the Adi Granth, the old book, to distinguish it from the later Dasam Granth, the book of the tenth Guru. It is more popularly referred to Granth Sahib as a mark of respect, and as Guru Granth Sahib to indicate that it enjoys the status of the Guru. For the fifth Guru Arjun, under whose guidance the Book was compiled, it was no ordinary compilation: 'The book is the abode of God.'[7] Conceived as a doctrine of living devotion to the one God or the Creator or The Truth (*Sat*), this religion later became a martial creed and took up the sword. During the seventeenth century the gurus entered into Mughal politics and unfortunately found themselves in opposition. Guru Nanak's successors started acting like worldly chiefs. This resulted in a radical transformation of this unworldly sect into a militant community. Consequently, religious passions were aroused. The first clash with the Mughals came when the Guru backed the wrong side at Jahangir's accession by supporting his misguided son Khusrow. The animosity climaxed when Aurangzeb executed Guru Tegh Bahadur in 1675. His successor, Guru Gobind, completed the transformation of the sect into a militant religious body distinct from both Hinduism and Islam. Though he submitted shortly before his death to Bahadur Shah, the conflict had been too bitter for reconciliation and the new community acquired a notable anti-Muslim bias, despite the fact that Sikhism profusely inducted many good principles of Islam into its own. For instance, the Islamic prohibition of alcohol was matched by a ban on tobacco, and meat was added to the permitted Sikh diet. The Sikhs had a holy book in the Granth Sahib or Adi Granth like the Qur'an of the Muslims. Sikhism eschewed idolatry and caste system. If the Muslims had religious warriors of *ghazis* in their rank, the Sikhs had their own holy warriors in the *akalis*.

In Bengal, the preaching of Chaitanya (1485-1533) gave rise to another syncretic sect which centered around the worship of a Satya-Pir (Truth-Saint). His disciples believed that Chaitanya was a reincarnation of the Hindu divine lovers Radha and Krishna together in one body. He cultivated the emotional side of *bhakti* through *kirtanas* or devotional songs sung with musical instruments and in ecstatic dance. His movement, however, remained local. Krishna bhakti was popularized by another saint, Vallabhacharya in Uttar Pradesh, Rajasthan and Gujerat. He developed the ceremonial side of *bhakti* in temples where the daily round of his activities were ceremonialized from the early morning when the Lord awoke till he went to bed at night for sleep. Another dervish, Daud Dayal (1544-1603) shared devotional beliefs and practices with sympathetic Sufis.

1. Rabindranath Tagore (trans.), *Songs of Kabir*, Quoted in *A History of India*, Volume One, Romila Thapar, Ch 13
2. Quoted in *Hindus: Their Religious Beliefs and Practices* by Julius Lipner
3. *South Asia: A Short History,* Hugh Tinker
4. *One Hundred Poems of Kabir*, translated by Rabindranath Tagore. Quoted in *The Oxford History of India*, Book IV, Ch. 3, Fourth Edition, Vincent A. Smith
5. *The New Cambridge History of India*, Vol. II.3, Ch. 2, ed. J. S. Grewal
6. M. A. Macauliffe, *The Sikh Religion*, I, Quoted in *A History of India*, Volume One, Romila Thapar, Ch 13
7. *The New Cambridge History of India*, Vol. II.3, Ch. 3, ed. J. S. Grewal

26
ARRIVAL OF THE GRAND MUGHALS

On the eve of the Mughals' arrival the Indian political scene was in disarray. Sultan Ibrahim Lodhi (1517-26) had lost the allegiance of his courtiers. In the intense struggle for power in the north, the Sultanate at Delhi had become totally oblivious of the presence and highhandedness of the Portuguese at the south-western coast. The Hindu masses were mainly occupied in agriculture in the villages. Devotion to idol worshipping was operating with full force and with all its paraphernalia. The brahmans were controlling the temples and schools, with no mitigating effect on the caste system. The elite class of both Hindus and Muslims came mainly from the land-holding group, who were ever ready to serve and please the local rajas, or to assume power of their own, whenever possible. Religious movements continued to spring up throughout the country. The Sufis, on the other hand, had brought Islam to the doorstep of the general population and by that time had converted a lot of people. At the time of the Mughals' entry into India the overall cultural and religious climate had become more open and tolerant of change. Several centuries of dominance of Muslim power had, on the one hand, led Hindu institutions to a reaction by strengthening popular devotional expression, and on the other, the Muslims of both north and south India had developed understanding and a fellow-feeling with the Indian society and even towards Hinduism. Mystics, and intellectuals, and even ordinary Hindu and Muslim folks were in quest of some form of synthesis between the two.

The long reign of the grand Mughals started on April 21, 1526, when "I placed my foot in the stirrup of resolution and my hands on the reins of confidence in God and marched against Sultan Ibrahim...whose army in the field was said to amount to a hundred thousand men and who....had nearly a thousand elephants..... The sun had mounted spear-high when the onset began, and the battle lasted till mid-day, when the enemy were completely broken, and routed. By the grace and mercy of the Almighty God this difficult affair was made easy to me, and that mighty army, in the space of half a day, was laid in dust." This was the account of the founder of the Mughal empire, Zahiruddin Babar, given in his memoir, *Babar Nama*.[1] But the intensely hot and humid climate of India was too unpleasant and unbearable for the army, his close companions and even for Babar himself, who admitted later: 'Hindustan has few pleasures to recommend it. The people are not handsome. They have no idea of the charms of frankly mixing together, or of sociable intercourse. They have no imaginative mind, no politeness of manners, no amiable feelings, no ingenuity in mechanical matters when planning or executing their handicraft works, nor skill or knowledge in their architecture.... Hindustan is a large country and has abundance of gold and silver. There are innumerable workmen of every kind, and for every sort of work and everything there is a fixed caste that has done that work or that thing from father to son until now. All artisans, wage earners and official workers are Hindus. In our country the wild folk have tribal names, but here those on farms and in towns are named like different tribes. Most of the inhabitants of Hindustan are pagans; they call a pagan a Hindu. Most Hindus believe in transmigration of souls'.

Babar had not risked his life and those of his followers in vain. And who would like to forsake a great country like India for a small principality of barren Afghanistan? But Babar would not also hold up those who wanted to go back to Afghanistan. He told them 'If there is any one amongst you who cannot bring himself to stay, he can depart. He has my permission'. In this moment of triumph and rejoicing the loyal followers too would not forsake their *padishah*. They decided to stay with him. Only Khoja Kilan, Babar's old friend, decided to go back home because of his physical condition. While departing, he inscribed the following in a light vein on the walls of his residence:

If safe and sound I pass the Sind
Shame on me if ever again I long for the land of Hind!

Babar's wittiness was not slow to a reply, which he promptly dispatched through a messenger to Khoja Kilan:

Babar, give hundred thanks to God most High,
Who gave you Sind and Hind and royal kingdoms,

If ever wearied by the fires of its sky
You long for cold, remember the frost and ice of Ghazni![2]

Such a reply was sent despite his own admission later in *Babar-Nama* that "This is quite a different world from our countries". In India "they have no good horses, no good flesh, no grapes or musk-melons, no good fruit, no ice or cold water, no good food or bread in their bazaars, no baths or colleges or candles or torches..."

Turmoil had engulfed the political life of India. The Sultanate lay shattered and a new power had arisen. It was not yet tested. The Hindu powers saw it fit to reorganize themselves in order to oust the Muslims from India for good. A confederacy was formed under the leadership of Rana Sanga, the Rajput ruler of Mewar. They hoped to banish the nascent power of the Mughals. Babar faced the confederate army in the battle of Khanua in March 1527. Though heavily outnumbered by the enemies, he emerged victorious, destined to strengthen the foundation of the long-lasting Mughal dynasty.

Babar's yearning for the life of his native land remained a dream, and he was forced, by circumstances, to pass the rest of his life on Indian soil till he died in 1530 leaving the throne to his eldest son Humayun. Babar was beyond sectarian feelings and quarrels, and loved to call himself a *qualandar* (carefree *dervish*). Babar left a will for his son, as authenticated by Professor R. Nath, a Professor at Rajasthan University, that it was *'incumbent that religious bigotries should be wiped off the tablet of the heart, and justice meted out to each religion according to its tenets...The temples and places of worship of whatever religion under the royal authority may not be desecrated.*[3]

When Humayun's brothers, Kamran and Askari, revolted in order to capture the throne and gave him enough trouble Humayun had to neutralize them by subjecting Kamran to a particularly sadistic blinding and Askari to a long period of harsh confinement before banishing him to Mecca. After overthrowing Humayun in the battle near Kanauj, Sher Shah assumed the kingship of Hindustan. In the short reign of five years he proved to be a very able administrator. He controlled the crime, developed a remarkable revenue-collection system, built the Grand trunk Road, and laid a network of caravan-sarais (inns) by the side of roads, where both Hindus and Muslims were served without distinction. Brahmans supplied water and cooked food for the Hindus so as their religious laws were not violated.

1. Zahiruddin Babar, *Babar Nama*, as translated by J. Leyden and W. Erskine. See *A New History of India* (Fifth Edition), Ch Eight, Stanley Wopert
2. *The Builders of the Mughal Empire*, Michael Prawdin
3. *The Indus Saga and the Making of Pakistan*, Aitzaz Ahsan

27
UNLETTERED PHILOSOPHER

Tolerance and love are preached by social reformers and religious teachers. Rulers and monarchs practice tolerance. After Asoka, it was the grandson of the founder of Mughal empire, Jalaluddin Akbar, that he both preached and practiced it. A boy king of thirteen at the death of his father Humayun, Akbar spent his youth learning to hunt and fight with no time to read or write. At least four tutors tried to teach the young prince to read, but they all failed. A recent analysis suggests that Akbar was probably dyslexic and thus physically unable to read.[1] But he developed the practice of having himself read to daily. His son Jahangir, commented in Tuzuk-i- Jahangiri: 'My father always associated with the learned of every creed and religion, especially with the Pundits and the learned of India, and although he was illiterate, so much became clear to him through constant intercourse with the learned and wise...that no one knew him to be illiterate, and he was so acquainted with the niceties of verse and prose compositions that his deficiency was not thought of.'[2]

Akbar was illiterate, and so were the prophets. Therefore, he thought, he also should have at least the qualities of a prophet. If not a representative of God on earth who could give a new religion, he at least could give a framework of laws and customs based on religion. This synergy might have been brought about to him by the circumstances of his birth and upbringing: born to a *sunni* father and a *shia* mother when they were on the run in a far away place at Omarkot in Sindh, taking birth in the house of a Hindu prince, nursed by a shrewd women Maham Anga and tutored by a trusted shia courtier Bayram Khan amidst *sufis* like Mir Abdul Latif. He thus gave his men the message of unity and a religion called *Din-i-Ilahi* (The Religion of God). The message of unity was well taken but not the religion, which did not travel probably beyond the confines of his court. It soon faded as a non-starter. What emanated from Akbar's heart was the desire to remove differences among the people of his country and to unite the believers of different faiths by breaking the traditional barriers among the religions. And the product of his political mind was the prolonging of the Mughal rule and unity of the country with the participation of all communities in the affairs of the state, specially the majority community. H. G. Wells says in *The Outline of History:*

"Akbar, next perhaps to Asoka, was one of the greatest of Indian monarchs, and one of the few royal figures that approach the stature of great men....

"His distinctive quality was his openness of mind. He set himself to make every sort of able man in India, whatever his race or religion, available for the public work of Indian life. His instinct was the true statesman's instinct for synthesis. His empire was to be neither a Moslem nor a Mongol one, nor was it to be Rajput or Aryan, or Dravidian, or Hindu, or high or low caste; it was to be *Indian*."[3]

Akbar's policy of religious toleration was both political and humane. He aimed at creating a cult of the ruler: a just ruler. It was a political necessity too. "On one occasion, when it was necessary to persuade the Raja of Jodhpore to abandon his intention of forcing the widow of his deceased son to mount the funeral pyre, Akbar rode two hundred and twenty miles in two days. In battle he displayed the utmost bravery. He led his troops in person during the dangerous part of a campaign, leaving to his generals the lighter task of finishing the war. In every victory he displayed humanity to the conquered, and decisively opposed any exhibition of cruelty. Free from all those prejudices which separate society and create dissention, tolerant to men of other beliefs, impartial to men of other races, whether Hindu or Dravidian, he was a man obviously marked out to weld the conflicting elements of his kingdom into a strong and prosperous whole."[4]

By this time the initial period of the Muslim rule in India was over and enough time had passed. A lot of assimilation had taken place and differences between the ruling and the subject races were in the process of fading away. The Muslims were no more outsiders in the land. It was Akbar's brilliance that he sensed the wind of change and recognized the pluralistic nature of Indian society. He realized that such a vast empire with a miniscule minority of the Muslims could not be governed without cooperation of the Hindus. He recognized that a Muslim regime, howsoever strong and brilliant outwardly, cannot survive in India unless it was buttressed by the intrinsic strength of the Hindus. Therefore, he was to become a leader, not of the minority group of the Muslims but a leader of all-India stature by treating the indigenous Hindu population as equal of his Muslim subjects. In 1562 Akbar abolished the practice of enslaving prisoners of war and their families, and of forcibly converting them to Islam. If a Hindu had been made a Muslim against his will, he was allowed to go back to his old religion if he wanted to, and, for that matter, anyone could go over to any religion he wanted. In 1563, when he learned at one of his hunting trips near Mathura that Hindus were subjected to a pilgrim tax while travelling to worship at sacred places in India, he abolished the tax immediately. It is unworthy for a worshipper of God, he declared, to levy a due on other worshippers when they wanted to worship Him. In 1564 he abolished the hated *jizya.* The symbol of discrimination was gone and Hindus started feeling comfortable as equal to Muslims. It is believed that in the beginning he had to face strong opposition of the ulema but later he prevailed. He castigated them for their medieval outlook. The abolition of *jizya* was one of the most important measures which won the support of the majority of India's population. One of the edicts of Akbar issued for a Jat clan in Muzaffarnagar near Delhi reads:

> By the present farman...., certain community councils in India which during the reign of the Muslim sultans, before my reign, were charged certain taxes, are now being excused. Each community council has my permission and is free to carry on its traditional functions, in my reign. Both Hindus and Muslims are one in my eyes, so I give freedom [of action] to those councils. They are exempt from the payment of *jaziah* [religious tax] and other taxes.
>
> *Issued in the reign of emperor of India, Emperor Akbar, 11th Ramzan, 989 Hijri [A.D. 1580]. Mandate issued by grand wazirs, Abul-Fazel and Raja Todar Mal.*[5]

Not only did he allow the Jesuits to build a church, he issued an order that 'if any of the infidels chose to build a synagogue, or an idol temple, or a Parsee tower of silence, no one was to hinder him'. He, along with his courtiers, began participating in the celebration of Hindu festivals of Dipavali and Rakhi and the Zoroastrian festival of Navroz, and even wore the Hindu sacred thread, and made it a point to drink only Ganga water, if possible. He declared cow slaughter an offence, possibly punishable by death. He adopted the Hindu custom by having himself weighed against gold, silver and grains, and giving alms to the poor. Wherever a local dispute involved two

Hindus, Hindu Law (*dharmashastra*) was applied. Decision of the village panchayat was final, unless appealed to the emperor. Akbar instituted *madad-i-m'ash* (sustenance grants) for brahman priests, jogis, and religious institutions. Two documents preserved in the Saivite shrine at Jakhbar, sixteen miles from Pathankot in the Punjab, confirm to this. It was the seat of meditation of Saivite Jogis. An imperial order issued in 1581 added fifty bighas of tax-free land to the parcel of *madad-i-m'ash* lands given ten years earlier in order to compensate for the loss of lands inundated and made useless. Since the Jogi Udant Nath had been "honored with admittance to the imperial court," he obtained confirmation of the earlier largess and the additional lands. In return he was to "remain occupied with praying for the permanence of the Conquering Dynasty while sustaining himself year after year with the entire produce from that (land)."[6] Other religious denominations also received land grants of Akbar. By such a policy of reconciliation he earned for himself the distinguished honour of being the first Muslim ruler to receive full allegiance of all the ethnic and religious groups living in India. His claim to rule, he felt, should be accepted by dint of reasons and not because of any superior force. It proved so durable that loyalty to the Mughal dynasty became the uniting force in the War of Independence against the British three centuries later in 1857, at a time when the Mughals were kings only in name for the preceding one hundred years.

In 1579, Akbar issued the Infallibility Decree by which he assumed the power to make final decision in any matter on which the ulema disagreed. He stopped paying annual subsidies to Mecca and Medina, substituted the Hejira calendar with his own reign and started reading the *khutba* at Friday Prayers. Some times he used mosques as storage places, or even destroyed some, but it does not mean that he was against his religion. He simply demonstrated that Islam was not the supreme religion of the land and that he was daring the authority of the *mullas.* When Akbar discovered that Muslim religious institutions and individuals held a large portion of the lands of the empire as tax-exempt religious grants, many of which were obtained or transferred to heirs illegally or fraudulently, he ordered in 1578 a thorough scrutiny and verification of titles of all land grants made on grounds of piety and religious charity. The lands which could not be authenticated were immediately resumed. Later he placed some restrictions on such grants and fraudulent inheritances. It was natural that tension between him and the ulema should grow into a full-blown political conflict. Afraid of Hinduism's resilience and absorptive power, and thus apprehensive of loss of Islamic identity of the minority Muslim population, the ulema were understandably alerted. Through taxes like *jizya* and provisions of the sharia they had intended to have a direct influence on state policies and to inflict harsh treatments on the idolaters. Orthodox Muslims came to the conclusion that the emperor had abandoned Islam entirely. A person like Shaikh Ahmad Sirhindi, could muster the courage to criticize him openly. As a protege of Abul Fazl at Akbar's court he was convinced that the emperor was opposed to the true path of Islam. Led by another religious personality, the Mulla of Jaunpur, the imams of the mosques instigated the congregation of Muslims to rise in revolt against the king. In 1581 rebellion flared in Bengal and Kabul. In the final decade of his reign, orthodox Muslim opposition mounted in the north but Akbar managed to suppress them all.

During the Sultanate period, Hindus were employed in large numbers in administration and even were active members of the war machinery, yet they were a subordinate group to the newly victorious Muslims. They had no say in the policy matters of the state. The majority of the Hindus were peasants and artisans. Their militancy was represented by the Rajputs. The concentration of Rajputs as a powerful group was found in Rajasthan; nevertheless they were scattered all over India both as farmers and chiefs. Therefore, Akbar first decided to woo the Rajputs, marrying the daughter of Raja of Amber (Jaipur) in 1562. What made this marriage special was the fact that the bride was allowed to continue practicing her religion as freely as before. Shortly thereafter he also married a daughter of Raja of Jaisalmar and a niece of Raja of Bikaner. These marriages won for Akbar the goodwill of the Rajputs. But Akbar was not a sage that he was ever ready to stoop low for conciliation and for winning his adversaries' allegiance. Rana of Mewar, a descendant of Rana Sanga, was adamantly opposed to striking a note of reconciliation with the Mughal emperor despite Akbar's diplomatic overtures. When Akbar realized that his attempts at reconciliation had resulted only in puffing up the Rajput's pride, he personally led the siege of Chitor in October 1567 and 'ordered the massacre of some thirty thousand of its defendants when it fell in February 1568. No prisoners were taken; only the massive regalia, Mewar's kettledrum and candelabra, were dragged back to Agra as symbols of the Mughal victory, which had broken the back of Rajput resistance. Ranthambore surrendered in March 1569, and Kalinjar that August. By November 1570, virtually all the chiefs of Rajasthan-except for the Rana of Mewar, who had fled to the hills-had sworn allegiance to Akbar.'[7] In return of their allegiance and loyalty the Rajputs were brought into the service of state. Not only this, they were now inducted into Akbar's inner circle of trusted counsellors. Rajput chiefs were appointed in high positions such as military commanders and provincial governors. Rajput states were given internal autonomy, and their nobles were treated at par with the Muslims in matters of state protocol. Raja Man Singh of Ambar, brother-in-law of the emperor, received the *mansab* of 5000. He became a general and governor of Kabul and Bengal. Rao Surjan Hara, the defender of Ranthambore, also became a governor. Akbar inducted in his court several other talented Hindus such as Todar Mal, Bhagwan Das, Birbal and Tansen. Todar Mal assumed the most important position in his administration as Revenue Minister and even officiated for a while as *Vakil* or Chief Minister, and Bhagwan Das became a general in the army. Birbal was made a poet laureate of Hindu poetry, at par with Faizi, the poet laureate of Persian. Tansen was given the lureateship of Indian Music. These appointments had profound effects on the formation of a homogenous society. Apart from the fact that Akbar's revenue collectors were ordered to remit taxes in afflicted districts, the sympathetic administration of that ministry, being headed by Todar Mal, led now to less coercion and brutality in general collection of revenue than in the past. Under Akbar's patronage young men were induced to study the northern Indian vernacular that had by then become India's national tongue. Translation of Persian and Sanskrit classics was undertaken. The most popular work was the translation from Sanskrit to Hindi of the epic Ramayana by Tulsi Das. Akbar's reign also produced another exponent of Hindi literature, Abdul Rahim Khanekhana, whose forte lay in writing on a wide variety of secular subjects.

Akbar recruited his nobility from diverse sources. It was a heterogeneous body of Sunnis, Shias, Hindus, Indian Muslims, Afghans, Arabs, Persians, Uzbeks, Chughtais, etc. No single ethnic or sectarian group was prominent or large enough to challenge the emperor. The *mansabdari* system of Akbar required from each title holder to raise and maintain a certain number of soldiers for the emperor to be drawn on in an emergency. It was divided into thirty-three ranks. Roughly 70 per cent of higher rank mansabdars were born outside of India. The remaining 30 per cent comprised Hindus and locally converted Muslims in equal proportion. Of the 416 top *mansabdars*, 47 were Rajputs.[8] These were Akbar's measures to make a deal with the Hindus, which imparted to the Hindu community a sense of belonging to the Mughal government.

It is said that around 1575 Akbar was undergoing a mystical experience. He spent whole days and nights in prayer. As religion was the main driving force in the separation of people from each other, he thought that as there was one ruler for all people, there should also be one religion. It should be a melting pot for shaping them into a single entity. Akbar himself expressed his views in the following terms: 'Although I am the master of so vast a kingdom and all the instruments of government are in my hand, yet since true greatness consists in doing the will of God, my mind is not at ease in this diversity of sects and creeds; and apart from this outward pomp of circumstances, with what satisfaction, in my despondency, can I undertake the sway of empire? I await the coming of some unknown man of principle who will resolve the difficulties of my conscience.' In a General Council of learned men and military commanders he addressed them: 'We ought, therefore, to bring them all into one religion in such a fashion that they be both 'one' and 'all', with the great advantage of not losing what is good in any one religion, while gaining whatever is better in another. In that way, honour would be rendered to God, peace would be given to the peoples, and security to the empire' In his passion for universal toleration he was helped immensely by the intellectuals of his court and his close associates like Sheikh Mubarak and his son, Abul Fazl, the chronicler and author of Ain-i-Akbari. Akbar declared that by taking from every religion that which appeals to reason, he might 'in this way open the lock, the key of which has been lost'. Abul Fazl writes: 'The Shahinshah's court became the home of the enquirers of the 'seven climes', and the assemblage of the wise of every religion and sect.'[9]

He often went into trances or in moods of depression or possibly under mild attack of epilepsy. To satisfy his spiritual quest, he constructed a large hall of worship at Fatehpur Sikri in 1575 where debates in religion and theology could be held. First the debates were confined to the King's own religion. Not satisfied, he invited after 1579 learned Jains, Hindus and Parsis to the debates. In 1580, Jesuits from Goa were asked to take part in them. Two priests, Aquaviva and Monserrate, came to Sikri primarily with the intention to instruct the king and his entourage in Christianity. Father Monserrate gives a vivid picture of a series of bitter disputations with the ulema, and according to him Akbar was noticeably sympathetic to the Christian point of view. The Jesuits became so optimistic that they thought that the monarch would embrace Christianity. Thus Akbar initiated a series of debates between the representatives of all religions of his realm. The debates dismayed him. He had thought that in this way the religious scholars would be able to understand each other's point of view which would create greater harmony. Instead they led to mutual incrimination and greater intolerance, which forced him to close the Hall of Worship. However, he continued such discussions privately. Listening to them he had found some good features in every religion. He tried to find a unifying code by culling the best features of the older religions, thus surpassing all of them and at the same time uniting them all together in one religion. And thus came into being his Din-i-Ilahi in 1582.

The new creed did not meet with the favour of Akbar's courtiers. It is said that only eighteen of them subscribed to it and that, too, only half-heartedly. Discouraged by such a low turn-out, Akbar did not press the general public to embrace his religious philosophy, but he was successful in making a point for them to see that the monarch was a firm believer in religious eclecticism. Many historians, as well as ulema, consider that by giving a new religion Akbar ceased to be a Muslim. In fact, Akbar never claimed himself to be prophet or representative of God. He only considered that 'the divine will manifests itself in the intention of kings', as has been the usual Islamic thinking. His Din-i-Ilahi was not a religion; it was a creed, a set of principles and opinions given to reason in various religions. It was the manifestation of the reverence the monarch had for all religions, as much as of the reverence for the monarch as a semi-divine personage by the followers of all religions, climaxing in a universal body of toleration, both political and religious. To his good luck, his name "Jalal-ud-din Akbar" suited to synthesize itself with the Islamic creed. It is said that he instituted a uniform court salutation as Allah-u-Akbar, with the dual meaning of God is the Greatest or God is Akbar.

During the fifteenth century a heretical Islamic sect had emerged. The founder, Sayyid Muhammad of Jaunpur (b. 1443) had declared himself as Mahdi, and had won a large following. Sayyid Muhammad disapproved the legalism and formalism of the contemporary ulema and prescribed ardent devotion, renunciation, and meditation. However, at the same time he indulged in the heretical pronouncement of rejection of the four schools of *fiqah* (interpretation of Islamic laws). In Gujrat and western India the Mahdawis were specially strong. When Akbar conquered Gujrat, he did not persecute either the leaders or followers of this heretical sect. Instead he permitted the Mahdawis saints to explain and defend their doctrines in religious discussions held at Fatehpur Sikri.

In 1605 Akbar lay ill dying. Prince Salim nearly lost the throne to Khusrow, his own seventeen-year-old eldest son, who rose in revolt against him a few months later. Two important nobles, Raja Man Singh Kachhawha of Amber and Mirza Aziz Koka, whose daughter was married to the young prince, failed to persuade the majority of the nobles to support Khusrow's claim to the throne. Another party, led by Sayyids of Barha, brought Salim to the dying emperor. Akbar invested him with royal turban and robes, and Humayun's sword, thus designating Salim as the heir to the throne after his death. After a week of mourning for the emperor's death, Salim mounted the throne in Agra fort and took the title of Nur-ud-din Jahangir Padshah Ghazi.

Jahangir was a free-thinking person, and not a very religious one. He rejected his father's Din-i-Ilahi, but throughout his life he adhered to Akbar's ideals of the co-existence of all religious communities. Given more to pleasure, he was satisfied with a policy of ease and tolerance. Being the son of a Hindu mother, he continued with the Hindu customs practiced by his father of *jharokha-darshan* (balcony appearance) and *tuladana* (weighment against gold and precious stones). Jahangir also took a lively interest in painting. He deputed the best of the artists, Bishandas, to Isfahan to execute a portrait of the Persian Shah Abbas.

After the armies of prince Khusrow had been routed at Lahore in 1606 the insolent prince was arrested attempting to cross the Chenab. Khusrow and his supporters had to suffer for their misdeeds. Khusrow was brought in chains before the monarch along with his confederates, Husain Beg and Abdul Aziz. The emperor himself describes the event in his memoirs:

"The Prince stood between them trembling and weeping. Husain Beg, suspecting that he would be made the scapegoat, began to speak sorrowfully but he was not allowed to continue. Khusrow was placed in custody. I then ordered the two villains to be enclosed in the skins of a cow and an ass respectively, and to be put on asses, their faces towards the tails, and to be paraded in this manner round the city. Husain Beg, who was enclosed in the cow's skin, lived only to the fourth watch, as the skin of that animal dries quickly, and then died. Abdul Aziz, who was in the ass's skin, which is less affected by moisture, survived a day and a night. Then he died....Having directed a number of sharp stakes to be set up in a double row, from the garden of Mirza Kamran to the gates of Lahore, I caused 700 traitors who had conspired with Khusrow against my authority to be impaled alive upon them. There cannot be a more excruciating punishment than this since the wretches lingered a long time in the most agonising torture before they died, and the spectacle of their agony was most frightful."[10]

The prince was paraded on an elephant to see for himself the writhing and shrieking of the victims. The king inflicted the pain of blinding his errant son so as to disqualify him permanently from the kingship. The prince later regained his sight. During the life time of Jahangir, Prince Khurram had him secretly killed and then concocted Khusrow's illness and death to the emperor.

When his other son Khurram revolted, he was chased for three years from Rajasthan to the Deccan, from there into Orissa, Bengal, modern Uttar Pradesh region and back into the Deccan. Exhausted, he sued for peace and was obliged to yield two of his sons, Dara Shikoh and Aurangzeb, as hostages to the emperor.

The most notable Muslim religious figure of the time, Shaikh Ahmad Sirhindi also did not fare well with Jahangir. He declared himself through his treatises and letters as *mujaddid-i-alf-i-thani*, the Renewer of the Second Islamic Millennium, which began in 1592-93. He claimed that he would be able to reverse the downward descent of Islam which had taken place in the days of Akbar. In his opinion the Commander of the Faithful, the emperor, had failed to command the Muslims of India. Jahangir, he had hoped, would take steps to reverse Akbar's religious policies, which he did not do. In order to face the storm of syncretism and absorption by Hinduism Shaikh Ahmad Sirhindi was now ready to provide an alternative sheet anchor by invoking the sovereignty of God. In his letters Sirhindi called for the humiliation of Hindus and their false religion. On the execution of Guru Arjun, taken by him as a Hindu, he commented as follows:

'These days the accursed infidel of Gobindwal was very fortunately killed. It is a cause of great defeat for the reprobate Hindus. With whatever intention and purpose they are killed, the humiliation of infidels is for the Muslims life itself.'[11]

Jahangir was alarmed at Shaikh Ahmad's growing popularity. In 1619, he summoned him to an imperial audience. In his memoirs Jahangir commented that Sirhindi "had spread the net of hypocrisy and deceit," enlisted disciples, and was leading Muslims to false belief and heresy. He was especially incensed by Sirhindi's claim to have surpassed the spiritual stage attained by the rightly-guided companions of the Prophet. At the audience Shaikh Ahmad was "extremely proud and self-satisfied with all his ignorance." He was then imprisoned in the state prison at Gwalior fort to permit his own confusion and "the excitement of the people' to subdue. On his release, the subdued Shaikh Ahmad Sirhindi traveled with Jahangir's entourage to the Deccan. But the damage had been done: his anti-Hindu sentiments undoubtedly contributed to the sharpening division and crack in the Hindu-Muslim unity which Akbar had so successfully cultivated and cemented.

Jahangir was respectful to holy men and sought their audience. But he was intolerant to those who posed danger to his rule or created dissension in society. For blessing his rebellious son, Khusrow, Jahangir banished an eminent sufi, Shaikh Nizamuddin Faruqui, to Transoxiana, who later died in Balkh. He imprisoned another religious leader Syed Ahmad Afghan, who was creating restlessness against the state in the Afghan community. Probably, due to some conspiracy of the Sunnis, his wrath fell on a prominent Shia saint, Qazi Nurullah Shustari, and had him flogged to death in spite of his old age of 70. Like Sirhindi, Abdul Haq Muhaddis Dehlavi also had incited the nobles and imperial officials to protest against the emperor's liberal policies. He was about to be banished that Jahangir died, and thus was spared the punishment.

Once Jahangir wanted to visit the venerated Vaishnava ascetic, Gosain Jadrup of Ujain, whom Akbar also had visited. When the ascetic did not turn up at the court at Agra despite several invitations, Jahangir himself went to the saint at his abode in 1616. A hole dug in the side of a hill near Ujain was the saint's dwelling place. The Emperor visited him several times later. Of his last visit in 1620 Jahangir commented:

"On Monday, the 12th , my desire to see Gosain Jadrup again increased and hastening to his hut, without ceremony, I enjoyed his society. Sublime words were spoken to between us. God Almighty has granted him an unusual grace, a lofty understanding, and excellent nature, and sharp intellectual powers, with a God-given knowledge and a heart free from the attachments of the world, so that putting behind his back the world and all that is in it, he sits content in the corner of solitude and without wants."[12]

When Jahangir's health declined rapidly by 1622, a tussle for the throne ensued. Jahangir's third son, Khurram, was married to Arjumand Bano, daughter of Nur Jahan's brother, Asaf Khan. Another prince, Shaharyar, was married to Nur Jahan's own daughter from her previous marriage with Sher Afghun. At the time of the Emperor's death on 29 October 1627 at Bhimbar in Kashmir, both Khusrow and Pervez were already dead. Among the two main contenders to the throne, Khurram, emerged successful. Khurram assumed the royal title of Shahabuddin Muhammad Shah Jahan and occupied the throne in January 1628. In 1629 he executed his brother Shaharyar, Khusrow's son Dawar Baksh, and two cousins, who were all involved in the fighting for the throne.

In the beginning Shah Jahan intended to present himself as a fervent Muslim, discarding the liberal and non-sectarian attitude of his father in the affairs of state and treatment with non-Muslims. In 1633, Shah Jahan began to impose restriction on construction and repair of churches and temples. When he learned that wealthy Hindus wished to complete construction of several unfinished temples at Benaras, he ordered that all recently built temples in the city be torn down.[13] After this initial flurry of destruction only prominent shrines encountered in the course of military campaigns suffered damage.[14] Towards the end of his reign Shah Jahan even gave his patronage to both local music and Hindi literature.

But such a policy did not last long. Probably it was just a facade or a strategy to appease the Muslim sentiments or to ward off unnecessary opposition of the religious fanatics in his realm. This policy was not based upon conviction. It was even discontinued. It is said that he came under the influence of his eldest son, Dara Shikoh, (1615-58), who was very enlightened in matters of religion. As compared to him, Shah Jahan's third son, Aurangzeb (1618-1707) was just his opposite, a very religious person, reflecting his own image sometimes as a bigot. Dara was a true follower of reasoning and moral sentiments, which were earlier demonstrated by his great grand-father, Akbar. In his young age he had come in contact with two liberal sufi shaikhs of Qadri order, Mulla Mir (d. 1635) and Mulla Shah Badakhshi (d.1661) as well as some Hindu mystics. He himself acquired the ideas of sufism. In this early phase of his mystical studies Dara compiled a hagiography of Sufi saints and a recounting of orthodox mystical beliefs.

Following the Qur'anic injunction that no land has been left without prophetic guidance, Dara Shikoh was convinced that the Vedas and the Upanishads constitute the concealed scripture mentioned in the Qur'an. The Upanishads, he considered, were the ultimate source of all monotheism, including Islam. With the assistance of brahman scholars, he translated the fifty-two Upanishads into Persian in a work titled Sirr-i-Akbar. He found that there were many common grounds in sufism and *vedanta*; and to establish this relationship he wrote a treatise by the name of *Majma-ul-Bahrain* (Mingling of the Two Oceans). To make it available to Hindu scholars he translated it into Sanskrit under the title *Samudra Sangam*. He maintained that the only difference between the Hindu doctrine of advaita and the Muslim sufi traditions was one of terminology. He argued that the essential nature of Hinduism was identical to that of Islam. He spent long years in Kashmir translating the Vedas and the Upanishads into Persian, and this translation led to a Latin version. It is believed that it left a deep impression two hundred years later on the mind of the great German philosopher, Schopenhauer.

1. Ellen Smart, *Akbar, Illiterate Genius*, Kaladarshana (1981), PP. 99-107. See *The New Cambridge History of India: The Mughul Empire,* Vol. I.5, Ch. 2, John F. Richards
2. *Tuzuk-i- Jahangiri*, translated by A. Rogers and edited by H. Beveridge. See *The New Cambridge History of India: The Mughul Empire*, Vol. I.5, Ch. 2, John F. Richards.
3. H. G. Wells., *The Outline of History*, XXXII
4. Schmit, Emil in Helmolt's *History of the World*, Quoted in *The Outline of History,* XXXII, H.G.Wells
5. M.C. Pradhan, The Political System of the Jats of Northern India, (Bombay, 1966). See *The New Cambridge History of India: The Mughul Empire*, John F. Richards, Vol. I.5, Ch. 4
6. B. N. Goswamy and J. S. Grewal, *The Moghuls and the Jogis of Jakhbar* (Simla, Indian Institute of Advance Study, 1967), pp. 51-52. See *The New Cambridge History of India: The Mughul Empire*, John F. Richards, Vol. I.5, Ch. 4
7. *A New History of India* (Fifth Edition), Ch. Nine, Stanley Wolpert.
8. *South Asia: A Short History*, Hugh Tinker; *A History of India*, Vol. Two, Percival Spear
9. *The Builders of the Mughal Empire*, Michael Prawdin
10. Lane-Poole, *Mediaeval India*, page 86-87, quoted in *The Indus Saga and the Making of Pakistan*, Ch 18, Aitzaz Ahsan

11. Yohanan Friedmann, *Shaykh Ahmad Sirhindi: An Outline of His Thought an a Study His Image in the Eyes of Posterity* (Montreal: McGill-Queen's University Press, 1971, p.40. See *The New Cambridge History of India: The Mughul Empire*, John F. Richards, Vol. I.5, Ch. 5 *
12. *Tuzuk-i- Jahangiri*, translated in S.A.A.Rizvi, Muslim Revivalist Movement *in India in the Sixteenth and Seventeenth Centuries* (Agra, 1965, p. 328). See *The New Cambridge History of India: The Mughul Empire*, John F. Richards, Vol. I.5, Ch. 5
13. Bedley, E., and Desai, Z.A., eds., *The Shah Jahan Nama of 'Inayat Khan*, (Delhi, 1990), p. 154; Sri Ram Sharma, *The Religious Policy of the Mughal Emperors* (London, Asia Publishing House, Inc., 2nd edition, 1962) pp. 86-87. See *The New Cambridge History of India: The Mughul Empire*, John F. Richards, Vol. I.5, Ch. 6
14. Sri Ram Sharma, *The Religious Policy of the Mughal Emperors*, pp. 86-87. See *The New Cambridge History of India: The Mughul Empire*, John F. Richards, Vol. I.5, Ch. 6

28
DEFEAT OF LIBERALISM

Tussle for the throne began in the midst of conflicting ideas, beliefs and intellectual make up of the two princes, Aurangzeb and Dara Shikoh. Both of them were obsessively bent upon to condition the affairs of state according to their own thinking, one radical and the other liberal. Consequently, the nobles and courtiers too came under a polarized situation. Such current of events dominated the later half of Shah Jahan's reign with full force. Dara Shukoh remained most of the time at the court in close personal contact with the emperor. His greatest supporter was his eldest sister, Jahan Ara, who had served as the mistress of the royal household after the death of her mother, Mumtaz Mahal. She had a similar temperament as that of her brother. In 1652, Shah Jahan sent Aurangzeb to the Deccan, while Dara stayed closer to his father as the governor of Punjab. The influence of Jahan Ara resulted in Dara emerging as Shah Jahan's favorite son and heir apparent by about 1653. But that was not the end of it. Aurangzeb seemed to have hated his elder brother from a very young age and coveted his father's throne. The conflict first came to a head when Aurangzeb was in the Deccan finalizing plans for the conquest of Bijapur and Golconda that he received the orders of the emperor not to go ahead with his plans. Aurangzeb was furious at it, and thought that his father's orders were given at the behest of Dara Shikoh who was at his side in the capital. Shah Jahan used to control the tension between the two, held them in check, and kept them from open warfare. Dara cared little for worldly glory and was thus neglectful of court intrigues. Further, Dara had presented himself to Muslims in general and ulema in particular as a non-practicing Muslim, thus losing their support and inviting the assault of the ulema. Dara was no match to his brother in shrewdness. Niccolao Manucci gives an eyewitness description of Aurangzeb as a prince:

"This prince was very different from the others, being in character very secretive and serious, carrying on his affairs in a hidden way, but most energetically. He was of a melancholy temperament, always busy at something or another, wishing to execute justice and arrive at appropriate decisions. He was extremely anxious to be recognized by the world as a man of wisdom, clever and a lover of the truth. He was moderately liberal, distributing rewards and conferring gifts wherever suitable. But above all, for a long time he pretended to be a faquir (*faqir*), a holy mendicant, by which he renounced the world, gave up all claim to the crown, and was content to pass his life in prayers and mortifications."[1]

In 1657, the aged Shah Jahan fell ill. The court at Delhi, which was rife with intrigues and tension because of the two princes, fell in a state of panic. Each side became overly active over the issue of succession. The turmoil was not, however, to remain confined to the capital; soon its reverberations were felt in the far corners of the empire. Shah Jahan regained his health after a year and tried desperately to help Dara emerge as the stronger contender for the throne. But being more of a mystic Dara spent little time in forging strategies to win the crown which appeared to be his due on account of his father's liberalism and affection to him. Aurangzeb manipulated his youngest brother, Murad, to join him and then marched north with a joint force to defeat the formidable imperial army under Jaswant Sing of Jodhpur at Dharmat in April. Dara tried to defend Agra but had to flee away. Aurangzeb was now encamped outside Agra. Fearing his own safety, Shahjahan shut the gates of the fort. Aurangzeb stopped the supply of drinking water from Jamuna. Shahjahan fell sick by drinking bitter water of the wells of the fort. He wrote a pathetic letter to his son:

Praised be the Hindus in all cases,
As they ever offer water to their dead.
And thou, my son, art a marvellous Musalman,
As thou causest me in life to lament for water.[2]

Later, Aurangzeb was successful in entering the fort. He now usurped the power of the king, imprisoned his father and then pursued Dara. He met Dara at Samugarh, several miles east of Agra. Dara was betrayed by his own Muslim generals like Uzbek Khalilullah Khan, while thousands of Rajput soldiers died for him. He fled towards Agra but was captured by an Afghan chief, Malik Jiwan, whose life Dara had once saved from execution. He was sent to Aurangzeb. The official ulema condemned Dara to death on grounds of apostasy from Islam and idolatry. On the night of August 30, 1659, Dara and his youngest son Sipihr Shukoh were slain. Dara's head was delivered from the victorious Aurangzeb to the imprisoned father. The dream of many that India would soon be blessed with another ruler as tolerant and liberal as Akbar was shattered. The course of history had now taken a new turn.

In July 1658, Aurangzeb assumed the kingship as also the title of Alamgir. He then turned promptly to the task of liquidating his remaining two brothers, Shuja and Murad, which he accomplished soon. The war of succession had amply demonstrated his cunning, ruthlessness and organizational ability. As a monarch he showed himself as a firm and capable administrator who retained his grip on power even up to his last days at the age of eighty-eight. Though ruthless, he was a highly pious Muslim, or probably the most pious among the Mughal rulers. He punctiliously observed the public rituals of Islam. Earlier Mughal kings used to drink wine, an act which is prohibited in Islam. Aurangzeb never drank liquor. His policies were generally directed to define the political culture of the empire consistent with his own ardent piety, and in exclusive Islamic terms. Not finding peace for what he had done with his father, which was in every way condemnable under the sharia and under the norms of Muslim society, he sent a mission laden with precious gifts to the ruler of Hijaz (modern Saudi Arabia) for a formal recognition of his regime. His first mission was unsuccessful but his second mission earned him the reward. Saqi Mustaid Khan reports in *Ma'asir-i-Alamgiri*:

"[Aurangzeb] used to send large amounts of money, for some years annually, at others once in two or three years, to the pious men living in retreat in those Holy Cities, and a large number of men in those Holy Places were permanently employed by him on daily stipends to act as his deputies in walking round the Ka'ba, bowing to the Prophet's tomb, reading the two copies of the Quran written by this pious Emperor with his own hand and presented to Medina".[3]

While settling down to business his first task was to present himself as a model Muslim monarch. The era of religious tolerance and the tradition of treating Hindus and Muslims equally that had been initiated by Akbar were now over. Whereas Akbar treated Hindus as equals Aurangzeb conscientiously tolerated them. Starting from the court, he discontinued *jharokha darshan* (balcony audience), abolished *navroz* and *dipawali* celebrations, dispensed with the services of court painters, and banned music, the last two being not encouraged by Islam. For governing the lives of his Muslim subjects he compiled an exhaustive digest of Islamic laws (*Fatawa-e-Alamgiri*) for the guidance of the qazis. At provincial capitals and large cities, he appointed censors (*muhtasibs*) of public morals who were charged with the responsibility of rooting out drinking, gambling and prostitution, and ensuring that Islamic laws were obeyed and proper prayers performed. He gratified the ulema with tax-free land grants, as also with liberal sums to repair and maintain mosques and religious charity. In 1690 all such land grants were made fully hereditary as another major concession to them.

Thereafter, Aurangzeb prescribed a series of disabilities for his Hindu subjects. The pilgrim tax levied on Hindus, which was abolished by Akbar, was reinstated. He issued an injunction against the propagation of Hindu faith. In 1665 he decreed that Muslims should be taxed at 2 1/2 percent of value on internal customs duties and Hindus at 5 percent, but the order was made ineffective by Muslim merchants, who smuggled goods belonging to Hindus. Thus Hindus were actually made to pay the lower rate of 2 1/2 per cent. A general edict addressed to provincial governors and revenue officers commanded the dismissal of Hindu officers and their replacement by Muslims.[4] In 1668 Hindu religious fairs were outlawed, and no new Hindu temple permits were issued, nor would royal permission be granted to repair rundown temples. In 1672 he reversed Akbar's policy and resumed all grants held by Hindus. Although not completely enforced in practice, the new policies were disliked by majority of the population but deemed as a sweeping victory by the Muslim ulema of the empire.

According to the author of *Ma'asir-i-Alamgiri*, when the emperor received the shocking reports from various provinces, specially from Benaras, that Brahmans were teaching their scriptures and idolatry publicly to which even Muslims were attracted, Aurangzeb issued a general edict in 1669 'to all the governors of provinces to destroy with a willing hand the schools and temples of the infidels; and they were strictly enjoined to put an entire stop to the teaching and practice of idolatrous forms of worship.'[5] Throughout the empire many such temples were destroyed by official action. The emperor's special targets were the renowned stone temples in the holy cities of Mathura and Varanasi. The great Kesev Rai temple at Mathura built at a cost of over three million rupees by Bir Singh Bundela was pulled down. The golden bejeweled idols were taken to Agra and buried under the steps of Jahan Ara's mosque. A new mosque was erected on the site of the razed temple. Admittedly, this action was an explicit statement of the emperor's view on idolatry. The emperor's message was simultaneously political and religious; it was also a rebuke to the Bundelas and their troublesome allegiance to the empire.[6]

Aurangzeb received many warnings that rebellion would spread across India if he persisted in his bias against the indigenous religion, but he stayed firm. He announced his most controversial measure in 1679. Aurangzeb re-imposed the hated jizya or poll tax on Hindus. Abolished by Akbar, this tax was not levied during the reigns of Jahangir and Shah Jahan. Aurangzeb himself could not levy this tax for twenty-one years of his reign. Many of his nobles had argued against this measure. A letter of protest was submitted to the emperor, ascribed by Sir J. Sarkar to Shivaji, which, after praising the tolerant conduct of Akbar, Jahangir, and Shahjahan, reads as follows:

"Such were the benevolent intentions of your ancestors. Whilst they pursued these great and generous principles, wheresoever they directed their steps, conquest and prosperity went before them; and then they reduced many countries and fortresses to their obedience. During your majesty's reign, many have been alienated from the empire, and further loss of territory must necessarily follow, since devastation and rapine now universally prevail without restraint. Your subjects are trampled under foot, and every province of your empire is impoverished, depopulation spreads, and difficulties accumulate....

If your Majesty places any faith in those books by distinction called divine, you will there be instructed that God is the God of all mankind, not the God of Muslims alone. The Pagan and the Muslim are equal in His presence. Distinction of colour are of his ordination. It is he who gives existence. In your temples, to His name the voice is raised in prayer; in a house of images, when the bell is shaken, still He is the object of adoration. To vilify the religion or customs of other men is to set at naught the pleasure of the Almighty. When we deface a picture we naturally incur the resentment of the painter; and justly has the poet said, 'Presume not to arraign or scrutinize the various works of power divine.'

In fine, the tribute you demand from the Hindus is repugnant to justice; it is equally foreign from good policy, as it must impoverish the country; moreover, it is an innovation and infringement of the laws of Hindostan".[7]

But he was as under pressure from the theologians to curb the infidels, as was hard pressed to raise the revenue. At the imposition of jizya, the capital became the centre of protests and demonstration. Hindus from the city and its surrounding districts gathered in large numbers in front of the emperor's balcony on the Delhi fort to protest the new tax. When Aurangzeb rode out from the fort to the Jama Masjid:

"....the Hindus crowded from the gate of the fort to the Jama Masjid in such a large number for imploring redress that the passage of the people was blocked. The money-lenders, cloth-merchants and shopkeepers of the camp Urdu Bazar (Army Market) and all the artisans of the city abandoned their work and assembled on the route of the Emperor... [Aurangzeb], who was riding on an elephant, could not reach the mosque. Every moment the number of those unlucky people increased. Then he ordered that the majestic elephants should proceed against them. Some of them were killed or trampled under the elephants and horses. For some days, more, they assembled in the same way and requested for remission (of the jiziya). At last they submitted to pay the Jiziyah."[8]

For the imposition of jizya a graduated system was adopted. The population was divided into three classes according to their resources: rich, middle and poor. People owning property worth ten thousand dirhams or more were classed as rich, those with property valued at two thousand dirhams or more as middle class, and those with property at less than two hundred dirhams as poor. Dirham, though not in use, was only denominated as a measure of value. The tax was collected in silver. According to J. N. Sarkar's calculations, the jizya for the three classes respectively was 13 1/3, 6 2/3, and 3 1/3 rupees, i.e. 6 per cent of the gross income of the poor, 6 1/4 per cent on the middle class, and 2 1/2 per thousand on the rich. Government officials and the priestly class were exempt.[9]

During the war of succession Raja Jaswant Singh Rathore of Marwar had lent his support to Dara. Later when Shivaji was in Aurangzeb's custody, his escape was facilitated with the complicity of Jaswant Singh. Suspicious of his loyalty Aurangzeb was not happy with him, although he had served as Aurangzeb's general till his death in 1678. So when Jaswant Singh died, Aurangzeb sent an army to Jodhpur so as to turn it into an imperial crown territory (*khalisa*). It was a measure to reallocate the kingdom in jagirs. En route, or when Jodhpur was occupied, the army indulged in iconoclasm.[10] When a son was born posthumously to Jaswant Singh, Aurangzeb refused to recognize the claim of this infant. He invested Indra Singh Rathore, son of Jaswant Singh's deceased elder brother, as the ruler of Marwar. Alarmed by this development, the Rajputs of Mewar and Jodhpur rose in joint revolt against Aurangzeb in 1681. A strong force was sent to subdue the Rajputs under the command of Prince Akbar. Instead of curbing them, Akbar, being a liberal himself and disgusted with his father's policies, turned against the emperor, joined hands with the Hindu rebels and declared himself the emperor. When Aurangzeb endeavoured to sooth his son's ambitions with promises and threats, the Prince replied to his father:

What good did you do to your father
That you expect so much from your son?
O thou that art teaching wisdom to mankind
Administer to thine own self what thou art teaching to others!
Thou art not curing yourself,
Then, for once, give up counseling others.[11]

Akbar sought the friendship of Shambhaji, the son of Shivaji, who had also risen in revolt against the emperor. He tried unsuccessfully to lure Shambhaji to march to the capital with a joint army of Marathas, Rajputs and his loyal Mughals. But the prince was no match to Aurangzeb's shrewdness and military genius. He had soon to flee away to the Deccan. Aurangzeb then personally marched to Deccan to subdue his son and control the Marathas.

Ajit Singh, son of Jaswant Singh, who was carried off by some loyal Rajputs beyond the reach of the emperor during his infancy, had become after twenty years the acknowledged leader of Marwar. A reconciliation was reached at last, and Ajit Singh was made a mansabdar of 3,500 in Aurangzeb's court. But when Aurangzeb died, Ajit Singh rose in revolt and drove the Mughal occupation force from Jodhpur. He destroyed those mosques which were erected since the Mughal occupation and forbade Islamic prayers in the city.[12]

In late 1687, the Jats revolted. They attacked the camp of Mahabat Khan, Governor of the Punjab, near Sikandra and then occupied Sikandra itself and desecrated the tomb of Akbar. Niccolao Manucci writes:[13]

"Already angered by the demands of the governors and faujdars for revenue, a great number of them [Jats] assembled and marched to the mausoleum of that great conqueror Akbar. Against him living they could effect nothing; they therefore wreaked vengeance on his sepulchre. They began their pillage by breaking in the great gates of bronze which it had, robbing the valuable precious stones and plates...of gold and silver, and destroying what they were not able to carry away. Dragging out the bones of Akbar, they threw them angrily into the fire and burnt them."

Manucci further says that it was 'the greatest affront possible to the house and lineage of Taimur-i-lang." Aurangzeb appointed the young Raja Bishun Singh Kachhwaha of Amber (Jaipur) as faujdar of Mathura and as Jagirdar of Sinsini, the Jat stronghold, and asked to restore normalcy. Bishun Singh suppressed the revolt.

Aurangzeb, the shrewd politician, administrator and fighter, had undergone a change of character in his last days. He had become an ascetic and a sage, spending long hours in prayers, fasting, and copying the Qur'an, and fearing for his accountability before his Creator. But his grip on power was never lost; it is said that his eldest surviving son in far Kabul never received a letter from his father without trembling. In 1707 the monarch, pious and terrible, adored and hated, breathed his last in his encampment in Ahmadnagar in the Deccan. His piety had made him live within what he earned by copying the Qur'an. He had a small amount saved from his earnings for his burial. His grave in the city he built in Central India, Aurangabad, has no dome or elaborate gardens like those of even minor potentates. With Aurangzeb ended the glorious period of the reigns of the Grand Mughals.

After Aurangzeb's death his eldest son Muazzam hastened from Kabul to secure his succession. In this process he had to vanquish and slay one brother, Azam, near Agra. He marched to the Deccan to eliminate the other brother, Kam Bakhsh. He was then able to occupy the throne as Bahadur Shah in 1707 at the old age of sixty-three. His reign is generally considered an era of little importance because it lasted only for five years as compared to fifty years of his father's. But it should not be forgotten that in this short period the able monarch took effective measures to restore the strength to the empire which was lost during Aurangzeb's long war in the Deccan. He was always on the march to settle the affairs of state. He neutralized the three inveterate enemies of the time, Rajputs, Marathas and Sikhs by making peace with them.

Another contest for the throne had begun even before Bahadur Shah's death in January 1712. Factional conflicts had become rampant in the imperial court. The leading contender of the throne was his second son Azim-us-Shan, who was the Governor of Bengal and Bihar. He died while caught in a quicksand in the Ravi, fleeing the victorious army of Zulfiqar Khan, the chief adviser of the emperor. Zulfiqar Khan then lent his support to the eldest prince, Jahandar Shah. The other two princes, Rafi-us-Shan and Jahan Shah were later defeated and killed. Jahandar Shah succeeded to the throne in March 1712. Jahandar Shah proved to be an incompetent ruler. His authority soon slipped into the hands of Zulfiqar Khan. For the first time Zulfiqar Khan began the tradition of persecuting those nobles who had sided with the defeated princes. He made his private official Sabha Chand as diwan (chief fiscal officer) of the imperial khalisa. In the broad policy of reconciliation, he got the jizya abolished just after nine days of the coronation of Jahandar Shah. Ajit Singh Rathore was appointed governor of Gujerat, and Jai Singh Kachhwaha was made governor of Malwa.

Jahandar Shah was a very weak king. He had an easy and lavish style of living. The imperial court became full of intrigues. At the same time his nephew Farrukh Siyar, the second son of Azim-us-Shan, had managed to survive as governor of Bengal. During the war of succession he had marched from Bengal in support of his father. But when he heard of his father's defeat and death, he crowned himself as king at Patna, then named as Azimabad. This thirty-year old nephew dethroned Jahandar Shah with the help of two powerful courtiers, Sayyid Brothers of Barha, Sayyid Husain Ali and Sayyid Abdullah. Jahandar Shah was put to death in the following year. The dead emperor was paraded through the streets of Delhi with his severed head impaled on a spear. Several princes of blood including Humayun Bakht, the ten year old brother of Farrukh Siyar, were blinded with red-hot needles. Sayyid brothers, became the king makers and the real power behind the throne. Later, the young emperor engaged himself in spying and intriguing against his benefactors, but the Syed brothers proved to be a greater power. Intending to teach a lesson to the inept emperor, Husain Ali marched from his viceroyalty over the Deccan at the head of an army which included some eleven thousand loyal Maratha soldiers of Balaji Vishwanath, Shauji's Peshwa. The conflict culminated in the deposition of Farrukh Siyar in 1719, who was blinded, thrown into prison and later strangled to death.

1. Niccolao Manucci, *Storia do Mogor or Mogul India,* I, 229, See *The New Cambridge History of India: The Mughul Empire*, John F. Richards, Vol. I.5, Ch. 7
2. *History of Aurangzeb I*, Jadunath Sarkar, See S. A. A. Rizvi, *The Wonder That Was India*, Part II, Ch. III
3. Saqi Mustaid Khan, *Maasir-i' Alamgiri*, p.525 as quoted in N. R. Farooqi, *"Mughal-Ottoman Relations: A Study of Political and Diplomatic Relations Between Mughal India and the Ottoman Empire: 1556-1748,"* unpublished Ph. D dissertation, University of Wisconsin, Madison, 1968, p.210. See *The New Cambridge History of India: The Mughul Empire*, John F. Richards, Vol. I.5, Ch. 8
4. S. Moinul Haq, *Khafi Khan's History of Alamgir*, Karachi: Pakistan Historical Society, 1975, translation of Muhammad Hashim Kafi Khan, *Mutakab-al-Lubab, p. 252*. See *The New Cambridge History of India: The Mughul Empire*, John F. Richards, Vol. I.5, Ch. 8
5. Sri Ram Sharma, The Religious Policy of the Mughal Emperors (London: Asia Publishing House, Inc., 2nd edition, 1962), pp. 130-131). See *The New Cambridge History of India: The Mughul Empire,* Vol. II.3, Ch. 4, ed. J. S. Grewal & Vol. I.5, Ch. 8; . See also *The Oxford History of India*, Vincent A. Smith, Book VI, Chapter 6
6. Sri Ram Sharma, The Religious Policy, p. 133. See *The New Cambridge History of India: The Mughul Empire,* John F. Richards, Vol. I.5, Ch. 8
7. See *The Oxford History of India*, Vincent A. Smith, Book VI, Chapter 6
8. [Moinul Haq, Khafi Khan, pp. 258-59] See *The New Cambridge History of India: The Mughul Empire,* John F. Richards, Vol. I.5, Ch. 8
9. S. A. A. Rizvi, *The Wonder That Was India*, Part II, Ch IV
10. D.B.Vohra, *A Panormic History of the Indian People*; Ch. Ten
11. *The Oxford History of India*, Vincent A. Smith, Book VI, Chapter 6
12. [Satish Chandra, Parties and Politics at the Mughal Court, 1707-1740 (New Delhi: People's Publishing House, 2nd ed., 1972) p. 29]. See *The New Cambridge History of India: The Mughul Empire*, John F. Richards, Vol. I.5, Ch. 12
13. Niccolao Manucci, *Storia do Mogor or Mogul India*, I, 229, See *The New Cambridge History of India: The Mughul Empire,* John F. Richards, Vol. I.5, Ch. 11. See also *The Oxford History of India*, Vincent A. Smith, Book VI, Chapter 6

29
SIKHS: FROM LOVE TO MILITANCY

Since the founding of the Sikh faith in the early sixteenth century, this community had flourished in the Punjab, drawing its followers mostly from hard working peasantry of Hindus as well as from Muslim stock. Sikhism, as a nascent religion, had not made inroads in the courts of Akbar and his Hall of Worship, although the third Guru, Amar Das, was patronized by Akbar. The fourth Guru, Ram Das, had served at Akbar's court. It was, however, Akbar, who had granted him some land between the rivers Sutlej and Ravi in the Punjab, not as the head of a religious movement but as a pious leader of a cult. On a piece of that land at Amritsar arose the great Harmandir guru-dwara (the Guru's House), which was to become the Sikh religion's sacred capital. During the ill-fated revolt of 1605, Prince Khusrow had a brief encounter with the fifth Sikh Guru, Arjun, at Gobindwal in Punjab. For Jahangir, Guru Arjun had erred by offering his blessings to the rebel prince and putting a saffron mark on his brow. Jahangir seemed already to be inclined unfavorably to this religious figure. In his memoir, Tuzuk-i-Janhangiri, he makes the following observation about the Guru:

"In Gobindwal, which is on the river Biyah (Beas), there was a Hindu named Arjun, in the garment of sainthood and sanctity, so much so that he had captivated many of the simple-hearted of the Hindus, and even of the ignorant and foolish followers of Islam, by his ways and manners, and they had loudly sounded the drum of holiness. They called him Guru and from all sides stupid people crowded to worship and manifest complete faith in him. For three or four generations (of spiritual successors) they had kept this shop warm. Many times it had occurred to me to put a stop to this vain affair or to bring him into the assembly of the people of Islam."[1]

Arjun suffered a fate like other followers of Khusrow. Jahangir "ordered them to produce him [Arjun] and handed over his houses, dwelling places, and children to Murtaza Khan, and having confiscated his property commanded that he should be put to death."[2]. "In the Sikh tradition, however, there is hardly any reference to Jahangir's order of capital punishment. Bhai Gurdas admires the incredible equanimity of Guru Arjun under unbearable torture, but he says nothing more. In the *Bachittar Natak*, composed in the last decade of the seventeenth century, there is a reference to the martyrdom of Guru Tegh Bahadur, but nothing about the martyrdom of Guru Arjun. In the late eighteenth century, it was believed that Jahangir imposed a fine of 200,000 rupees which Guru Arjun refused to pay and he was tortured. Already in the 1640s the author of the *Dabistan-i-Mazahab* had stated that Jahangir imposed a heavy fine on Guru Arjun which he was not in a position to pay, and consequently he was tortured in hot weather and he died. It was generally believed that the person responsible for torturing Guru Arjun was the *diwan* of Lahore. All this evidence suggests that the capital punishment was commuted into heavy fine."[3] It was Guru Arjun who had completed the temple and named its city Amritsar (Pool of Immortal Nectar) for its tank filled with "sacred" well water. He guided the compilation of the Sikh scripture, Granth Sahib, which was deposited in Amritsar's temple. "In this vessel" wrote Guru Arjun of his book, "you will find three things-truth, peace, and contemplation."

Arjun's young son, Hargobind (1595-1644), was now installed as the sixth Guru of the Sikhs. Before his death Guru Arjun had already established a Sikh treasury at Amritsar where tithes and offerings from the Sikhs between Afghanistan in the west and Bengal in the east were collected. Encouraged by this arrangement and partly in reaction to Arjun's persecution, the immature Hargobind adopted a style bordering on royalty. He constructed a high platform opposite the Harmandir and he called it Akal Takht, 'the immortal throne'. He built a fort called Lohgarah and held court as if he were a raja or a prince. He wore two swords, one symbolizing his spiritual authority and the other his temporal power. He hunted with his retainers like a raja. He began to train his disciples in military style self-defence. Alarmed, Jahangir moved to quash this young Sikh leader's pretensions. Hargobind was arrested for non-payment of his father's fine, and imprisoned in the state prison at Gwalior for two years (1609-1611). Eventually satisfied with the justifications given by Guru Hargobind for his interests and activities, the emperor released him from the prison. Upon his release, Hargobind shifted his household along with the institutions of Sikh religion from Amritsar to Kiratpur in the Himalayan foothills.

He established his court in the fashion of those Rajput rulers who had fled away in the hills in similar circumstances. He spent his time strengthening his military resources, converting the pacifist faith of its founder into a militant order. He continued to receive offerings from his followers in the plains. But subsequently he did not cause any trouble to the monarch. So his withdrawal went almost unnoticed, hence there was no further conflict during Jahangir's reign. During Shahjahan's reign, however, the Guru came into conflict again with the emperor and gave a tough fight to the Mughal army. The Guru died a peaceful death in 1644.

Janhangir's harsh treatment of the Sikh Gurus appears to have stemmed more from their perceived political threat than from hostility to their religious doctrines as such. Jahangir did not seem to know of Sikhism as a religion. This is why Jahangir referred to Guru Arjun as a Hindu, and for that matter, a heretic Hindu. But Jahangir's treatment of their Gurus had turned the Sikhs into inveterate enemies of the Mughals.

Before his death Guru Hargobind had bypassed the claims of his two living sons to the guru-ship. He had named Hari Rai, son of his prematurely deceased eldest son, as his successor, who had become the seventh guru. In Aurangzeb's time again a political misstep was taken by the Guru. Hari Rai (1644-61) and Dara Shikoh were friends. When Dara fled from Delhi during the war of succession, Hari Rai emerged from his mountain abode to meet him in Punjab, and offered him his support and aid to realize his claim to the throne. In this political struggle, the Guru had again put the stake on the wrong horse. Once victorious, Aurangzeb demanded of him to send his eldest son, Ram Rai, as hostage to Delhi. In the new company, the young man was conditioned to the values and institutions of the Mughal court. He turned out to be a loyal follower of the emperor. His manner and conduct won him Mughal friendship. Aurangzeb gave him land in the Siawalik hills later known as Dehradun. It was natural for him to lose his father's support, and he was bypassed for the Guru's *gaddi*. Shortly before his death in 1661, Hari Rai designated his younger son, Har Krishen, as his successor, although a faction of the Sikhs was supporting Ram Rai as the successor. He had also Aurangzeb's blessings with him. But Har Krishen too was forced to seek Aurangzeb's's favor in Delhi, where he died of smallpox in 1664. Hari Rai's granduncle, Tegh Bahadur (1621-75), became the ninth guru. By accepting his nomination as the Guru, Tegh Bahadur had given affront to Aurangzeb who had intended to arbitrate in the matter of succession. Even then, had he stayed in his chosen place for the new centre of Sikkhism, Makhowal, Aurangzeb might have ignored the affront. First, to avoid confrontation with Ram Rai, who enjoyed the emperor's support as the Sikh leader, Tegh Bahadur left for eastern India and later returned to the Punjab. Second, for the next ten years, Tegh Bahadur spent his time vigorously in organizing and proselytizing throughout the Punjab and as far east as Bengal and Assam. 'The news-writers of the Mughal empire were bound to send reports of this response. Guru Tegh Bahadur was making a public demonstration of his convictions at a time when the emperor was bent upon discouraging such demonstrations. Whereas the emperor could use the power of the state in support of his policy, the Guru could rely on moral courage inherited from a long line of illustrious predecessors to defend the claims of conscience.' Courting his own martyrdom, he nominated his son Gobind Das as his successor in July 1675 and moved out of his territory of Makhowal. He was arrested as he entered the Mughal territory of Ropar, along with five companions, and was brought to Delhi. While the monarch was in Hasan Abdal (in Punjab, Pakistan), Tegh Bahadur was tried at the qazi's court, convicted of blasphemy, sentenced to death and executed in November, 1675. There was widespread anger among the Sikhs. While Aurangzeb was returning from Jami mosque of Lahore in October 1676 two brickbats were thrown at him The accused were handed over to the law enforcement authorities, but no reprisal was made against the community.[4]

Gobind Rai (1666-1708), Tegh Bahadur's son, became the tenth Guru. He vowed to avenge his father's murder. Generally he was kept on the run but he was successful in forging his community into an "army of the pure" (*Khalsa*) in 1669. He took his new surname as Singh or "lion". This name was also adopted by his close associates. From this time onward the Sikhs emerged as a close knit community and a force of toughened fighters. He believed that the use of physical force in defence of good was sanctified by God:

Having created Durga, O God, You destroyed the demons. From You alone did Rama receive his power to slay Rawana with his arrows. From You alone did Krishna receive his power to seize Kansa by the hair and to dash him on the ground.

He declared himself as the last guru. He forged a new brotherhood of the Sikhs, called Khalsa. The Khalsa was to be the heir of everything he possessed, because he himself owed everything to them. After him, the majority will of the Khalsa would represent the Guru. As the sign of their faith the Khalsa brotherhood were obliged to wear five things, beginning with 'K' in Hindustani language: they vowed never to cut their hair (kaise), to keep a comb for their hair (kangha), to wear a steel bracelet on the wrist (kara), always to carry a sword (kirpan), to sport a wrestler's shorts (kachchha). It is said that Guru Gobind Singh had more than twenty thousand loyal supporters in his retinue at one time, but Mughal armies continued to outnumber and harass him. In the last days of Aurangzeb the Guru wrote an impassioned and spirited letter to him. He justified his position on moral grounds and pointed out a breach of faith on the part of the monarch. Aurangzeb, who was at that time in the Deccan, ordered the governor of Lahore, Mun'im Khan, to conciliate the Guru at all costs and to persuade him to meet the emperor personally. Guru Gobind refused the help offered by the governor, but proceeded anyway to meet the emperor. On his way to the Deccan, when he was in Rajasthsan he heard the news of the death of the emperor. How satisfying it was for the Guru to at least outlive his hated rival, the monarch, by a year and a half! In the ensuing war of succession, Guru Gobind Singh supported the victorious Bahadur Shah. This time the Guru's political acumen paid dividend. The bond of friendship between the two grew stronger and when the emperor marched to confront his brother Kam Baksh in the Deccan, Guru Gobind Singh accompanied him in the royal entourage.

Following Guru Gobind's death in 1708, the Sikhs resumed militant action against Mughal garrisons in the Punjab under the leadership of Banda Bahadur. In 1709 he stormed the town of Samana in Sirhind, overpowered the *faujdar* of Samana, killed its inhabitants in thousands and razed the town to the ground. "For eight or nine months, and from two or three days march from Delhi to the environs of Lahore, all the towns and places of note were pillaged by these unclean wretches, and trodden under foot and destroyed. Men in countless numbers were slain, the whole country was wasted, and mosques and tombs were razed."[5] Another historian, W. Irvine, describes his atrocities in these terms: "The scavengers and leather-dressers and such-like persons, who were very numerous among the Sikhs, committed excesses of every description. For the space of four days the town [Sirhind] was given up to pillage, the mosques were defiled, the houses burnt, and the Muhammadans slaughtered; even their women and children were not spared.... Not a soul dared to disobey an order, and men, who had often risked themselves in battle-fields, became so cowed, that they were afraid even to remonstrate. Hindus who had not joined the sect were not exempt from those oppressions".[6] By 1710 he had captured a large part of north India and made his own administrative arrangements. Only Lahore, Delhi and a few Afghan towns held out. In 1715, his army had to surrender before the imperial forces. Banda and his followers, numbering about 700, were taken to Delhi, where they were executed in 1716.

The Sikhs developed the doctrine of Guru-Panth, which ensured the right of every Sikh to fight, to conquer and to rule. Deriving power from God through the grace of the Gurus, every individual Sikh chief was authorized to assert sovereignty against outsiders. In the second half of the eighteenth century, the political vacuum created by the disintegration of the Marathas was gradually filled in northern India by the Sikhs. The result was that a number of Sikh principalities arose between the Jamuna and Sindh rivers. But the Sikh states conformed to St Augustine's definition: 'What are states, but robber bands, and what are robber bands but little states'[7] In 1799, a process of unification was started by Ranjit Singh virtually to establish an empire. In 1839 Ranjit Singh died. Within ten years of his death, the British took over his empire as they had done with others in India.

1. Jahangir, *Tuzke Jahangiri*. See *The New Cambridge History of India: The Mughul Empire*, John F. Richards, Vol. I.5, Ch 5
2. Jahangir, *Tuzke Jahangiri*. See *The New Cambridge History of India: The Mughul Empire*, John F. Richards, Vol. I.5, Ch 5
3. *The New Cambridge History of India: The Mughul Empire*, Vol.II.3, Ch 4, ed. J. S. Grewal; *The Oxford History of India*, Book VI, Ch. 7, Vincent. A Smith
4. *The Wonder That Was India*, Pt. II, CH. III, S. A. A. Rizvi; *The New Cambridge History of India: The Mughul Empire*, Vol.II.3, Ch 4, ed. J. S. Grewal
5. Kafi Khan quoted in Khushwat Singh, *A History of the Sikhs*, See *The Mughul Empire*, Vol. I.5, Ch 12, John F. Richards. Also see The Oxford History of India, Book VI. Ch. 7, Fourth Edition, Vincent A. Smith
6. See *The Oxford History of India*, Book VI, Ch. 6, Fourth Edition, Vincent A. Smith
7. *A History of India*, Vol. Two, Ch. 10, Percival Spear

30
MARATHAS: RISE AND FALL

A very important episode of Aurangzeb's time, which has attracted considerable attention of historians and politicians alike, is that of the Marathas' struggle to carve a niche of their own to rule. It was not a religious movement, nor did it represent an effort for revivalism of Hindu culture. It was basically a political and armed struggle to establish a regional kingdom by a Hindu chief, Shivaji (1627-80). For that purpose Shivaji had to contend with the Deccan Sultanates as well as with the Mughal might. Contests for territory have been commonplace, without any consideration of religion. Hindus have fought with Hindus and Muslims with Muslims and have indulged in cross-alliances when necessary. Aurangzeb did not stop cooperating politically with Hindu princes and Shivaji did not mind having a Muslim ally when the sultan of Golconda supported his campaign in Southern India. In 1681 Aurangzeb virtually transferred his capital to the Deccan where he spent the rest of his life in camp, to successfully annex the two remaining Muslim kingdoms of Bijapur and Golconda in 1686-7, as also trying somewhat fruitlessly to crush the Maratha rebellion. It was only when Hindu-Muslim animosity was fanned during the nineteenth and twentieth centuries that the Mughal-Maratha conflict provided a convenient tool to be represented as Hindu revivalist movement against Muslim dominance. Such a relationship between the two could only be created by over-stretching the facts and imagination. Aurangzeb and Shivaji came to be perceived as protagonists of Islam and Hinduism respectively and their confrontation helped to highlight this fact. Since the whole episode is often given such a connotation, a description of the events will be appropriate.

The Marathas, a hardy and rough-hewn people, lived mainly in the western Ghats spilling across Deccan up to central India. Consisting mainly of sudra class peasantry, they had no history of their own. In the fourteenth and fifteenth centuries they were living peacefully under the Muslim Bahmani kingdoms. In the seventeenth century Maratha chiefs took service with the local Muslim states. However, it was the ambition of one man—Shivaji Bhonsle (1621-80)—that awakened in them a sense of belonging to the land and an identity to their community. Shivaji's grandfather, who was the member of a prominent Maratha family, had named his two sons Shahji and Sharifji after a Muslim saint named Shah Sharif, whom he deeply venerated. Shivaji's father, Shahji, was a fief-holder of Ahmadnagar, a fief around present-day Pune bordering Bijapur. He was the first important Maratha figure to make his presence felt in the politics of the Deccan by transferring his allegiance first from Ahmadnagar to Bijapur, and then to the Mughal emperor Shah Jahan when he advanced into the Deccan, accepting a Mughal mansab in 1630. When Shah Jahan returned to the north in 1632, he went back to his allegiance to the original overlord of Ahmadnagar. He carved out an independent enclave for himself. But his hold on it proved short-lived, as he had to surrender soon to a joint Bijapur-Mughal army. Thereafter he was banished from Pune. Shortly before the birth of Shivaji he had taken a new wife. He abandoned his first wife and the son.

Shivaji was cared and groomed by his devout Hindu mother. He decided early in his life at freeing Maharashtra from the control of both the Mughals and Bijapur. He mastered the art of guerilla warfare, gathered around himself a band of loyal companions, and took to ambushing the military caravans in the countryside of Maharashtra. But like his grandfather he generally remained respectful to Islam during his campaigns. Khafi Khan, who has termed Shivaji in his writings as 'a sharp son of the devil', and 'a father of fraud', mentions about his special virtues as follows:

"In fine, Fortune so favoured this treacherous worthless man that his forces increased, and he grew more powerful every day. He erected new forts, and employed himself in settling his own territories, and in plundering those of Bijapur. He attacked the caravans which came from distant ports, and appropriated to himself the goods and women. But he made it a rule that wherever his followers went plundering, they should do no harm to the mosques, the Book of God, or the women of any one. Whenever a copy of the sacred Quran came into his hands, he treated it with respect, and gave it to some of his Musalman followers. When the women of any Hindu or Muhammadan were taken prisoners by his men, and they had no friend to protect them, he watched over them until their relations came with a suitable ransom to buy their liberty. Whenever he found out that a woman was a slave-girl, he looked upon her as being the property of her master, and appropriated her to himself. He laid down the rule that whenever a place was plundered, the goods of poor people, copper money, and vessels of brass and copper, should belong to the man who found them; but other articles, gold and silver, coined or uncoined, gems, valuable stuffs and jewels, were not to belong to the finder, but were to be given up without the smallest deduction to the officers, and to be by them paid over to Sivaji's government".[1]

The decrepitude of the state of Bijapur had tempted Shivaji to add to his father's holding on his own account. He rose to occasional rebellions and land grabbing activities. Bijapur sent its general Afzal Khan to curb the rebel. Shivaji, while embracing Afzal Khan in a friendly ploy, pulled out his stomach with an iron claw attached to his fingers. In 1660, Shaista Khan, the governor of the Mughal Deccan, swept aside Maratha resistance, occupied Pune and took up residence there. Later, Shivaji made an attempt on the life of Shaista Khan, by entering deep inside his harem. In 1664, he sacked the Mughal port as far-off as Surat where only the English merchants successfully defended themselves in their warehouses. In one of the most minute records of the East India Company it is mentioned that an Englishman named Smith saw Shivaji seated in a tent and engaged in ordering the cutting of the heads and hands of those who concealed their wealth.[2] After plundering Surat, Shivaji killed its wealthiest merchant, Baharji Bohra, seized the Mecca-bound ships and exacted ransoms from the pilgrims on board. The Mughal emperor was now alarmed. Aurangzeb deputed one of his ablest generals, Mirza Raja Jai Singh Kachhwaha of Amber, to destroy Shivaji and thereafter invade and annex Bijapur. Jai Singh soon secured his capitulation and forced Shivaji to sign a treaty in June 1665, ceding four-fifths of his territory and promising to serve the emperor loyally. Shivaji then accompanied Jai Singh with his11,000 troops to the abortive Mughal campaign to Bijapur. It seemed for the moment that Shivaji's career had come to an end, for he agreed to present himself at Aurangzeb's court at Agra with the promise of a Mughal mansab in return. He did so, taking with him offerings of gifts of submission. But he was furious at his treatment. The reward was not as high as he had expected. At the imperial court he was asked to stand with the mansabdars, in order of precedence, behind Jaswant Singh, whom he had previously defeated. Further, the Mughals considered 5,000 to be a very high rank for a new entrant like Shivaji. But he expected a mansab of at least 7,000 because of his political standing and prestige in the Deccan.

Sensing Shivaji's reluctance to compromise he was put under house arrest. Palace intrigue prevented Aurangzeb from resolving the misunderstandings. Before the Emperor could take further action, Shivaji escaped wearing a deception to the Deccan on 28 August 1666. He quickly re-captured most of the forts he had ceded to the Mughals. Shivaji made peace with the Mughal governor of the Deccan, Prince Mu'azzam, and got a mansab of 5,000 for his son, Shambhuji. He was allowed a free hand to conquer Bijapur. Shivaji remained at peace with the Mughals from 1667 to 1669 during which time he consolidated his power. In October 1670 the Marathas again attacked Surat and plundered it mercilessly. Sparing the English, Dutch, and French factories, the Muslim and Hindu traders were totally destroyed.

In 1674 Shivaji assumed the royal status, without reference to the Mughal emperor. This was the first time in generations that a regional monarch had become the head of a parallel government. In the meantime the most revered Hindu theologian at Varanasi, Gagga Bhatta was persuaded to declare that Shivaji was not a sudra, but a lapsed kshatriya, a Rajput. Gagga Bhatta traveled to the Maratha capital where he purified Shivaji and invested him with the sacred thread and Vedic verses reserved for the twice born castes. At the royal consecration on June 6, 1674, Gagga Bhatta raised the royal umbrella over Shivaji's head and hailed him as a Siva Chhatrapati (Lord of the Four Quarters). Shivaji devised two new types of tax: one was *sardeshmukhi* at the rate of 10 per cent of the annual yield for the homeland (*svarajya*) of the Marathas (as an additional tax for Shivaji being a hereditary *deshmukh*, chief), the other was *chauth* levied on conquered lands beyond the *svarajya*, which was to be paid forcibly at a higher rate of 25 per cent for Maratha 'protection'.

As a fighter his genius lay in outwitting the Mughals with guerilla tactics, and as a leader of the people in welding the caste-conscious brahmans and sudras, into a harmonious whole. He wanted self-rule and full freedom to practice his own religion in the land of his birth, Maharashtra, which he achieved. Shivaji was hailed by his followers as the founding father of the Maratha 'nation' but reviled by the Mughals as a Deccan 'mountain rat'. The Muslim states of Bijapur and Golconda, which had long opposed the Mughal power, gladly allied themselves with this Hindu Raj. However, during the 1680s Aurangzeb was able to destroy the last independent Muslim kingdoms of the Deccan. Shivaji became the master of a compact and well-organized kingdom in western India at the time of his death in 1680. But soon the Maratha kingdom lost its moral standing. The hardy patriots became toughened raiders notorious for their rapacity and ruthlessness, showing themselves as more of a scourge than an inspiration. They were to spread this reputation all over India, and their name came to be dreaded by Muslims as much as by non-Maratha Hindus. Maratha leadership was not accepted by Hindu India because the Maratha had made themselves hated. They became too bitter and aggressive to be acceptable as national leaders, hence they lacked the power to impose themselves permanently on the whole country. In 1689, Aurangzeb's forces captured Shivaji's successor, Shambhaji. He was offered his life in return for his forts. But as he used abusive language to the captors, he was tortured and killed, along with a dozen of his close companions. Aurangzeb took Shambhaji's seven-year old son Shahu and his mother into his imperial palace, and made him a mansabdar of 700. The Maratha bid for an empire, probably wishing to replace the Mughals' with their own Raj, was in effect defeated before it began by the octogenarian Aurangzeb. Maratha independence had survived but at the price of the soul of Maratha nationalism.[3]

Bahadur Shah did not pursue a belligerent policy vis-a-vis the Marathas. On the advice of the trusted noble, Zulfiqar Khan, he released Shahu (Shivaji II) and sent him back to his own country, and left him to fight his own war against the rebel Maratha diehards. Embroiled in their own civil war the Marathas were unable to create trouble for Mughals. The Maratha civil war was ended by the wise policies of Balaji Vishvanath (ca.1660-1720), who had become Shahu's Peshwa in 1714. In return for their loyalty to Sayyid Husain Ali and the imperial Mughals, the Marathas were officially recognized and given power to collect tax (*diwani*) over the land they actually controlled. Shahu was given a mansab of fifteen thousand cavalry to serve the emperor upon call and thus became a member of the Mughal bureaucracy. In return, the Marathas were given permission to collect both *sardeshmukhi* and *chauth*, and asked to pay one million rupees annually to the imperial treasury. They were given a free hand over all of Shivaji's old territories and those which were conquered from Khandesh and Berar, including the Maratha lands in Mysore and those along the coasts around Tanjore and the Carnatic. This agreement implied a free hand given to the Marathas to conquer more lands even from the Mughal territory, whose boundaries were undefined, reaching even up to the environs of Agra and Delhi. It was the dawn of a century of unprecedented Maratha power and expansion at the expense of neighboring Mughal provinces. They felt so strong as to even ignore the annual payment they owed to the emperor. Maratha expansion had, in fact, been so rapid that during Balaji Baji Rao's peshwa-ship Poona became the bureaucratic headquarters of a loose-knit confederacy. There were four extremely powerful generals, each of whom carved out his own dynastic domain: the Gaekwar in Baroda, Holkar at Indore, Sindia in Gowaliar, and Bhonsle at Nagpur. In 1741, Orissa was a part of Bengal province. Bhonsle attacked Orissa, and in one year reached near Calcutta. He even ignored the Peshwa's demand for the share of the Orissan revenue. In the meanwhile, the Nawab of Bengal, Ali Vardi Khan, appealed to the Peshwa for help. Balaji's army moved against the fellow Maratha invaders under the treaty with the Mughals. After forcibly taking back the money owed to the Mughal treasury Balaji chased Bhonsle back to Nagpur.

During the crumbling years of the Mughal empire, the remaining aspiration of the Marathas was shattered at the battlefield of Panipat in 1761 at the hands of Ahmad Shah Abdali of Afghanistan. The Maratha confederacy dissolved in warring fragments. For the time being, Mahadaji Scindia seemed likely to repair the disaster. In 1770 the Marathas became so powerful that they occupied Agra and Mathura. In 1771 Mahadaji Scindia captured Delhi and invited the emperor Shah Alam to return to his capital from Allahabad, where he was forced to live under British supervision. He promised the emperor to restore him to his old supreme position. In 1785 the powerless Mughal emperor made him the general administrator of the Mughal empire. In that capacity Mahadaji even demanded from British the emperor's share of the revenues of Bengal. He needed money to maintain a large army in order to control the Rajputs, Sikhs, Jats and Rohillas (an Afghan clan), each having their respective ambitions, in northern India. He was busy fighting the Rajputs, that in 1788 the Rohilla chief, Ghulam Qadir, sacked Delhi and blinded the hapless Mughal emperor. The incident was reported thus by a contemporary source :

"He [the Rohilla}, sent for the dethroned king and all the princes of the royal family to the audience chamber; on their arrival, he sternly commanded Shah Aulum to discover his concealed treasures; in vain did the king plead his degraded state, and the consequent inability to conceal even the smallest article. Inflamed by a continual debauch, which had thrown him into a paroxysm of rage, the tyrant threatened his sovereign with instant loss of sight; What! exclaimed the suffering prince, What! Will you destroy those eyes which for a period of sixty years have been assiduously employed in perusing the sacred Koran?

"Regardless of the pathetic appeal, the Rohilla, with characteristic inhumanity, commanded his attendants to seize the king. Having thrown him on the floor, the ferocious ruffian implanting himself on his bosom, transfixed with a poignard the eyes of his venerable sovereign! On the completion of this horrid deed Gholam Cadir ordered the king to be removed to a distant apartment. The miserable Shah Aulum, pale and bleeding, was conducted to his retreat; there, in all the bitterness of anguish, to contemplate on his now ruined fortunes."[4]

Mahadaji rushed to the rescue of the emperor but it was too late. He pursued the Rohillas, captured Ghulam Qadir, and tortured him to death. Though the emperor's agony had been avenged by his Maratha ally, the poor king survived another twenty years, bearing the marks of his oppressor. With Mahadaji's death in 1794 the Maratha empire itself withered away. The Marathas passed away from the Indian political stage unsung.

1. *The Oxford History of India*, Book VI, Chapter 6, Fourth Edition, Vincent A. Smith
2. See *The Oxford History of India*, Book VI. Ch. 6, Fourth Edition, Vincent A. Smith
3. *A History of India*, Vol. Two, Percival Spear
4. W. Francklin, *The History of the Reign of Shah Aulum*, reprint 1988, page 176, quoted in *The Indus Saga and the Making of Pakistan*, Ch 18, Aitzaz Ahsan

31
MUGHAL IMPACT

The process of integration of the two major communities, Hindus and Muslims continued during the times of the Mughals. Both communities continued borrowing eagerly from each other. Both were coming to an understanding that the ethnic mix had come to stay, and as such they were ready to accommodate each other and to adopt the institutions, and social and religious norms of each other. Culture is always in process of evolution, slow or fast, unnoticed or conspicuous. The Muslims had begun acclimatizing with Indian society and culture, and they were being Indianized in turn. The process of integration was somehow facilitated by the policies of the Mughal rule, whose quick and universal acceptance promoted a new culture. The moulding of the Indian culture was probably the finest achievement of the Mughals. It made a long lasting impact, so much so that even today it is referred to as the '*Mughlai*' culture, which reflected itself in the language, literature, art, architecture, dress and manners. The process of integration was somehow facilitated by the policies of the kings. The Mughal monarchs 'regarded the ruled as a flock or herd to be tended and exploited rather than converted or persecuted.' They became universal symbols of power and remained a stable unifying force for two centuries. There may have been temporary set-backs but the tempo was never lost. According to Percival Spears: "Another characteristic of Mughal rule was tolerance. Tolerance was not absolute, and was subject to considerable variations. There were times, notably in the reign of Aurangzeb, when the ruler aspired to be the head of an Islamic state rather than the Muslim head of an Indian state. But even so, though some discrimination was practised such as the imposition of the *jizya* on non-believers and the occasional demolition of temples, tolerance was the general rule. Temples received grants as well mosques, and were rarely demolished without a political motive. The emperor intermarried with Rajput families and Hindu customs were countenanced at court. It may be said that in any case religious tolerance was an Indian tradition."[1]

A secular-minded race, the Mughals were, according to Sardar Panikkar, 'kings by profession', more interested in ruling than propagating religion. "The Mughals considered themselves Islamic rulers....But their ruling ethos was non-communal and led to the emergence of a cross-communal service class. This was a development actively encouraged. Akbar's successors continued this tradition of drawing upon differentiated symbols of legitimacy to serve as Hindu *Maharajah* and *Padishah-i-Islam* simultaneously. Cleavages rested on class rather than religious lines; prevailing standards were aristocratic rather than communal. Among those who participated in the court culture, communalism was regarded as bad manners."[2]

B. N. Pande explains it as follows:

'Destiny had ordained that the Mughals would play this unifying role. So strong was this tradition among the Mughals that even Aurangzeb could play the bigot only half-heartedly, and with considerable restraint.'[3]

The power structure, even in the heyday of the Mughals, was more of a hierarchic nature than administrative. There existed various levels of power, which most of the time emanated not directly from the state but locally. The Mughal kings achieved universal dominance in the country, yet the real authority of the State did not belong to them but to the local Hindu rajas and heads of villages who virtually controlled the whole country. A warrior could overrun his neighbors, collect revenue from villages and get recognition from the imperial court as the Raja. Or anybody, Muslim and Hindu alike, could build up large landholdings from his own resources and then assume the position of the local authority. But all aspirants to power, big or small, had to obtain such titles and rights from the emperor. Apart from being Rajas of their respective lands, Hindu princes were generally holder of *mansabs* at the imperial court. Even Sikhs and Marathas, not happy with the Muslim rule in India, had to seek their own legitimacy as ruling authorities from the Mughal sovereign. In 1714, The Maratha king Shahu had to walk barefoot to make obeisance at the tomb of the Emperor Aurangzeb at Khuldabad. At the end of the eighteenth century the Maratha warlord, Mahadji Scindia, received the title of Regent Plenipotentiary of the empire. To obtain the blessings of the crown in their endeavor to strengthen their political authority around Delhi, the Sikhs had to make ceremonial offerings to the throne in 1783. Even when regional viceroys founded their own ruling dynasties like in Bengal, Hyderabad, Awadh and the Carnatic, they never dared to challenge emperor's ultimate authority or assume imperial titles. Only Tipu Sultan of Mysore, uneasy as a newcomer with the traditions of the Indo-Persian nobility, took up the title of emperor. But even then he maintained a respectful communications with the imperial court. Even the Europeans trading from seaports regarded the Mughal emperor as among the great kings of the world. During the most expansive period of empire building, the British too maintained the form of imperial grants and participated in the rites of Mughal authority-at least down to 1848. Richard Wellesley, Governor General, 1798-1805, warned his aides to show respect to the Emperor as 'almost every class of people...continue to acknowledge his nominal authority.'4

Perhaps the most lasting of the influences of the Mughals was in administration. The Mughals gave India an all-pervading ordered administration. The semi-sacred imperial authority of the monarch, apparatus of government, administrative concepts, nomenclatures, regalia and dress, introduced by them was also adopted by local rajas and nobility, and even by the Marathas who were fighting to get rid of the Mughal political influence. In the Muslim administration of Carnatic, Hindu officers were invested with such designations as *mufti*, *kazi*, and *kotwal*. In the Hindu state of Benaras and the Jat state of Bharatpur, Muslim officers were policy makers and revenue collectors. The Marhatas adopted the Mughal system of revenue collection in place of the dreaded system of *chauth* collection. Under the leadership of Mahadji Scindia the Mughal elements in the Maratha regime became more marked. His army was composed of as many Muslim as Hindu soldiers. In the early nineteenth century the Sikh rulers of all-Punjab appointed Muslims as judicial officers in the city of Lahore. Coinage of various local rulers came out of mints with the Mughal emperor's name prominently displayed.[5]

The British administrative system in the country, and even that of the independent India of today, owe a great deal to what the Mughals had done in this regard. "To Akbar it is necessary to give the same distinctive attention that we have shown to Charlemagne or Constantine the Great. He is one of the hinges of history. Much of his work on consolidation and organization in India survives to this day. It was taken over and continued by the British when they became the successors of the Mogul emperors. The British monarch, indeed, used as his Indian title the title of the Mogul emperors, *Kaisar-i-Hind*. All the other great administrations of the descendants of Jengis Khan, in Russia, throughout Western and Central Asia and in China, have long since dissolved away and given place to other forms of government. Their governments were, indeed, little more than taxing governments; a system of revenue-collecting to feed the central establishment of the ruler, like the Golden Horde in South Russia or the imperial city at Karakorum or Peking. The life and ideas of the people they left alone, careless how they lived-so long as they paid. So it was that, after centuries of subjugation, a Christian Moscow and Kieff, a Shiite Persia, and a thoroughly Chinese China rose again from their Mongol submergence. But Akbar made a new India. He gave the princes and ruling classes of India some inklings at least of a common interest. If India is now anything more than a sort of ragbag of incoherent states and races, a prey to every casual raider from the north, it is very largely due to him."[6]

Persian, the court language, became the administrative language of the country. It turned into a symbol of prestige for the Hindu nobility and ministerial class and a tool of promoting careers of the youth. "From that time Persian became the diplomatic language throughout India, the language of the Rajput courts like French in Henry III's England and the stock-in trade of the clerical Hindu. When the missionary Swartz went on a mission to the Hindu raja of Tanjore in the extreme south of India in the eighteenth century, they conversed in Persian. Hindu students in Delhi commonly took Persian as one of their degree subjects to the outbreak of the Second World War."[7] The beauty of the language was so intense that it embraced the local vernacular in its fold. This marriage of love between Persian and Hindustani languages, occasioned by mixing of the Mughal and Turkish army with the local population in bazaars, gave birth to a new language called Urdu (from Turkish word 'Ordu' meaning army, and its English version 'horde'). This language, even after half a century of post-Independence Hindi domination in academia, is holding its own so tenaciously that even today it may be termed as the lingua franca of north India. Its most forceful and conspicuous presence is found in the songs and dialogues of Indian films captivating the masses.

In the development of painting and calligraphy the Mughal monarchs had a personal role to play. Beginning with Akbar, a Mughal-Rajput alliance was forged in the artistic expression through paintings. The result was a school of painting specializing in a hybrid Indo-Persian style creating a new style of Mughal miniatures with delicate lines and soft colours, with figures of royalty adorned sometimes with a halo. In such pieces of art there was little distinction in either dress or appearance between the Mughal royalties and their Hindu nobles and chiefs. Hundreds of painters were employed at court by Mughal kings and honored with mansabdar rank. Apart from the presence of famous Persian calligraphers and artists in the imperial court, like Khwaja Abdul Samad, Aqa Rida of Heart, Abul-Hasan, and Mansur, most of the great artists were Hindus: Daswanath, Basawan, Lala Kesu, Haribans, Manohar and Bishandas. The portraiture work of Bishandas was of such an excellence that Jahangir deputed him to Isphahan to paint the Persian emperor.

Architecture too was not left untouched. It started with 'almost pure Persian phase in a building like Homayun's tomb (1560) through the Indo-Muslim style of Akbar's day to its apotheosis in the Taj Mahal, which could have been built nowhere else but in India and not without the background of Persian influence'. Mughal forts and palaces at Delhi, Agra and Fatehpur Sikri are reminiscent of the beautiful sandstone palaces of the local rajas. Their adornment with beautifully carved beams, brackets and columns is foreign to India, but this combination has produced a new Mughal-Hindu style of architecture

The ruthlessness, as demonstrated by the Mughals, appeared to be the need of the time. However, it did not pertain to governing day to day affairs of the state. It was generally used in the context of suppressing the sub-continental culture of rebellion or in case of princes and aspirants to the throne, who dared 'touch the sceptre'. Torture and execution, bereft of any judicial process, seemed to be the only deterrent to rebellion. The following accounts of the French doctor, Bernier, who visited the court of Aurangzeb and had seen the gruesome wars of succession, show why such procedures were deemed necessary.

'My readers have no doubt condemned the means by which the reigning Mughal attained the summit of power. These means were indeed unjust and cruel; but it is not perhaps fair to judge him by the rigid rules which we apply to the character of European princes. In our quarter of the globe, the succession to the crown is settled in favour of the eldest son by wise and fixed laws; but in Hindustan the right of governing is usually disputed by all the sons of the deceased monarch, each of whom is reduced to the cruel alternative of sacrificing his brothers that he himself may reign, or of suffering his own life to be forfeited for the security and stability of the dominion of another. Yet even those who may maintain that the circumstances of country, birth, and education afford no palliation of the conduct pursued by Aurangzeb, must admit that this Prince is endowed with a versatile and rare genius, that he is a consummate statesman, and the great King."[8]

Aurangzeb's decided to publicly humiliate and then kill his captive brother Dara Shikoh:

"In private session with his grandees, Aurangzeb now invited pro and con arguments. For the moment it seemed that Dara would be taken to Gowalior state prison, but the debate centered on the question of whether or not there should be a humiliating parade through Delhi's streets. A few nobles counselled caution: it could only spatter mud on the royal family to make a degraded spectacle of the prince, and there was even the possibility of a riot or rescue attempt. The opposition countered with blunt insistence: Dara had to be exposed to public gaze in order to terrify the mob with the reality of Aurangzeb's power; besides, only seeing was believing, and nothing less than an open display could make it quite clear that Dara was incontrovertibly a prisoner. Aurangzeb finally decided that future fake Daras must be prevented from stirring up trouble. Dara and his son Sipihr Shikoh would be dragged in squalor under military guard through the main thoroughfares of central Delhi, for every Indian to see".[9]

1. The Mughals and the British, Ch. XXV by Percival Spear in The Cultural History of India, edited by A.L.Basham
2. Dr. Henny Senderin, *Kashmiri Pundits* (collected in R.E.Frykenberg, ed., *Delhi through the Ages*, 1986), quoted by M.J.Akbar in Nehru: *The Making of India*, Ch 2
3. Quoted by M.J.Akbar in *Nehru: The Making of India*, Ch 2
4. *The New Cambridge History of India*: Vol. II.1, Ch 1, C. A. Bayly
5. *The New Cambridge History of India*: Vol. II.1, Ch 1, C. A. Bayly
6. Wells, H.G., *The Outline of History*, XXXII
7. *A History of India*, Vol. Two; Percival Spear
8. Bernier, Quoted by Lane-Poole in *Aurangzeb*, page 63-64, see *The Indus Saga and the Making of Pakistan*, Ch.18, Aitzaz Ahsan
9. Waldemar Hansen, *The Peacock Throne: The Drama of Mughal India* (1972) 372, quoted in *The Indus Saga and the Making of Pakistan*, Ch 18, Aitzaz Ahsan

32
CHRISTIANITY COMES TO INDIA

For five hundred years of war and destruction, Jews were looking for a Messiah, who was to redeem mankind by restoring the fabulous glories of David and Solomon and bringing the whole world under the firm Jewish heel, when in the reign of Tiberius Caeser about 2000 years ago arose out of Judea such a teacher. He was Jesus of Nazareth, son of Mary and Joseph. He was a penniless teacher, who wandered about the dust in the sun-bit country of Judea, living upon casual gifts of food. He was a person of intense personal magnetism. He was to liberate the intense realization of the righteousness from that exclusive narrowness with which it was so extraordinarily intermingled in the Jewish mind. 'The Jewish idea was and is a curious combination of theological breadth and an intense racial patriotism.' Contrary to expectations, and being unhappy with many of such ideas and practices of his native Jewish faith, Jesus started preaching a new but profound doctrine: the loving Fatherhood of God and the coming of the Kingdom of Heaven. 'For whosoever shall do the will of my Father which is in heaven, the same is my brother and sister, and mother.' (Matt. xii. 46-50). In the name of universal brotherhood, Jesus had denounced tribal patriotism and family loyalty. This doctrine was a bold and an uncompromising demand for a complete change and cleansing of the life of the struggling race. The Jews had believed that God was a righteous god, but at the same time a trading god, who had made bargain with Abraham to bring the Jews a predominance in the earth. Jesus taught that God was no bargainer, there were no chosen people, and no favourites in the Kingdom of Heaven. God was the loving father of all life, and all men were brothers. There are no privileges, no rebates, and no excuses in the Kingdom of Heaven. In the parable of Good Samaritan Jesus cast scorn on glorifying oneself and minimizing the righteousness of other creeds and other races. Among his best known teachings are: "love thy neighbours" and "turn the other cheek" to the enemy who hit you on one cheek. He also denounced private riches.

" And when he was gone forth into the way, there came one running, and kneeled to him, and asked him, Good master, what shall I do that I may inherit eternal life? And Jesus said unto him, Why callest thou me good? there is none good but one, that is, God. Thou knowest the commandments, Do not commit adultery, Do not kill, Do not steal, Do not bear false witness, Defraud not, Honuor thy father and mother. And he answered and said unto him, Master, all these things have I observed from my youth. Then Jesus beholding him loved him, and said unto him, One thing thou lackest: go thy way, sell whatsoever thou hast, and give to the poor, and thou shalt have treasure in heaven: and come take up the cross, and follow me. And he was sad at that saying, and went away grieved: for he had great possessions.

"And Jesus looked round about, and saith unto his disciples, How hardly shall they that have riches enter into the kingdom of God! And the disciples were astonished at his words. But Jesus answered again, and saith unto them, Children, how hard is it for them that trust in riches to enter into the kingdom of God! It is easier for a camel to go through the eye of a needle, than for a rich man to enter into the kingdom of God."(Mark x. 17-25)

When Jesus appeared as a teacher he was thirty years old. He went about the country for three years spreading his doctrine. But when he reached Jerusalem he was accused of trying to establish a strange kingdom in Judea. He was tried upon this charge and crucified together with two thieves. Due to the miraculous circumstances of his birth, the Christians believe that he is the Son of God, sent on this earth to save mankind from their sins and that he has redeemed mankind by being crucified on the cross for the sins of his followers. Christians believe in the original sin, and that Jesus died in their place to save them from that sin. They generally believe that Jesus is a part of the Holy Trinity: God the Father, Jesus the Son and the Holy Spirit. These are three distinct Persons, but one God. Thus, believing in the divinity of Jesus Christ, they worship Jesus as the living God and pray for divine forgiveness and blessings and salvation from him. Later on, all Christendom was torn by disputes about the Trinity. [1]

There are a multitude of forms of Christianity which developed either because of disagreements on dogma, adaptation to different cultures, or simply personal tastes. The most prominent division arose four hundred and eighty-two years ago when a monk in Germany,

Martin Luther, nailed his legendary attack on Roman Catholic Church practices on a church door. This act of conscience triggered the Protestant Reformation Movement. The result was the wrenching division of Christianity, and more than a century of religious wars that killed hundred of thousands. Lutherans believe that faith alone, an acceptance of God renewed every day, ensures eternal salvation. The Catholic Church believes that salvation comes from the sum total of faith and good works—that a life of devotion and service on earth earns the faithful the key to heaven.

Christianity entered into India as early as the first century. It is believed that St. Thomas arrived in India around the year 52 AD and established a number of Syrian churches in Malabar. Today the Syrian Christians in Kerala proclaim themselves as belonging to the sect which was founded by St. Thomas. With missionary zeal he went inside the country reached the east coast at a place near Madras city, which was subsequently called Bet Thuma or House of Thomas. He started preaching from that place. Unfortunately, it was not taken kindly by the people who killed him in 68 at a place called Maylapur near Madras. The west coast, being situated on the main trade route of east Asia and China, was host, apart from the Christians, Muslims, Zoroastrian and Chinese, also to the Jews. At Cochin, a small Jewish community also believe that their religion took an implant there in the first century.

1. H. G Wells writes in *The Outline of History*: "There is no clear evidence that the apostles of Jesus entertained that doctrine. Nor does he give his claim to be the "Christ" or his participation in the godhead any such prominence as one feels would have been done had he considered it a matter of primary significance. Most outstanding is the statement (Matt. xvi. 20), 'Then charged he his disciples that they should tell no man that he was Jesus the Christ'! It is difficult to understand this suppression if we suppose he considered this fact was essential to salvation."

33
PORTUGUESE SAGA

Trade interest of Europe in India is very old specially for commodities like spices and textiles. Greek and Roman reports on trade with India were amply available on which the later days Europeans formed their image of India. Hegel observed thus in *History of Philosophy*: "The quest for India is a moving force of our whole history. Since ancient times all nations have directed their wishes and desires to that miraculous country whose treasures they coveted. These treasures were the most precious on earth: treasures of nature, pearls, diamonds, incense, the essence of roses, elephants, lions, etc., and also the treasure of wisdom. It has always been of great significance for universal history by which route these treasures found their way to the West, the fate of nations has been influenced by this.'[2] After the fall of the Roman Empire and the rise of the Muslim Arabs, direct contact was lost, but trade continued to be carried indirectly thorough middlemen. Later in the Middle Ages the intensity of trade increased, but it also had to face two major threats: Mongol and Turkish invasions both from land and sea up to Egypt, and the monopoly of trade shared by Egyptians and Venetians. 'Crusading zeal against the Muslims and commercial zeal against spice monopolists were the motives which sent Columbus to America in 1492 and Vasco da Gama to Calicut in 1498'. Vasco da Gama arrived at the port of Calicut on a small flagship San Gabriel on May 27 as the explorer of trade and for cultural expansion on behalf of the Portuguese monarch, who had full backing of the exclusive Papal Bull (decree) and was styled, 'Lord of the Navigation, Conquest and Commerce of Ethiopia, Arabia, Persia and India'. Europe had found a southern direct passage to the East, a phenomenon which was soon to strike a Christian blow on Arabs, Turks, and Mongols. In India, it initiated an era of European penetration and conquest that would last for four and a half centuries. For the Portuguese, it was to herald an era of their domination of the Indian Ocean for another century.

At the time of Vasco da Gama's arrival, Calicut was a port thriving with the activities of Arab, Hindu, and Chinese merchants and seamen. Coming from all parts of Asia and Eastern Africa they purchased pepper and ginger of Malabar and gave in return gold, ivory, silks, and jewels. On his arrival, Vasco da Gama at once acknowledged the sovereignty of Vijyanagar, the Lord of South India under whose tutelage the Zamorin (Chief) was ruling at Calicut as 'King of the Mountains and the Sea'. Vasco da Gama in his reply to the Zamorin of Calicut said that he came to seek 'Christian and spices'. By all accounts it was a very successful venture. It gave birth not only to the Portuguese empire in India, but also opportunities to the Portuguese to give enormous boost to their trade, persecute the Muslims and Hindus alike, and spread their religion and culture in the area under their control. "The Christians whom da Gama did find in Malabar-the so-called Syrian community—had been peacefully settled there for more than a thousand years. So had the Arabs, whose presence surprised and dismayed him. Unconnected with the Muslim sultanates to the north, they were favoured by the Hindu Zamorin, whose dependence upon Arab commercial activity made him the only Indian ruler to react to first sign of Portuguese aggressiveness. He also had links with the Sultan of Egypt, whose well-gunned vessels came to the aid of the Zamorin's outmatched coastal navy and put the Portuguese enterprise in some danger. The expeditions that followed Vasco da Gama failed to take Calicut, but established their first small strongpoint at near-by Cochin."[3]

When Portugal resounded with the news of 3000 per cent profitability of da Gama's trade, an armada of ships was immediately assembled. It sailed under the command of Pedro Alvarez Cabral in March 1500. On reaching Calicut, he forced the Zamorin, in a show of strength, to sign a treaty of peace and friendship with Portugal. 'The era of friendly Indo-Portuguese collaboration was followed by a longer period of bitter conflict and hatred. For, soon after leaving Calicut, Cabral plundered a Muslim ship laden with spices, and in retaliation the "Moors" attacked the Portuguese factory and killed all the Westerners they found living there. Vasco da Gama returned with a fleet of fifteen heavily armed ships in 1502 and blasted the port until it was all but reduced to rubble. Then he captured several Muslim vessels and cut off the hands, ears, and noses of some eight hundred "Moorish" seamen, sending the lot to the *zamorin's* palace for his highness's "curry". Such orgies of piracy and plunder served to secure Portugal's direct route to the East and assured an uninterrupted supply of pepper and cloves.'[4]

In 1509, Affonso Albuquerque was deputed as the Captain General to work as the custodian of Portuguese interests in the East. He was to become the master architect of Portugal's Indian empire. He was 'a strategist of no mean vision and a religious fanatic whose hatred of Islam was almost as great as his knowledge of the Indian Ocean.' The first important act of his masterly command was to wrest control of the strategic Goa in 1510 from the sultan of Bijapur. He then forced the sultan of Gujerat to cede Diu to the Portuguese. In 1511 he took control of Malacca in the East Indies after a hard-fought battle, and then of Macao, an island off the Chinese coast. He then established a strategic base at Ormuz at the entrance of the Persian Gulf. He seized Socotra Island to control the traffic and trade from Red Sea. In a masterly move he made Goa the capital of the Portuguese eastern empire from where the Portuguese supervised Malabar and all other strong points. Thus he achieved full control of the spice trade at its source in the East Indies and on the traffic of the Arabian Sea, which was now subjected to a Portuguese licensing system. It soon came to be known as the Golden Babylon of the East.

The Portuguese, who were fighting the Moor in North Africa, had entered India with the same zeal and hostility towards all Muslims. Goa's population was mostly Hindus. Albuquerque cut their taxes in half 'after doing no less to the bodies of every Muslim soldier and official or overlord he could find.' Viceroy Albuquerque wrote his king, Dom Manoel, 'I do not believe that in all Christendom there will be so rich a King as Your Highness, and therefore, do I urge you, Senhore, to strenuously support this affair of India with men and arms, and strengthen your hold in her, and securely establish your dealings and your factories; and wrest the wealth of India and business from the hands of the Moors.'[5] Albuquerque's hatred of Islam was so fierce that he dreamed of diverting the Nile in order to dry up Egypt and of stealing the remains of the Prophet from Mecca. No Muslim was permitted to hold any office, no matter how humble, in Albuquerque's imperial regime, though Hindu "police" (*sipahi*, later sepoy) were readily employed. Western Europeans learned long before the British arrived how best to exploit the communal conflicts and social divisions within India's fragmented, pluralistic society.[6]

In the beginning, the Portuguese were totally occupied with mastery over sea, trade and traffic. They showed no signs of territorial ambition to expand inside India. They maintained very good relations with the ruler of Vijayanagar, Krishnadeva Raya (1509-30), who himself needed a trade outlet from Goa as also a source of military supplies. Vijaynagar was in continuous state of conflict with the Muslim sultanates of the Deccan. The enemy of Muslim powers was a natural ally of Albuquerque, so he warmly solicited the friendship of its ruler. It resulted, temporarily, in non-prosecution of Hindus. Initially, they satisfied their ambitions of infusing Christian culture and of making a permanent presence by inter-marrying and producing a hybrid community of Roman Catholic Portuguese Goans. This community, they thought, would be committed to the Portuguese settlements and provide a self-perpetuating garrison. However, their control of the sea irked the Mughals and other Muslim rulers, specially because of the tax the Portuguese levied on trade from the port of Surat and on the pilgrim traffic to Makkah. Often they spilled over from the Portuguese settlements and formed communities of their own which tended towards disorder and piracy. Such incidents, one at Surat at the time of Jahangir in 1613, and the other at Hugli was suppressed by Shah Jahan in 1632. "In seizing and retaining their strong points they acquired a reputation for cruelty and perfidy because their practice on both these points was below the current Indian standard. They were deeply impregnated with the idea that no faith need be kept with an infidel. It was from this period that the word *feringi* (lit. *farangi*, frank) acquired the opprobrium of which echoes may still be heard today. In religion they were intolerant to the extent of allowing no Hindu temples in Goa and introducing the Inquisition (1560), both measures which can be regarded as sub-standard from the Indian standpoint, and they advertised this trait in their rough handling of the Syrian Christians of Malabar to secure their submission to Roman supremacy."[7]

The Portuguese were men of the Catholic renaissance. "Sixteenth-century Protestant and Catholic clergy and governments agreed with each other in holding that it was the prerogative of a local government to dictate the religion of its subjects (*cuius regio, eius religio*). Dissenters must migrate or else run the risk of being put to death-probably by being burnt alive."[8] With the crusading zeal to convert India's "heathen" population to Catholicism, the first Jesuit missionaries arrived in 1542. The Jesuits were members of the Society of Jesus set up in 1534 by the Spaniard, Ignatius Loyola, to propagate the Roman Catholic faith. In 1548 Francis Xavier had to write back to Ignatius Loyola that "all these Indian nations are very barbarous, vicious, and without inclination to virtue, no constancy of character, no frankness." Xavier soon found the converts interested less in Christianity and more in free ration. Anyway, the number of converts, combined with offspring of intermarriages (Luso-Indians), made the population of Goa so much Catholic dominated that Inquisition was introduced in Goa in 1560. But it appeared that Portuguese trade and power was linked with the prosperity of Vijyanagar. In 1965, the Deccan sultanates of Ahmadnagar, Bijapur, Bidar, and Golconda joined together to declare a war against Vijayanagr, which had employed in its vast army 2000 Turkish cavalrymen. Vijayanagar was reported to have armed nearly a million soldiers in its defense. But it proved no match to the united Muslim force; the Hindu army at Talikot was slaughtered and Vijayanagar was plundered and destroyed. The Portuguese were now left weak and languishing for lack of trade. They now lived in the midst of a frightening prospect of being kicked out by the newly enriched and emboldened Muslim Sultans of the Deccan. But the Sultans did not drive the Portuguese out of India.[9]

1. H.G.Wells, *The Outline of History*, Ch. XXVIII
2. G.W. F. Hegel, Vorlesungen uber die Ohilosophie der Geschichte (Stuggart, 1961) pp.215ff, quoted in *A History of India* ,Hermann Kulke & Dietmar Rothermund.
3. *India: A Concise History*, Ch. Seven, Francis Watson
4. *A New History of India* (Fifth Edition), Stanley Wolpert
5. *The Commentaries of the Great Affonso d'Albuquerque, Second Viceroy of India*, trans. from the Portuguese ed. Of 1774 by W. de Gray Birch, *A New History of India* (Fifth Edition), Ch. Ten, Stanley Wolpert
6. *A New History of India* (Fifth Edition), Ch. Ten, Stanley Wolpert
7. *A History of India*, Vol. Two, Percival Spear
8. Arnold Toyanbee, *Mankind and Mother Earth*
9. *A New History of India* (Fifth Edition), Stanley Wolpert

34
PROSELYTIZING WITH PROFIT

The quest of the English for a short passage to India had begun as early as the fifteenth century. A cartographer, named Sebastian Cabot, formed a company for this purpose in 1551. In 1583 some merchants sent a boat named Tiger to test the Portuguese blockade of the sea, but they were captured and taken prisoners to Goa. One of them was Ralph Fitch who wrote back home:

"Here be many Moors and Gentiles. They have a very strange order among them—they worship a cow and esteem much of the cow's dung to paint the walls of their houses. They will kill nothing, not so much as a louse, for they hold it a sin to kill anything. They eat no flesh, but live by roots and rice and milk. And when the husband dieth his wife is burned with him if she be alive:...In the town they have hospitals to keep lame dogs and cats, and for birds.....Goa is the most principal city which the Portugals have in India...Here be many merchants of all nations"[1]

The Mughal army was a mighty one but it did not have the support of a naval force. For the protection of annual passage of the pilgrims to Makkah the only choice for them was to seek the costly services of the Portuguese, and that too in spite of their bigotry. Between 1607 and 1611, the English Captain Hawkins, who had become a companion of Emperor Jahangir and had also obtained a mansab of 400, tried hard to seek privileges at Surat. His efforts bore no fruit as the Mughals appeared not to affront the Portuguese. But when the Company's ships defeated the Portuguese at an estuary off Surat in 1612 it came as a breath of fresh air to the Mughals. The English now appeared as a better alternative to the Portuguese. The Mughals were now willing to talk, and thus arrived Sir Thomas Roe, the new ambassador from King James's court, with costly presents in 1616. Even then it took more than two years to convince the emperor and to obtain permission from him in 1619 for East India Company to build a factory at Surat. In return, the English would provide protection to the commercial and pilgrim sea traffic from the Portuguese. The table was turned and Coḿpany tacitly became the maritime auxiliary of the empire.

Sir Thomas advised the Company to rest content with the profits to be derived from 'quite trade', and not to seek territorial expansion like the Portuguese. In the 1680s, the Surat Council of the company brought themselves in a state of belligerence towards the Emperor Aurangzeb on an ill advice from the Company's president at London. The Mughals seized their factory. Fortunately, the emperor pardoned the Company after an apology and a promise of a respectful behaviour. The factory at Surat was restored. In addition, the Company was allowed a new settlement in Bengal. A piece of land was allotted to them, on which arose Fort William in 1696, and which subsequently became the city of Calcutta. The first foot-holds of the British on both eastern and western sides of the Indian soil were thus established. By this time public opinion in Europe had come to believe that its civilization was superior to all others'. Thus, apart from the motive of seeking trade profits, markets and raw materials for their burgeoning industries, capture of new territories began to be considered holy in order to impart 'the inestimable benefits of civilization'. Like other European powers elsewhere, the British in India thus came to stay for a long time as rulers.

The British got a firm hold on the administration of India after their victory in the battle of Plassey in 1757. After the displacement of Mughal rulers, we find an array of administrators, Governor Generals, parliamentarians, intellectuals, evangelists, public debaters, all having their own opinions and perceptions of India and its people, as also on how best to govern the new colony. At the core of all debates was the belief in the superiority of western civilization; all others were regarded as either static or in decay. It was considred a great disservice to humanity to withhold recognition of the immense contribution of western enlightenment, learning and rationality in precipitating the march forward of India in that direction. Intellectuals like Thomas Babington Macaulay, who was a member of the Supreme Council of India from 1834 to 1838, expressed his opinion in his *Minutes on Educational Reforms in India* of February 1835 as follows: "I am quite ready to take the oriental learning at the valuation of the Orientalists themselves. I have never found one among them who could deny that a single shelf of a good European library was worth the whole native literature of India or Arabia. The intrinsic superiority of the Western literature is, indeed, fully admitted by those members of the Committee who support the Oriental plan of education"[2] Everyone seemed eagre to shower the blessings of the British rule on India. Under the force of arguments of Burke, British Parliament had committed itself in the late eighteen century to promote the country's welfare. Many were of the opinion that introduction of western Christianity in this eastern country will catalyze the process of self-reformation. Thus, annexation of Indian territories, which was considered 'bad' under Pitt's India Act of 1784, later came to be considered 'good'. There were also some servants of the Company, who were imbued with liberal ideas and were aware of the susceptibilities existing below the surface of the Indian society. They believed in the slogan: 'Let us, therefore, calmly proceed in a course of gradual improvement'. But there were Conservatives too who, like Warren Hastings, believed in leaving things as they were because the contrary could be a perilous course.

It is said that Clive founded the British state in India, Hastings made it politically viable, Cornwallis gave it a definite form, and Bentinck took upon himself the administrative task of reforming the Indian society. Since the British had established themselves at the expense of the Muslim power it would not appear illogical that their first measures should be to cripple the Muslim elite and general populace both economically and politically; and to counterbalance this act they had to push up and puff up the Hindus. In 1765, Clive secured the revenue license for Bengal from the weakened emperor Shah Alam II. The zamindars taxed the peasantry as much as they could, and after paying a fixed sum as revenue to the Government kept a portion thereof for their own living. One of the important measures taken by Warren Hastings (1774-1785) was to set up the Asiatic Society of Bengal in 1784. Its linguistic and archaeological researches helped in the rediscovery of India's past civilization. It "brought into being a new concept of Hindu golden age as a legacy for the rising Indian intelligentsia." He established Calcutta Madrasah in 1782. He got the traditional Hindu and Muslim laws translated and codified for the benefit of British judges adjudicating civil disputes between the Indians. Warren Hastings himself learned Persian and Urdu, and asked two of his British assistants to produce a Bengali grammar and an English translation of Bhagavad-Gita. As for Lord Cornwallis who was sent to India as Governor-General in 1786, two of his acts are most noteworthy. First, he undertook the cleansing of administration, because in his own words: 'Every native of India, I verily believe, is corrupt'. So, all Indian officials drawing a salary of more than 500 pounds a year were dismissed with the sole exception of the 'incorruptible judge of Benaras', Ali Ibrahim Khan. Such positions were now reserved exclusively for the British. To root out corruption he raised the salaries of low-paid employees. But some time later, it was Lord William Bentinck (1825-35), who had to dismiss from service two of his Residents on corruption charges, which caused a furor in the official British circle. The second important act of Cornwallis was to introduce Permanent Settlement in 1793 in the province of Bengal. Under this arrangement zamindars (landlords) were given permanent and hereditary rights on government lands for collection of revenues on behalf of the Government. This arrangement changed fundamentally the nature of power and seriously affected Hindu-Muslim relations in the province. Under the settlement, the British acquired the right to seize a zamindar's land and auction it for non-payment of dues. Subsequently, in the years of draught and flood when zamindars were unable to pay the revenue to the British, their deeds were auctioned and taken over by Hindu money-lenders and bankers of Calcutta, who emerged as the new generation of absentee landlords. Many of the old Mughal aristocrats were thus displaced.

It goes to the credit of Bentinck that, for the purpose of reforms and removing inhuman practices from the society, he dared even touch the Hindu faith. Bentinck placed a ban on *sati* in 1829 for 'the good of mankind'. Earlier, even Lord Wellesley's concern about this practice was disregarded and a decision repeatedly postponed. Despite the extremely inhuman and cruel nature of this practice even the Muslim emperors had not interfered with the faith of their subjects, but the British Governor General cared less for the ire of the orthodox Hindus, if it led ultimately to humane results. Bentinck also abolished *thugee,* a cult of highroad violence. Its votaries had held the belief that the robbing and strangling of unsuspecting travellers had the sanction of goddess Kali. Thus the era of government intervention into the area of holy rituals was initiated, and the British Raj no longer remained merely a group of plundering merchants. Another important step of far-reaching effects taken by Bentinck in 1835 was to replace Persian with English as the official language. English was also to be used in the higher law-courts, while regional languages were to be used in the lower courts. With the down-gradation of Persian language, the Muslims shunned English language, but the Hindus, in general, did not show any aversion to this change. As they had earlier learned Persian, which was a foreign language, so they easily switched over to learning another. The knowledge of English had become necessary for all who had to establish relations with the government. With the reluctance to learn the new language, Muslims were left far behind in the services of the State, and were alienated in the emerging society with a westernized culture. The collapse of the Muslim power, which had begun in the eighteenth century had now turned into a steep decline. The Muslims as a class had lost both office and wealth.

The Evangelists and Radicals both were horrified at the state of idolatry in India and believed in their duty to preach the gospel 'whose light would dissolve the mists of superstition and cruelty enshrouding the Indian people'. Here were the millions who were so far denied the chance of Christian salvation. It was due to the tough stand taken by the Conservatives that had held up missionary activity in the Company's territories. When the renewal of the Company's charter was being discussed in 1793 influential persons like Wilberforce had tried hard to obtain permission for missionary activity in India, but such a move was promptly defeated in the House of Commons. By 1813 things had changed and both the Company's monopoly on trade and ban on missionary activity were abolished. The Charter Act of 1813 forced the Company to permit Christian missionaries to come to India under license. But the Act provided at the same time that the missionary activity was to be carried out without government support. The campaign against idolatry resulted in the withdrawal of governmental patronage of certain Hindu temples and festivals. By the middle of the century there was, in addition to the British, a flood of American and other European missionaries. Apart from evangelical and pastoral work, they opened a net-work of colleges and hospitals and carried out other philanthropic work on the strength of the newly acquired wealth from the Industrial Revolution. The British Prime Minister Palmerston himself said that he 'firmly believed' that 'God meant England to (Christianize) India...Till India is leavened with Christianity she will be unfit for freedom." In 1855, on the occasion of a dinner party given in honour of Lord Canning, the newly appointed Governor General, Palmerston further said: "Perhaps it might be our lot to confer on the countless millions of India a higher and holier gift than any mere human knowledge."[3]

English education was considered for long as an important tool of imparting knowledge on Christian religion. As far back as 1792 Sir Charles Grant had maintained that in this way the Indians would be 'instructed in the nature and perfection of the one true God'. By the

Charter Act, Pound 10,000 was set aside annually for 'imparting to the Native population knowledge of English literature and science through the medium of English language'. The Bible was introduced not only in missionary institutions but also in Government schools and colleges, which imparted both Christian ethics and western ideas. Their teachings were often insensitive and offensive. R. C. Majumdar writes in the History and Culture of the Indian people:

"All the evils and abuses of Hinduism, real and fancied, were painted in the most lurid colour, while the blessings of Christianity were described in glowing phrases, and the salvation offered by it was held out in the most attractive form before the youthful pupils in their most impressionable age. No wonder that the Deputy Inspectors of schools were popularly known as native clergymen. Not only educational institutions, but even public prison houses were used as instruments for conversions to Christianity. Gopi Nath Nandi, a Bengali convert and clergyman, has thus recorded his experience: 'The prisoners in the jail were also daily instructed in Christianity and general knowledge by a Christian teacher, and every Sabbath morning the Gospel was preached by me. This privilege was granted by our pious magistrate.... The judge and the magistrate, as well as other gentlemen, took a deep interest in the mission, and helped us with their prayers, good advice, and pecuniary aid. When the number of native converts began to increase, six of them, at the suggestion of the late Honourable Mr. Colvin, became small farmers' ... Filthy abuses of Hindu gods and goddesses formed the main plank of the public preaching and propaganda of the Christian missionaries. The missionary preaching was rendered more odious to the people by the official assistance rendered to them. Sir Syed says that the civil and military officers helped the missionaries. The latter openly preached in mosques and abused other religions, and because a chaprasi or policeman accompanied them, no one dared object for fear of authorities."[4]

These measures created discontent and a dread in the minds of all classes of people, Hindus and Muslims alike, that the British Government was determined to convert the Indians to Christianity. The result of missionary activity was the gradual formation of a large Christian community spread all over India. Drawn mainly from the lower castes this body was at first of little significance, but it grew steadily in weight as well as in numbers and is now recognized as one of the regular constituents of Indian society.

The story of proselytizing by colonial masters is not unique to India, although it has not been done in as coercive a way as in other colonies. A news item published in the newspaper, Toronto Star of Canada dateline Canberra, August 27, 1999, describes how children of the Aboriginals and Natives were snatched away in Australia and Canada from their parents for this purpose.

Australia 'regrets' treatment of Aboriginals

CANBERRA, Australia (AP)—The Australian Parliament recognized 200 years of injustice to the country's indigenous people yesterday and expressed regret for "the blemished chapter" in the nation's history.

The historic moment came the same day as an Aboriginal women taken from her mother at birth lost a legal battle considered crucial for Australia's so-called "stolen generation."

From 1910 until the 1970s, 100,000 Aboriginal children were taken from their parents under the belief that Aborigines were doomed and saving the children was the only humane alternative.

Light-skinned Aboriginal children were seized and handed out to white families for adoption. Dark-skinned children were shuffled off to orphanages.

Two years after Australia's Prime Minister John Howard refused to apologize to Aborigines taken from their families, he presented a motion in parliament that he called an attempt to reconcile black and white Australians.

"The mistreatment of many indigenous Australians over a significant period represents the most blemished chapter in our national history," Howard said yesterday, reading the motion to parliament.

Parliament expressed "its deep and sincere regret that indigenous Australians suffered injustices under the practice of past generations, and for the hurt and trauma that many indigenous people continue to feel."

The opposition Labour party failed to strengthen the motion to include the word "sorry."

The vote culminates a long and often bitter campaign to gain government recognition of the Australia's indigenous people........

Aboriginal reaction was mixed: some leaders said nothing short of the word "sorry" and compensation to those in the stolen generation was acceptable.

"The apology has to be one that is unreserved and that has a commitment to restitution for hurt and trauma that was caused to, and continues to be suffered by, the stolen generations," a coalition of Aboriginal rights group said........

In Canada, federal officials have estimated that from the 1920s to the mid-1980s, some 125,000 native students were taken from their families and sent to residential schools. There they were denied access to their language and culture and many endured physical and sexual abuse.

The federal government has apologized and set up a $350 million "healing fund" for counselling.[5]

1. J.C. Locke, *The First Englishmen in India: Letters and Narratives of Sundry Elizabethans*, London: G. Routledge and sons 1930, quoted in *A New History of India* (Fifth Edition), Ch. Ten, Stanley Wolpert
2. *Great Britain: Foreign Policy and the Span of Empire*, Vol. 3, Ed. Joel H. Wiener
3. Reginald Reynolds, *The White Sahibs* & Penderel Moon, *The British Conquest, See The Making of India: A Historical Survey*, Ch. 3 Ranbir Vohra
4. R. C. Majumdar, *History and Culture of the Indian People,* Vol. IX, Ch. XIII
5. *Toronto Star,* dated August 27, 1999

35

SECOND WAR OF INDEPENDENCE

By the early nineteenth century the weakened country had accepted the foreign regime as its fate on the condition that the socio-religious fabric of society, both Hindu and Muslim, was left untouched. Reaching the middle of the nineteenth century, however, the Indian society came deep in the throes of political, social and religious tension and stress. The reasons were many but the most severe and immediate irritant was the Doctrine of Lapse introduced by the Governor General, the Marquess of Dalhousie (1848-56). He considered native rule as another name for misgovernment. Direct British rule, in his opinion, was much superior and better for the governed in India. His Doctrine would thus bring those princely states under the British governance whose rulers would die without leaving direct heirs. The custom of adoption so far practiced would be disregarded. In the course of eight years Dalhousie annexed eight states including two Maratha states and one Muslim state of Oudh on this pretext. To crown it all, he gave notice to the Mughal emperor at Delhi that his title as the sovereign of India would lapse at his death

Then another provocation, though small but of serious nature because of religious sensitivities, put fuel on the smoldering restlessness of both Hindus and Muslims. The flame was up in the sky, and a war of independence against the British started. The incident which flared it up related to the local soldiery under British employ. They had to bite off the end of a cartridge, greased with animal fat, for loading the Enfield rifle. It was rumored that it was filled with fat of cows, which was taboo for Hindus, and with that of pigs, taboo for Muslims. Both were now convinced that a calculated and concerted assault was being made on their religions. It was an impiety that no sepoy was prepared to commit. When some of them refused to load new rifles, three regiments were summarily disbanded during the early months of 1857. On 9th May, at the height of his haughtiness a Colonel at Meerut Cantonment decided to test the courage of his native subordinates and to make an example of them if they dared challenge and disobey his orders. To his satisfaction or otherwise he found such disobedient men too under his command. He lined up the first eighty-five, and following British practice, asked their peers to pass judgement upon them. As a result, they were manacled and sentenced to ten-years behind bars. Resenting the punishment meted out to them, all the three regiments based at Meerut rose up in revolt the next day, killed their British officers, released the prisoners, and headed for Delhi. They seized Delhi, which at that time was denuded of British officers, on 11th May with the help of the local garrison, and proclaimed the eighty-two year old Bahadur Shah as the real Emperor of India. At that time the king was a prisoner of the British. On August 27, the Emperor issued a Proclamation recognizing the joint struggle of Hindus and Muslims to get rid the country of the British rule: *It is well known to all, that in this age the people of Hindoostan, both Hindus and Mohammedans, are being ruined under the tyranny and oppression of the infidel and treacherous English. It is therefore the bounden duty of all the wealthy people of India...to stake their lives and property for the well being of the public. With the view of effecting this general good, several princes belonging to the royal family of Delhi, have dispersed themselves in the different parts of India.*[1] The Bengal Army of 128,000 sepoys had risen in revolt and had acquired control of most of the cantonments from Patna to Jhansi and Ajmer. Soon the revolt of the sepoys turned into 'a full-scale Anglo-Indian war'. It flared up throughout northern India and the command was taken over by civilian leaders. Princes, zamindars and other power-holders took up the command in their respective areas. They were generally deprived of their power and position by the British. Most notable among them were the deposed Rani of Jhansi; dispossessed Begum of Oudh; Nana Saheb, the adopted son of the ex-Peshwa and aspirant to the Peshwa's *gaddi*; Tantia Topi of Gwalior; ex-zamindar Kunwar Singh of Bihar; and Khan Bahadur of Rohilkhand, another dispossessed scion. The British administration could not hold grounds and became virtually non-existent in north and central India. The British had to rely on their military reserves in India and, in the meanwhile, sent for re-enforcement from Britain. In September they recovered Delhi with the help of a Sikh force, which marked the beginning of the end of the War. Kanpur was soon recovered by the British, but a day too late when captive British women and children were slaughtered. Towards the end of September, Luckhnow was retaken, which marked the end of revolt in four months before the sea-borne enforcement from Britain could arrive. Extreme savagery from both sides during the revolt and vendetta after the victory were amply demonstrated. Rani of Jhansi was killed in the battle. Tantia Topi was captured and hanged. Nana Saheb escaped.

Undoubtedly it was a national revolt, but the British too had their own local support on the Indian soil. Despite the fact that the natives had the fighting spirit they had no unified war leadership except that of a symbolic figurehead of the Mughal emperor. They had no concerted fighting strategy or plan, and also no vision of the future: what was to happen if they succeeded in overthrowing the foreign rule. The uncertainty was their nemesis. On the other side were zamindars and talukdars, who were fashioned into bulwarks of the Empire. They had been pampered, and were beneficiary of the new arrangements, specially of the Permanent Settlement in Bengal. In a feudal system, the cultivators would only obey what the landlords would tell them to do; so the zamindars asked them not to lend support to the rebels. This is why the new Bengali zamindars remained aloof in this revolt, while the dispossessed talukdars of Oudh were in the forefront of the rebellion.

As a result of the victory of the British, the Mughal monarchy was abolished and the aged emperor was exiled to Rangoon. It was 'the total extinction of a dynasty, the most magnificent that the world had ever seen.' Administration of India was brought directly under British Government, and Queen Victoria became the Empress of India. Viceroy, not a Governor General, would thus be heading the Government in India. Henceforward, the first and foremost task for the British was to safeguard against any future large-scale uprising. This could be achieved primarily in two ways: control the Indians by pleasing them as far as possible and keep them divided so that they could not be able to unite against the British government again. On 1st November, 1858, Queen Victoria issued a Proclamation, which declared "it to be our royal will and pleasure that none be in anywise fovoured, none molested or disquieted, by reason of their religious faith or observances, but that all shall alike enjoy the equal and impartial protection of the law; and we do strictly charge and enjoin all those who may be in authority under us that they abstain from all interference with the religious belief or worship of any of our subjects on pain of our highest displeasure."[2] Missionaries were instructed to cut back their attempts at conversion. Rejecting Dalhousie's Doctrine of Lapse and wooing the princes of India, it further said that "all treaties and engagements made with them" would be "scrupulously maintained". Indians would be given opportunities to serve the Indian

Government at levels appropriate to their "education, ability and integrity". Special measures would be taken to "stimulate the peaceful industry of India."

1. The Azamgarh Proclamation, reprinted in 1857 in India, ed. Ainslie T. Embree, (Boston: D. C. Heath and Company, 1963, pp. 1-3, See Stanley Wolpert Wolpert, *A New History of India*, Ch. Fifteen

2. Quoted in Stanley Wolpert, *A new History of India* Ch Sixteen, (Fifth Edition)

36
DIVIDE ET IMPERA

If the British had to govern such a large country as India, as also other colonies around the world, the population of the British Isles could not be able to provide the necessary manpower. At that time there were only 40,000 Englishmen amidst a native population of close to three hundred millions, yielding a ratio of 1 to 7,500.[1] Administration could only be run through the support of the local population. So a loyal corps of civil servants was a necessity. Another task was to restrain the local population from uniting against the British. The first step to 'divide and rule' was provided by separating the 562 "princely states", the first loyal segment, from the rest of India. They were specially mentioned as a favored class in the Queen's Proclamation, by allowing them to enter into direct treaty relationship with the Crown and dignifying them with such pompous titles as *Daulat-i-Inglishia* (Treasure of the British Empire) and *Indar Mohindar* (Lord of Lords). A British Resident was, however, posted in each princely state as a guardian of the Imperial interest.

Since the Indian empire had been snatched away from the Muslims, they were naturally bitter. They were considered by the new rulers as enemy of the first rank. Regarded as the mainspring of rebellion by the British, therefore, the Muslims had to be punished. For generations they had been soldiers and administrators, but with the onset of British supremacy their numbers had dwindled. In English education, they were already lagging behind. They were thus further neglected, and the result was that among the Indians, who were to play an increasing part in the public life of the country in association with the British, Muslims were less in proportion to their population particularly in important fields like education, commerce, and local bodies. A civil servant, W. W. Hunter, wrote in 1868: "After the Mutiny, the British turned upon the Mussalmans as their real enemies so that failure of the revolt was much more disastrous to them than the Hindus...In every district the descendant of some line of Muslim prince is sullenly eating his heart out in a roofless palace and weed-choked tanks. The Mussalmans are excluded from the army and the law. The judiciary was either Anglicized or Hinduized; while Permanent Settlement led to wholesale eviction of Muslim landlords."[2] Till 1851 there were more Muslim lawyers on the rolls of the Calcutta court than Hindus and Christian combined, but between 1852 and 1868 only one Muslim lawyer entered the rolls. Their share of government jobs sank to as low as 11.7 per cent in 1867 and less than 7 per cent by 1887. After winning the War of 1857 the British allowed the Hindus to re-enter the deserted city of Delhi in October 1857, but allowed the Muslims only in August 1859, by which time the best properties had been settled.[3]

Immediately after the war was over, the Company appointed a commission of enquiry on the uprising: why this happened and what was to be done to preserve the British power in future? Lord Elphinstone, a very experienced civil servant of the Company and the then governor of Bombay, sent a note to the commission: '*Divide et impera* was the old Roman motto, and it should be ours. I might perhaps hesitate to express my conviction so decidedly if I were not able to show that my views upon this subject are entirely in accordance with those of the Duke of Wellington.'[4] The Secretary of State, Sir Charles Wood, in a letter of March 3, 1862 to Viceroy Lord Elgin, instructed:: 'We have maintained our power by playing off one part against the other, and we must continue to do so..... Do what you can, therefore, to prevent all having a common feeling.' And, again on 10 May, Wood wrote: 'We cannot afford in India to neglect any means of strengthening our position. Depend upon it, the natural antagonism of races is no inconsiderable element of our strength. If all India was to unite against us, how long could we maintain ourselves?'[5]

Combined with official or unofficial oratories, the administrative policies and actions were so maneuvered that subsequently the Indian nation really felt divided, not in two but in many. Several British writers on India, some occupying high government positions, perpetuated a repertoire of such images, construing Islam as an emblem of repellent otherness, 'the faith of a body of savage marauders and conquerors, who swept over the land...in a series of cruel raids, bringing rapine and destruction in their train.'[6] For instance, the Governor of Bengal put forward his views that the...*ethnic pageant which passes across one's vision as one travels over India is made up of many tableaux. There is one such tableau which at once arrests attention because of the many points of contrast which it provides with the rest of the procession...It is a tableau in which we see represented a religion, a civilization and culture, and an outlook differing profoundly in all material respects from those of Hinduism.*[7] European intellectuals romanticized the 'golden age of Hinduism'. Organizations like Theosophical Society, which was founded by Madam Blavatsky and Colonel Olcott in 1875 in New York and was influenced by Hinduism and Tantric Brahmanism, encouraged Hindu revivalism. Its headquarters was transferred in 1882 to Adyyar near Madras, and for a brief period Blavatsky moved to India. Hindu revivalist movement like Arya Samaj was in close touch with the Society. Even the native writers and reformers, many of whom grudgingly came to terms with the Muslim presence, accepted the knowledge about the Muslims and Muslim rulers from medieval chroniclers, selectively translated by British historians. The existence of Islam in India was termed as a break in the continuity of Vedic religion and culture. Many of the various strands of Hinduism which had sprung up at that time focused on reconstructing a national tradition so as to achieve a solidarity based on a glorious past. And the national tradition envisaged was a Hindu tradition, in which Muslims had no place.[8]

1. *A Panormic History of the Indian People*, Ch. Twelve, D.B.Vohra
2. W.W. Hunter, quoted in *Nehru, The Making of India*, M. J. Akbar, Ch. 4
3. *Nehru, The Making of India*, M. J. Akbar, Ch. 4
4. *Nehru, The Making of India*, M. J. Akbar, Ch 4
5. *Nehru, The Making of India*, M. J. Akbar, Ch. 4
6. W. Crooke, *The North-Western Provinces of India: Their History, Ethnology, and Administration*, pp. 258-9, See *Legacy of A Divided Nation*, Mushirul Hasan
7. *India:A Bird's Eye-view*, p.214, Ronaldshay, See *Legacy of A Divided Nation*, Mushirul Hasan.
8. *A History of India*, Hermann Kulke Rothermund . & Dietmar

37
MOVEMENTS: GOOD, BAD AND UGLY

Western ideas and ways of life spread through English education and administrative measures created a ferment in the minds of the Indians. They were neither in a mood to reject them because they appeared liberal and enlightened, nor they were ready to embrace those novel and foreign concepts of life, although they had accepted the foreign rule as a normal historical process. This state of agitation caused the mushrooming of movements both against the foreigners and their ideas, and in favour of transforming the traditional Indian society into a new mould by borrowing good points generously from them. Another poignant aspect of these movements, however, was to alienate the two major segments of the Indian society, Hindus and Muslims, from each other. Albiruni had observed in the eleventh century that the Hindus always thought '*that there was no country but theirs, no nation like theirs, no king like theirs, no religion like theirs, no science like theirs*.' So the presence of those who were non-Hindus always created impurity. Though Muslims had been socially Indianized, the existence of Islam as an unabsorbed religion on the Indian soil was an easy target for creating irritation. Therefore, at this point of time, when Muslims were no more in power, the environment was most appropriate to arouse the dormant sentiment of otherness through religious and nationalist movements.

The first of the Indian religious movements was that of Raja Ram Mohan Roy (1772-1833), son of a zamindar of Bengal. He had great interest in religions, and in order to understand their teachings in their source-language he mastered Sanskrit, Arabic, Persian, Latin, Greek, and Hebrew. He joined the Company's service and rose to the highest rank open to an Indian. He realized that there were better norms in the western culture which might be of value in reforming his own society. He was ready to welcome external influences in Hinduism if they were not contrary to the spirit of reason. He devoted his life to socio-religious reform and to mitigate racial differences. He launched a movement by the name of Brahmo-Samaj (Divine Society) in 1828 in Calcutta, which aimed at focusing the best elements of Hinduism, Christianity and Islam for theistic and ethical reforms. He recognized Christ and Muhammad as great religious teachers, but this idea did not find favour with majority of the Hindus.[1] The primary aim of the movement was to reform Hinduism and to rid it of idol worship, caste, and discrimination against women. Roy attacked the idolatrous practices of the Hindus, which according to him contradicted the monotheism of the Vedanta. He considered that all social institutions and customs should be judged on the touchstone of reason as expressed in the Upanishads, and which should be the basis of Hindu religion. The movement converted many young Hindus to serve as beacons of change. He travelled to Britain where he pleaded for abolition of sati against a petition by some brahmans not to interfere with the faith. It was due to his unflinching support that Lord Bentinck was able to achieve the objective of abolition of sati. In his aspiration to modernize India he fully shared Bentinck's belief in the English language as 'the key to all improvements'. He founded a number of schools and native newspapers. His efforts and support helped in developing an Indo-British dialogue for the sake of enlightenment. He earned the title of the 'Father of Modern India' by his countrymen. Ram Mohan Roy achieved the honour of being the ambassador of Mughal Emperor at the court of St. James at London, where he died in 1833.

In 1875, Swami Dayanand Saraswati (1824-83), a Sanskrit scholar and a Hindu ascetic from Gujrat, launched the Arya Samaj (Society of the Aryans) in Bombay. It was a drastically reformed version of Hinduism designed to hold its own against any challenge from the West, but mainly as the standard bearer of Hindu communalism. It found inspiration through the four Vedas and recognized them as the sole scriptural authority and depository of all knowledge. To impart congregational solidarity to Hindus he spoke of the necessity of a 'Vedic Church' on the pattern of Christianity. This movement opted for introducing a new element in its creed and that was of re-conversion to Hinduism of all who had given up their religion. It was called *shuddhi*, and which was to be implemented, if necessary, by force. Cow was also to be protected. In a letter of November 1875 to Madame Blavatsky, the founder of The Theosophical Society, Dayanand said: 'As night and day are opposed to each other, so are all religions opposed to one another'. He claimed that among the religions the only true and shining religion is Hinduism.[2] To advocate his thesis Dayanand also met Muslim leaders including Sir

Syed Ahmad Khan and insisted that all should accept the authority of the Vedas for a common cause, and any action to be taken on an all-India level must include the Hindu mould. Dayanand made intemperate references to Islam. He called the Qur'anic paradise "a grove of prostitutes." His celebrated text, Satyarth Prakash, was the basis of anti-Islamic polemics. His ideological successors like Pandit Lekh Ram, Swami Sharaddhanand and Lala Lajpat Rai, also subjected the Quran to severe criticism. It was as much a disrespect of the religion of the main contending community of India as also a ploy to lure back Muslim converts to Hinduism. Combing the past history of India, his movement tried to discover evidence of Muslim atrocities against the Hindus. Though this movement did not have any impact on the thinking of non-Hindus, it gave a new sense of Hindu identity and awakened the spirit of Hindu nationalism. This movement gained immense popularity and provided a stimulus to the development of nationalistic political activism specially in Punjab and western U.P. It played an important part in creating intolerance and spreading antagonism between Hindus and Muslims, Christians and even Sikhs, and became instrumental in generating physical and riotous clashes between Hindus and Muslims.

In 1876, Surendranath Banerjea (1848-1925), who had earlier been expelled from the ICS cadre on flimsy grounds, formed the Indian Association at Calcutta with the aim of uniting the races and ethnic groups of India on the basis of common political interest and aspirations. He laid special emphasis on promotion of friendly relations between Hindus and Muslims. To involve the grass roots in national movements it was thought essential that masses be educated to generate a strong body of public opinion. He suggested: 'We have a very useful institution among us, the Hindu Mela. Now why not make it an Indian Mela?' While founding his Association, Surendranath Banerjea declared "In the name...of a common country, let us all, Hindus, Muslims, Christians, Parsees, members of the great Indian Community, throw the pall of oblivion over the jealousies and dissensions of bygone times and, embracing one another in fraternal love and affection, live and work for the benefit of a beloved fatherland".[3]

One of the great spiritual leaders of Hinduism was Ramakrishna Paramahamsa (1834-1886). He passed many years in meditation and trance at the temple of Dakshineshwar in Bengal. His message was that the inherent truth in all religions is the supremacy of the same

God, who is one and many. According to him, God has a form and can be recognized by symbols, and that he may also be without form and conceived as a universal spirit. His vision and doctrine were given concrete shape by his favorite disciple, Swami Vivekananda (1863-1902), who shot into fame in 1893 with his soul-stirring address to the World Parliament of Religions in Chicago which presented Vedanta to the western world as a potential unifier of mankind. He told the Hindus of India that they were infused with the divine energy that sustained the cosmos. Thus it was their divine duty to strive fervently for the common good. He launched a social service organization, Ramakrishna Mission, named after his spiritual mentor. The movement restored the self-confidence of Hindus in their religion and culture, and quickened their sense of national pride and patriotism. Vivekananda combined Hindu ethical values in politics, which reinforced Hindu nationalism rather than Indian nationalism.

It was also a very difficult period for the Muslims of India. While they were facing the challenge of syncretism of Hinduism for long they began now facing the new assault of western rationalism. Their predicament was further aggravated by the loss of political power to the British. Two movements had thus been started, which in nature were quite different from each other. The first began at a very early stage of English domination, which arose more because of the helplessness felt by the Muslims on account of the decline of the Mughal imperial power. To strengthen itself, Indian Islam had to turn itself to religion for inner renewal. As in the time of Akbar and Jahangir, Sheikh Ahmad Sirhindi had stared a movement, during this period another theologian Shah Wli-ullah of Delhi (1703-62) maintained that the loss of political power could be adequately compensated by turning to the power of God. This movement later branched out in two directions. One became political, hence militant in outlook. In religion it turned out to be puritan and was called 'Wahabi' from the Arabian movement of the same name and nature. Its leader Syed Ahmad of Bareilly regarded India as a land of war because it was under infidel rule. He also directed his activities against the Sikhs who were the chief Muslim oppressors of the time. He laid his life in the battle with the Sikhs in 1831. His followers, based at Patna, gave the British government the hell of a time. They were virtually destroyed in the 1860s, when the Wahabi leaders were brought to trial at Ambala (1864-5) and Patna (1868-71). This episode gave the finishing touch to the Islamic resistance to the alien rule. The other branch was more concerned with reformation of Islam and was thus peaceful. It concentrated itself in purging the Islamic society of Hindu practices. The leaders of this movement were Sheikh Karamat Ali and Haji Shariat-ullah in eastern India.

The second movement was started at a later stage when the British had gained full control over India and the Mughal power was totally shattered. It stood more for renovation in Islamic society and acceptance of western rationalism in order to enable the Muslims to rejoin the current stream of Indian political and social life from which they had been alienated. This was started by Syed Ahmad Khan (1817-1898), which is described separately.

It was now the turn of the scholars and writers, who with their writings were generally fanning racial hatred. A number of them came forward with the dual focus on glorifying the past of Hinduism on the one hand and bringing out the picture of oppression of Hindus and degradation of Hindu society under Muslim rule on the other. According to them, the Muslims had been abductor and rapist of Hindu women, destroyer of temples and idols, and killer of sacred cows. Muslims imparted nothing good, materially or spiritually, to India, but only bonded it in slavery and degradation. Islam itself had no spiritual and ethical qualities, instead it was a sensual, immoral, irrational and bigoted religion, an antithesis of the ideal religion of Hinduism. They depicted the resistance and political struggles of the Hindu rajas as a fight between Hinduism and Islam. In this regard the writings of the following Marathi, Hindi, and Bengali writers are noteworthy: Gopal Ganesh Agarkar (1856-95), Hari Deshmukh (1823-92), Vishnushastri Chilunkar (1850-82), Bharatendu Harishchandra (1850-85), Partap Narain Misra (1856-94), Radha Charan Goswami (1859-1923), Kishorilal Goswami (1866-1932), Aravinda Ghose (1872-1950), Bal Gangadhar Tilak (1857-1920), and Bankim Chandra Chaterjee (1838-94). Specially, Bal Gangadhar Tilak, who was a fiery Hindu nationalist, 'blazed the trail for extremism'. In 1893 he started using the Ganesh festival to preach militant nationalism and later developed the Shivaji cult as a symbol of Hindu resistance to Muslim rule. Bankim Chandra Chaterjee, created a furor in the subsequent political struggle for freedom through the controversial song of Bande Mataram (Hail to the Mother) of his novel, *Ananda Math* (1882). It was a story full of hatred and invectives for the Muslims, a tale of the Hindu militants who defeated Muslim army to restore the Motherland to the Hindus. Another self-proclaimed liberal and a humanist, Nirad C. Chaudhuri, was 'repelled' by the thought of living in a province (Bengal) where Muslims would be a dominant social and cultural entity. When Italy attacked Tripoli in 1911 and when Turkey joined the German side in the First Word War, he was filled with ecstasy 'so that the Muslims would be taught a lesson'.[4] But there were also enlightened Hindu writers like Bhudev Mukhopadhyay (1827-94), who questioned such allegations and pointed them as inspired through the mischief of British historians. He emphasized on the common ties that bound Muslims with the rest of the population. In modern days, however, a scholar like R.C.Majumdar declares: "The basis of national unity in India is Hindu religion. Hindu nationality embraces all the Hindus of India irrespective of their locality or language. The Hindus are destined to be a religious nation.'[5]

1. Ranbir Vohra, *The Making of India: A Historical Survey*
2. *South Asia: A Short History*, Hugh Tinker
3. *The Making of India: A Historical Survey*, Ranbir Vohra
4. *Legacy Of A Divided Nation*, Mushirul Hasan
5. R. C. Majumdar, quoted in *Nehru: The Making of India*, Ch. 4, M. J. Akbar, and in *The Making of India: A Historical Survey*, Ranbir Vohra

38
SEEDING THE 'TWO-NATION'

Considering the strong possibility that one class or community might, by virtue of its superior numbers, wealth or education, come to dominate India's nascent democratic institutions, successive Viceroys changed the position of pushing up the Hindus in the social and political life of India, and began supporting a policy which was less anti-Muslim. Though in minority, the Muslims were in no way a lesser entity. They still wielded considerable power locally, hence they could not be alienated for long. It was, therefore, appropriate that they be enlisted 'as allies and auxiliaries.' To boost the morale of the Muslims, fortunately the person of Syed Ahmad Khan came in handy. He was born in the nobility of Delhi in 1817 and lived up to 1898 reviving the sagged spirit of the Muslims of India. In his zeal to work for the interest of the Muslims, he became unfortunately instrumental in weakening the spirit of Indian nationalism. In the aftermath of the great revolt of 1857 Muslims of India lay prostrate. Muslim nobility was now destitute. Sharing the common Muslim prejudice against the West, Syed Ahmad was averse to learning English. But family circumstances soon changed, as his brother, father and grand-father died in quick succession. To earn a livelihood, Syed Ahmad Khan joined the British judicial service in 1837 as a reader and rising in the service retired as a Sub-Judge in 1876. He was also knighted. In 1878 he joined the Viceroy's Legislative Council. He was regularly consulted by the British as he remained the unquestionable leader of Indian Muslims till his death. Along with Sir Syed, Muslim landlords and princes were viewed as blocs of potential support for the Crown Raj, and they were assiduously cultivated and regularly consulted by the British. The Muslim community might, after all, serve as an effective breakwater of tidal waves of national opposition and as 'the twin props of British rule'.[1]

In 1857 Syed Ahmad was posted in Bijnor, which was ceded to the British by the rulers of Oudh in 1801. During the uprising, Nawab Mahmud Khan seized control of Bijnor on May 20, 1857, and offered Syed Ahmad Khan a position in the new administration. He not only turned the offer down but also saved the lives of the likely-to-be massacred British community by his diplomacy and influence. He emphatically declared: 'By God, Nawab Sahib, I say that British sovereignty cannot be eliminated from India.'[2] It was the affirmation of his faith in the supremacy of the English. Deeply convinced of the resilience of British power, he firmly supported the British cause during the subsequent events. He became a devotee of the British. Syed Ahmad was tormented by the plight of the Muslims. The community had lost its pride and confidence after a century of stagnation, 'whose leaders had degenerated from emperors to caricatures'. He himself was an image of that downfall. Being extremely troubled about the future of the community, and eagre to pull them out of the political and social backwater, he found a solution. He came to the conclusion that as the British had shown the ability to destroy the Muslim power, in order to overcome this misfortune the Muslims had only to learn the ways of the British themselves. Indian Muslims must make terms with the west. Only that would help them in regaining much of the lost strength and providing them with the best survival techniques. What Ram Mohan Roy had done for Hindus, Sir Syed did for Muslims.

Considering education as the primary agent for the rehabilitation of Muslim position and fortune, he launched his movement from that point. But no progress could be made in that direction unless the British mistrust and prejudice against the Muslims, created during the War of Independence were blunted and eventually turned into a support. Therefore, he became 'India's first human bridge between Islamic tradition and Western thought'. Sir Syed proposed reforms in Indian Muslim thought designed to lure the community to come out of the old Perso-Arabic shell and enter into competition with other Indians for the privileges offered by the Anglo-Indian power. This led him to stress on the importance of studying western sciences. He emphasized on the commonality of Islamic and Christian ideas with their common Judaic heritage. In 1860, Syed Ahmad Khan issued his booklet, *The Loyal Mohammedans of India*. Through his publications, he stressed on the similarities between Christianity and Islam, and wrote: 'Without flattering the English, I can truly say that the natives of India, high and low, merchants and petty shopkeepers, educated and illiterate, when contrasted with the English in education, manners and uprightness, are as like them as a dirty animal is to an able and handsome man.'[3] He founded a Translation Society in 1864, which enabled Muslims to gain knowledge of Western works. In 1872, Sir Syed observed: 'It cannot be expected that Mohammedans who are made of much sterner material than the Hindus will adapt themselves so readily to this changing age. Let us have time, let us live, work and wait.' In the meanwhile, he pinned his hopes on the Pax Britannica to maintain a balance between the 'two races'[4]. His greatest achievement was the establishment in 1875 of the Mohammedan Anglo-Oriental College in Aligarh whose foundation stone was laid by the Viceroy himself. The Viceroy made a personal contribution of ten thousand rupees to the project. The focus of education in this college was to combine a British-type curriculum with a grounding in Islamic culture so as to "make the Mussalmans of India worthy and useful subjects of the British Crown". Later raised to the status of a University, this institution remained the premier educational centre of higher education for Muslims of India and a churning mill of Muslim leadership in pre-Independent India.

Sir Syed's efforts met with outstanding success. The concept of Muslim-British cooperation, which had looked odd a few years ago, turned into an idea of inter-dependence. For such a scheme to be operative in the context of India of that time it was only natural that his political and social philosophy should be conditioned by the religious divide. Though not anti-Hindu in his outlook and rather claimant of equality in treatment to both the communities, he was obsessed with the idea of improving the welfare of only the Muslims. He was simply indifferent to Hindu interests. As such he had, at times, to oppose a policy which would go in favour of Hindus. At one point Sir Syed even opposed the induction of Indians into the Civil Service because it would only bring 'Bengali babus' in the government. Up till now Sir Syed had considered Hindus and Muslims as "belonging to the same nation", but when in 1893 it came to giving some rights of franchise to the native people for electing representatives to local bodies he even showed an attitude which may be termed as undemocratic. Sir Syed expressed his fear that "the system of representation by election means the representation of the views and interests of the majority of the population.... [which] would totally override the interests of the smaller community."[5] His argument was that under universal franchise the Muslims would be outvoted. Since the Hindus outnumbered the Muslims by three to one, in any scheme of national voting the majority community will vote for the candidates of its own community, hence Muslim candidates will have less chances of being elected. 'It would be like a game of dice, in which one man had four dice and the other one.' According to him, a democratic regime meant majority rule, which would definitely be a Hindu rule. Therefore the British cannot be dispensed with immediately. In 1888, he founded the United Indian Patriotic Association with an appeal to both Hindus and Muslims to counteract the false impression in England that the whole Indian nation is at the back of the Indian National Congress. The Association aimed at preserving "peace in India and strengthen the British rule; and to remove those bad feelings from the hearts of the Indian people, which the supporters of the Congress are stirring up throughout the country and by which great dissatisfaction is being raised among the people against the British Government." As radical he was in matter of religion, so Sir Syed was a conservative in politics. For him, political rights 'were more important than religious traditions, and so long as the Muslims lived freely under British rule they would remain good subjects.' He never accepted the Congress as a truly national organization. He insisted that "India is inhabited by different nationalities", and termed the fight for freedom by the Indian National Congress in the capacity of a representative body of all Indians as an experiment which was "fraught with dangers and suffering for all the nationalities of India, especially for the Muslims." He argued that English-style representative institutions could not fit in the context of India, where elections would be contested not on a basis of personalities or parties but purely on community or 'communal' lines.

Writing in 1888 under the topic, the 'Present State of Indian Politics' in the newspaper Pioneer, he said: 'I have often said that India is like a bride whose two eyes are the Hindu and the Mohammedan. Her beauty consists in this - that the two eyes be of equal lustre'. So beautifully said, this statement was definitely a pointer towards the existence of two equal nations living in India. He further argued: 'Suppose that all the English...were to leave India...? Is it possible that under these circumstances two nations - the Mohammedans and the Hindus - could sit on the same throne and remain equal in power? Most certainly not. It is necessary that one of them should conquer the other and thrust it down....Probably they [the Muslims] would be by themselves enough to maintain their own position. But suppose they were not. Then our Muslim brothers, the Pathans, would come out as a swarm of locusts from their mountain villages and make rivers of blood to flow from their frontier on the north to the extreme end of Bengal'.[6] Sir Syed's thinking and arguments fully suited the British aims and policies that led directly to a community based politics, the demand for separate electorates and eventually to the creation of a separate country, Pakistan, in 1947. And in the political process of creating two nations, his Aligarh Muslim University acted as an 'intellectual cauldron'.

1. F. C. Robinson, *Consultation and Control: The United Provinces' Government and its Allies*, 1860-1906, Modern Asian Studies 5,4 (1971). See *A New History of India* (Fifth Edition), Stanley Wolpert
2. *Nehru, The Making of India*, M. J. Akbar, Ch 2
3. *Nehru, The Making of India*, M. J. Akbar, Ch 2
4. *South Asia: A Short History*, Hugh Tinker
5. Ranbir Vohra, *The Making Of India: A Historical Survey* Ch. 5, Quoted in Anil Seal, *The Emergence of Indian Nationalism*.
6. *South Asia: A Short History*, Hugh Tinker

39
BEGINNING OF THE POLITICAL VOICE

The British population of India had looked narrowly on the locals and treated them with contempt. For instance, they even challenged some liberal policies of the Government. By an Act of 1872, Indians in the British Judicial Service could not try cases involving Europeans, even for minor offences. In 1883, Law Member, Sir Courtney Ilbert, introduced a Bill on Criminal Jurisdiction to remove that racial restriction. The small community of the British immediately organized protests, and through newspapers attacked the Viceroy, Lord Ripon, who was fully in favour of the Bill. They declared boldly that "nigger natives" were not "the peers or equals" of Englishmen.[1] The Viceroy ultimately had to capitulate. A simmering tension was all pervasive, and a reaction from the natives seemed inevitable.

At that time a retired British civil servant, Allen Octavian. Hume (1829-1912), who had seen the excesses as a District Magistrate at Etawah during the 1857 uprising, was tormented by the prospects of another mayhem on national scale. He had special interest in the study of religion, was inclined towards theosophy, and thus had been in touch with local people, specially Hindu rishis and holy men. He was warned by them of a social disturbance of great magnitude. He started searching for a national forum through which "the picked men, the most highly educated of the nation" could "secure greater freedom...a more impartial administration (and) a larger share in the management." This could throw some cold water on the brewing unrest. He wrote to the graduates of Calcutta University that if only fifty men could be found 'with sufficient power of self-sacrifice, sufficient love for and pride in their country, sufficient genuine and unselfish heartfelt patriotism to take the initiative, a new India could be theirs'. In 1885, Hume established an organization, named Indian National Congress, with the support of Surendranath Banarjea. Hume remained General Secretary of the Congress from 1885 to 1906, as also its only full-time official. In the beginning, the aim of this organization was to give vent to the social and political feelings and aspirations of the people. Since this process was prone to create more frictions instead of removing them, emphasis was later laid on instilling a sense of unity and all-India patriotism in the people. While addressing the second session of the Congress in 1886, Dr Rajendarlal Mitter said: 'For long our fathers lived and we have lived as individuals only or as families, but henceforward I hope that we shall be living as a nation, united one and all to promote our welfare and the welfare of our mother-country.' But any political organization, association or movement, which was to be established in those days had first to affirm loyalty to the British Raj, lest its own existence was put into jeopardy. The President of that session, Dadabhai Naoroji, prompted the crowd to endorse the idea that Indian National Congress was to be another stone in the foundation of stability of the British government. Another leader, Pherozeshah Mehta, had already expressed this sentiment earlier in 1883 in connection with Ripon's Ilbert Bill: 'If I entertain one political conviction more strongly than any other, it is that this country in falling under British rule has fallen into the hands of a nation than which no other is better qualified to govern her wisely and well.'

Despite its projection as a national platform, the Congress had failed to attract Muslim community in substantial numbers. Sir Syed, as the acknowledged leader of Muslims, had advised them not to indulge in political movements which advocated a system of public representation based on majority votes. "The Muslims of the north had a long tradition of being the ruling race. They were not prepared to become the understrappers to the new Congress politicians. Sir Sayyid's active supporters were all Muslims of the traditional official class; they enjoyed the patronage of the Muslim aristocracy and the princes; but it was they who worked to create organisations. The farthest Sir Sayyid would go towards recognising the new situation of political organisation and agitation was to create a Mohammadan Educational Congress in December 1886 (the term 'Conference' was substituted for the suspect 'Congress' in 1890). In putting forward the Muslim point of view, Sir Sayyid was considerably influenced by British collaborators, specially Theodore Beck of the Aligarh College, and Colonel G.F.I. Graham, his biographer."[2]

At the 1906 session of the Congress Dadabhai Naoroji declared that swaraj or self rule was the goal of the Congress. But up to the first decade of the twentieth century, the Indian National Congress failed to make an impact and thus to be taken seriously by the British. The result was that the nationalist sentiment in the Congress began to turn anti-British. The extremists in the Congress lost faith in the British claim that they were guiding India toward self-government. Discarding the policy of collaboration they, therefore, took the path of confrontation. At the 1907 session, the Congress was divided between the moderates and extremists. Unfortunately at this moment the extremist leaders, led by Bal Gangadhar Tilak, thought it fit to exploit Hindu religious sentiments in order to make this organization more fiery. He looked nostalgically on Hindu's past glory and made Shivaji, struggling against the Mughals, as his ideal. Anti-Muslim sentiments had already been sufficiently aroused by the country-wide Hindu religious and revivalist movements. But this element could not achieve much success. Extremist leaders were expelled from the Congress. But the fact that the composition of its leadership remained overwhelmingly Hindu painted the Congress as a Hindu communal party, even though many Congress leaders were genuinely committed to secularism. Pure secularism was beyond the mettle of Congress leaders. In a society, which was held together by the bonds of caste and tradition of religious ghettos, no social reform could be introduced and no political unity forged without consideration to religion. It was not easy for them to detach their dharmikta (religiosity) from politics. Sometime later even the politician of the stature of Mohandas Karamchand Gandhi succumbed to this charm. Congress leaders therefore failed to create a true national solidarity. This was an opportune moment for the British to weaken the Congress and to undermine its claim to represent the "Indian nation". The British now started patronizing, beside the Muslims, also Sikhs and Schedule Castes, who saw it fit to take advantage of their patronage by working outside Congress. The British were now rightly pointing towards the Congress that it was not a representative national body but a communal one, having no moral justification for presenting the case on behalf of all Indians.

In the early twentieth century, the moderates had taken control of the Congress. It remained non-communal with its declared objective to achieve responsible self-government for India. Though its membership comprised both moderates and extremists like Gopal Krishna Gokahle, Surendranath Banerjea and Bal Gangadhar Tilak, yet the composition of its leadership continued to remain predominantly Hindu. The dread of a majority rule did not go away from the minds of the Muslims and an alarm sounded in their ears every time such a demand was made.

1. *A New History of India* (Fifth Edition), Ch. Seventeen, Stanley Wolpert
2. Hugh Tinker, *South Asia: A Short History*

40
BIRTH OF COMMUNALISM

Despite the fact that there was a spate of religious and nationalist movements, in the late nineteenth century the political spirit was still moderate, liberal and non-racial. In 1899, Lord George Nathaniel Curzon, a young man dedicated to the cause of the British Empire, was appointed Viceroy of India. He had been Under-Secretary of State for India in 1891-2 and Under-Secretary for Foreign Affairs from 1895 to 1898. He claimed to have India's interest at his heart. At that time the Congress was the only political body of some stature. Both the British government and the new Viceroy considered the Congress so potentially dangerous that it might one day mobilize the whole nation against the Raj. He was determined to uphold "the unchallenged supremacy of the paramount power" of the Crown. Curzon did not hide his dislike towards the Congress. He stated that 'one of my great ambitions while in India is to assist [the Congress] to a peaceful demise.'[1]

At that time the Bengal Presidency covered 190,000 square miles. It also included the whole of Bihar and Orissa and contained more than a quarter of the total population of the country. Curzon thought that if the British could not control the most powerful province of Bengal, which was their real power base, they would be weakened everywhere in India. If Bengal had the ability to challenge the Raj, better break it up. And the pretext was there. The province was too large to administer efficiently, so it should be broken up on the lines of the avowed policy of the *Raj*: 'divide and rule'. The partition of Bengal should be effected in such a way as to divide the people too. So it had to be done on communal lines: Hindus to be in majority in the western half and Muslims in majority in the east. As a result, the new Muslims province would 'invest the Mahomedans in Eastern Bengal with unity which they have not enjoyed since the days of the old Musalman viceroys and kings", as Curzon himself admitted.[2] On 3 December 1903, the formal scheme of partition, called the Risley Paper (after Sir Herbert Risley, Home Secretary, Government of India) was published. It is true that complaints about the unwieldy administration of Bengal had been voiced earlier also, and a proposal of division too was made, but it was not given serious considerations. Ultimately, the province was divided into East and West Bengal in 1905. A new province of East Bengal with thirty-one million people was created with Dhaka as its capital. Assam was merged with this new province. In the West Bengal of forty-seven millions Bengalis became a minority amongst Biharis and Oriyas. If Bengal was at all to be divided the best course would have been to separate Bihar and Orissa from it, which were linguistically different from Bengal. This step was, in fact, taken in 1919. But Curzon's consideration was beyond purely administrative; his hidden agenda was to weaken the nationalist movement in India and to drive a wedge between the two major communities. Curzon's unambiguous explanation sent to the Secretary of State for India, John Brodrick, in London on February 21, 1905, was: Calcutta is the centre from which the Congress part is manipulated throughout the whole of Bengal, and indeed the whole of India. Its best wirepullers and its most frothy orators all reside here. The perfection of their machinery and the tyranny which it enables them to exercise are truly remarkable....They dominate public opinion in Calcutta; they affect the High Court; they frighten the local Government of India. The whole of their activity is directed to creating an agency so powerful that they may one day be able to force a weak government to give them what they desire'.[3]

There was an uproar and widespread agitation. The Hindu intelligentsia and political class of Bengal as well as the whole countryside, including the Moslem Chronicle, were deeply stirred. It put the Indian National Congress in the forefront of opposition. They saw in this scheme a bid to undermine their cultural, economic and political cohesion and to raise the Muslims of East Bengal as a counterpoise. They decided to organize a resistance movement based on the concept of swadeshi (self-reliance and self-sufficiency). It gave birth to terrorism as well as to communalism. The terrorists were now imbued with a religious duty, i.e., liberation of the motherland. For this purpose they considered assassination as a sacred offering to goddess Kali. The British, on the other hand, were not slow to crush anti-partition demonstrations with ruthlessness. Up till then Hindus and Muslims had their religious and social differences, but by and large they had managed to coexist with little violence. From 1906 onwards, communalism spread over the entire subcontinent. Both communities increasingly came to be identified with their religions, and ethno-nationalism became a unique feature of Indian political and social life. The Congress itself was split between the hawks and doves at its Surat meeting in 1907. The division of Bengal caused communal rioting between Hindus and Muslims in India. It started in Bengal in 1906-1907 during an attack by Muslims on pro-swadeshi Hindus.[4] Then there were incidences of bomb attacks by natives. On April 10, 1908, the first bomb to take British lives was thrown by young Khadiram Bose apparently on the District Magistrates of Muzaffarpur, Douglas Kingford, who was notorious throughout Bengal for the pleasure he took in sentencing political offenders to flogging. In this incident two English ladies died instead, because their closed carriage resembled that of the magistrate. The British did not lag behind in this combat. One young English corporal in a fit of excitement shot the first native he met. Viscount Morley, the liberal Secretary of State, inquired of Minto, "What happened to the corporal?...Was he put on his trail? Was he hanged?...If we are not strong enough to prevent murder, then our pharisaic glorification of the stern justice of the British Raj is windy nonsense."[5] Other incidents of attack took place on the magistrate of Nasik, the Governor of Bengal and the Viceroy himself. An aide of the Secretary of State was assassinated. Hindu Mahasabha soon adopted a programme of *Shuddhi* for conversion to Hinduism of persons belonging to foreign religions and re-conversion of those who had adopted foreign religions. Curzon, who left India in 1905, was convinced that he would get away with his scheme. He was convinced that the Bengalis 'howl until a thing is settled and then they accept it'. But the howling this time would force no less a person than the King-Emperor himself to announce at a Darbar held in Delhi in 1911 that the partition of Bengal would be annuled. Viceroy Lord Hardinge carried it out the same year, and admitted at the same time that: 'the political power of the Bengali has not been broken'.

1. Curzon Papers in India Office Library. See *The Making of India: A Historical Survey*, Ranbir Vohra
2. *Nehru: The Making Of India*, M. J. Akbar, Ch 8
3. Curzon to Brodrick, February 21, 1905, Curzon Papers in India Office Library. Quoted in *Nehru: The Making of India*, M. J. Akbar, Ch 8
4. *South Asia: A Short History*, Hugh Tinker
5. Stanley Walport, *Morley and India*, 1906-1910 (Berkley and Los Angeles: University of California Press, 1967), p. 120, See *A History of India*, Ch. 19, Stanley Wolpert

41
COMMAND PERFORMANCE

In the India Council Act of 1892, the germ of an elective principle had already been placed. Muslim leaders had generally kept aloof from the Congress. Lord Minto's appointment as the Viceroy in 1905 became the occasion to encourage the Muslims to form their own political party from whose platform they could express their apprehension of the British style election. Any Government to be formed or any sort of representation in Viceroy's Council based on territorial election would, it was felt, give the Muslims a representation weaker than their relative numbers and the importance they wielded. One, Khwaja Yusuf Shah of Amritsar wired Nawab Mehdi Ali Khan (Mohsin-ul-Mulk), Secretary of Aligarh College, to wake up from his political "sleep" and organize a Muslim deputation to Simla.[1] In August 1906, he wrote to W. A. J. Archbold, the Principal of the Mahomedan Anglo-Oriental College, who was a friend of Minto's private secretary, J. Dunlop Smith: 'Although there is little reason to believe that any Mohammedans, except the young educated ones, will join that body [the Congress] there is still a general complaint that we [Aligarh people] take no part in politics and do not safeguard the political rights of Mohammedans.' He further proposed that a memorial be submitted to the Viceroy 'to draw the attention of Government to a consideration of the rights of Mohammedans.'[2] On 9 August 1906 Archbold wrote to Dunlop Smith at Simla: 'If the Muhammadans were informed (privately) that a deputation would be received and a statement made, what would happen would be that representatives of Muhammadans from various parts of India would come to Simla and present a carefully drawn petition.'. Dunlop Smith wrote, not to Archbold, but directly to Mohsinul Mulk (Nawab Mehdi Ali,1837-1907) on September 13, that 'His Excellency will have much pleasure in receiving the Deputation'.[3]

It was then decided by important Muslim leaders to send a special mission to Viceroy, Lord Minto to present a petition on behalf of India's Muslims. The text of the address was prepared by Nawab

Mohsinul Mulk, S. H. Bilgrami and W. A. J. Archbold. Sir Sultan Muhammad Shah Aga Khan, GCIE, the would-be leader of the delegation, confirmed in a note to Smith: 'I have also asked him (Mohsinul Mulk) not to move in any matter before first finding out (from J. Dunlop Smith) if the step to be taken has the full approval of the government privately.'[4] By 18th September the text of the petition was finalized and presented to Lord Minto at the Viceregal Lodge in Simla on 1 October by a deputation comprising the following thirty-five self-appointed representatives of 62 million Muslims consisting of nobles, jagirdars, talukdars, lawyers, zamindars and merchants: The Aga Khan, Prince Bakhtiar Shah of Mysore; Malik Omar Hyat Khan of Tiwana; Khan Bahadur Mian Mohomed Shah Din of Lahore; Maulvi Sharfuddin of Patna, Khan Bahadur Syed Nawab Ali Chowdhry of Mymensingh; Nawab Bahadur Syed Amir Husain Khan of Calcutta; Naseer Husain Khan Khyyal of Calcutta; Khan Bahadur Mirza Shujaat Ali Beg; Syed Ali Imam and Nawab Sarfraz Husain Khan of Patna; Khan Bahadur Ahmad Mohiuddin Khan of Carnatic family of Madras; Maulvi Rafiuddin Ahmad and Ebrahimbhoy Adamji Peerbhoy of Bombay; Abdur Rahim of Calcutta; Syed Allahdad Shah of Sind; Maulana H. M. Malak of Nagpur; Khalifa Syed Muhammad Hussain and Col. Abdul Majid Khan, both members of Patiala government; Khwaja Yusuf Shah, Mian Muhammad Shafi and Shaikh Ghulam Sadik of Punjab; Hakim Ajmal Khan of Delhi; Munshi Ihtisan Ali, Syed Nabiullah, Maulvi Syed Karamat Husain, Syed Abdulraoof, Munshi Abdul Salam Khan, Khan Bahadur Muhammad Muzammil Ullah Khan, Muhammad Ismail Khan, Sahabzada Aftab Ahmad Khan, Maulvi Mushtaq Husain, Maulvi Habibul Rahman Khan and Maulvi Syed Mahdee Ally Khan of the United provinces; and Nawab Syed Sirdar Ali Khan of Hyderabad. The thirty-sixth person, Nawab Salimullah Khan of Dhaka (d.1915) could not join the deputation due to his illness. Strangely, the Persian Consul-General based at Murshidabad was also present.[5]

After the normal courtesy of emphasizing 'the incalculable benefits conferred by the British rule', the delegation expressed the same old fear about what democracy would mean for Muslims; it was likely 'among other evils, to place our national interests at the mercy of unsympathetic majority'. As such, Muslims 'should never be an effective minority'. Therefore, Muslims be elected only through Muslim electorates. Disregarding the numerical size of the Muslim community the British should go beyond the numbers in conceding them representation and other rights bearing in mind the 'political importance' that community had commanded only a hundred years earlier and 'the value of the contribution which they make to the defence of the Empire.' Having been slow in accepting Western education, they were feeling uneasy to see Hindus rising to positions of prominence in all fields, including administrative and judicial services. Thus, they demanded that there should be a guaranteed percentage of jobs in the services for them and promotion without competitive examinations; and that this principle be extended to local government bodies.[6]

The viceroy did not ask them to establish their credentials. Instead, Lord Minto welcomed them 'heartily to Simla', and said, 'Your presence here today is very full of meaning.' He expressed gratitude 'for the opportunity you are affording me of expressing appreciation of the just aims of the followers of Islam and their determination to share in the political history of our empire'. He pointed out that the new province of Eastern Bengal was yet another reward for the Muslim loyalty. Igniting the fire of divisiveness he called them as 'descendants of a conquering and ruling race'. Recognizing the unrest prevalent in India he observed that it was only the work of the educated elite, who were at that time mostly Hindus. He further said, "in any system of representation...in which it is proposed to introduce or increase an electoral organization, the Mahommedan community should be represented as a community and you justly claim that your position should be estimated not merely on your numerical strength but in respect to the political importance of your community and the service it has rendered to the Empire...I am entirely in accord with you"[7]. He further observed: 'I am as firmly convinced, as I believe you to be, that any electoral representation in India would be doomed to mischievous failure which aimed at granting personal enfranchisement, regardless of the beliefs and traditions of the communities composing the population of this continent.'[8]. Dispelling their worry about the imminent democracy he said: 'the Mohamedan community may rest assured that their political rights and interests as a community will be safeguarded in any administrative reorganization with which I am concerned.'[9]

After the meeting, Dunlop Smith sent Lady Minto a note saying: 'I must send Your Excellency a line to say that a very, very big thing has happened today. A work of statesmanship that will affect India and Indian history for many a long year. It is nothing less than the pulling back of sixty-two millions of people from joining the ranks of the seditious opposition.'[10] Soon a controversy arose: if this spectacle was an arranged one, because it was a subject described later by Lady Minto in her diary as: 'Quite a Command Performance!' It was taken as a phrase which implied that the delegation was performing by command. The Englishmen defended it as a normal phrase about a pompous show where princes, nawabs and nobles were in the best of their garments and regalia. It was a general practice by courtiers and noblemen in London to attend the 'Royal Command Performance' opera in best of their dresses and decorations whenever it was called by the royal command. [11] Whether the British planned the Simla deputation that way or not, or if it was a command performance or a self-thought program by Muslims, the fact remains that the Muslims had been encouraged in this way to embrace a separate identity for themselves. It paved the way for establishing the first organization with a political manifesto designed for the Muslims on an all-India basis. Thus within three days of the deputation the Muslim elite took another major decision: they were to set up a political party, restricted to Muslims only, based on the Nawab Salimullah Khan's scheme for an All-Indian Muhammadan Confederacy. The president of the first session, Nawab Viqar-ul-Mulk Mushtaq Hussain (1841-1917) announced, "Time and circumstances made it necessary for Mohammedans to unite in an association so as to make their voice heard above the din of other vociferous parties in India and across the wide seas to England."[12] A resolution was passed on December 30, 1906, 'that a Political Association styled the All-India Muslim League be formed', with the objectives of promoting 'feelings of loyalty' and to 'protect and advance the political rights and interests of the Musalmans of India'. Thus was born the All India Muslim League in Dhaka. The Aga Khan continued generously to support the League, and in 1908 its executive committee rewarded him with the honorary title of permanent president. Its initial membership consisted mainly of titled nobility and landlords. Pampered by British Raj, Muslim League received assurances of a separate electorate for Muslims and a weightage to compensate for their minority status.

1. William Harcourt Butler to Harry, September 1906, *Harcourt Butler Papers,* India Office Library, London, Eur. Mss. F 116/24. See *A New History of India* (Fifth Edition) Ch. Nineteen, Stanley Wolpert
2. *South Asia:* A Short History, Hugh Tinker
3. *Nehru: The Making of India*, M. J. Akbar. Ch. 8
4. *Nehru: The Making of India,* M. J. Akbar, Ch. 8
5. *Nehru: The Making of India,* M. J. Akbar, Ch. 8

6. *Nehru: The Making of India*, M. J. Akbar, Ch. 8
7. Shan Muhammad, *The Growth of Muslim Politics in India*. See *The Making of India: A Historical Survey*, Ranbir Vohra; *Nehru: The Making of India*, M. J. Akbar, Ch. 8
8. *The Great Divide*, Ch 2, H. V. Hudson; *Nehru: The Making of India*, M. J. Akbar
9. *A New History of India* (Fifth Edition) Ch. Nineteen, Stanley Wolpert; *Nehru: The Making of India*, M. J. Akbar, Ch. 8
10. *Nehru: The Making of India*, M. J. Akbar, Ch. 8; *The Great Divide*, Ch 2, H. V. Hodson
11. *The Great Divide*, H. V. Hodson, Ch 2
12. *A New History of India* (Fifth Edition) Ch. Nineteen, Stanley Wolpert

42

DIVISIVE ELECTORATE

Lord Minto was true to his promise. Whereas the British had turned a deaf ear for many years to the demands of the Congress for increased representation towards self-government, they acceded to the demands of Muslim League almost as soon as it was made. In this regard a major scheme of reform came in the shape of the Indian Councils Act of 1909. At the second reading of the Indian Councils Bill in the house of Lords on February 23, 1909, the secretary of State Viscount Morley argued thus:"But the Mahomedans protested that the Hindus would elect a pro-Hindu upon it, just as I suppose in a mixed college of seventy-five Catholics and twenty-five Protestants voting together the Protestants might suspect that the Catholics voting for the Protestants would choose what is called a Romanising Protestant and as little of a Protestant as they could find. Suppose the other way. In Ireland there is an expression, a "shoneen" Catholic—that is to say, a Catholic, who though a Catholic, is too friendly with English Conservatism and other influences which the Nationalists dislike. And it might be said, if there were seventy-five Protestants against twenty-five Catholics, that the Protestants when giving a vote in the way of Catholic representation would return 'shoneens.'...

"The Mahomedans demand three things. I had the pleasure of receiving a deputation from them and I know very well what is in their minds. They demand the election of their own representatives to these councils in all the stages, just as in Cyprus, here, I think, the Mahomedans vote by themselves. They have nine votes and the non-Mahomedans have three, or the other way about. So in Bohemia, where the Germans vote alone and have their own register. Therefore we are not without a precedent and a parallel for the idea of a separate register...

"To go back to the point of the registers, some may be shocked at the idea of a religious register at all, of a register framed on the principle of religious belief. We may wish , we do wish-certainly I do—that it were otherwise. We hope that time, with careful and impartial statesmanship, will make things otherwise. *Only let us not forget that the difference between Mahomedanism and Hinduism is not a mere difference of articles of religious faith. It is a difference in life, in tradition, in history, in all the social things as well as the articles of belief that constitute a community.*[1] Do not let us forget what makes it interesting and even exciting. Do not let us forget that, in talking of Hindus and Mahomedans, we are dealing with and brought face to face with vast historic issues, dealing with some of the very mightiest forces that through all the centuries and ages have moulded the fortunes of great States and the destinies of countless millions of mankind. Thoughts of that kind are what give to Indian politics and to Indian work extraordinary fascination, and at the same time impose the weight of no ordinary burden."[2]

The Bill was passed and became the second India Councils Act, 1909. It is popularly known as the Morley-Minto Reforms after the names of the incumbent Secretary of State and Viceroy. Through this Act, the legislature was expanded to accommodate more non-official members, and direct election was to be held. It gave the Muslims the right of separate electorates whereby some of the seats were reserved for Muslim members to be elected only by Muslim voters. The electorates were divided into four categories: (1) General Electorates, composed of non-official members of the provincial legislative councils that elected fifteen members; (2) Landholders Constituencies, in which two of the six elected seats were reserved for Muslims; (3) Chambers of Commerce in Bengal and Bombay returning one member each; and (4) Separate Mohammedan Constituencies in Eastern Bengal, Bengal, United Provinces, Madras, and Bombay that elected six members. The electorate was initially a miniscule minority of upper-class Indians. They received franchise rights by virtue of the municipal property taxes they paid or the amount of higher education they had completed. The plea for introducing a separate or communal representation for Muslims was that in a system of property franchise, poverty would prevent Muslims from having an influence in general constituencies in proportion to their numbers. Now voting was made easier for them. A Muslim could become a voter if he paid tax on an income of only Rs 3,000 per year while a Hindu had to have an income of Rs 300,000. Similarly, in the graduate category, a Muslim needed to be a graduate of only three years' standing, while a Hindu required thirty.[3]

However, with this Act one of the most notable chapters was added to the history of India, which had a very far-reaching effect on the life of the country and caused an incalculable harm to the national unity. By this Act, an active process of division of the country had started. It was not only the division of communities but also their sub-divisions. Though obviously intended to detach the Muslims from the mainstream of Indian nationalism it was a dream come true for the Muslim League, but for the Congress the so-called 'Reforms' was a rude betrayal. Muslims now wore a new socio-religious identity, like a caste or a tribe, separate from the main stream of Indian nationhood, and contended with others for patronage and privileges. The era of communal politics had begun. It was the first official nail in the coffin of Indian nationalism. The constitutional principle of separate electorates remained an integral part of the Indian political life right up to 1947, and was abandoned by both India and Pakistan immediately after Independence. The secular foundation of Indian nationalism continued to be undermined through a judicious mix of concessions and guarantees in later years. The Government of India Act of 1919 produced still new divisions; communal representation was enlarged to include also Sikhs in Punjab, Europeans, Anglo-Indians, and Indian Christians. The Hindus were further divided by giving communal representation to non-brahmans in Madras and Marathas in Bombay. In 1935, another Government of India Act added the category of Sikhs, Indian Christians, Europeans, labor, universities, landlords, commerce and industry. To crown it all, the earlier Muslim category was further divided by infusing in it a new category of 'backward tribes'. The term "general population", continued to be essentially Hindu.

1. Note: This argument was a delineation of the ideological contours of the future Pakistan, which was so tenaciously put forward a few years later by Muhammad Ali Jinnah in pressing for the break-up of the country. See Ch. 45 'Watershed' below.

2. Great Britain: The Span of Empire, The Age of Imperial Expansion, 1852-1913, Ed. Joel H. Wiener, Chelsea House Publishers in association with Mc Graw Hill Book Co.

3. *Nehru: The Making of India*, M. J. Akbar, Ch. 8

43

ARCHITECT OF UNITY AND SEPARATION

It was the year 1906 that saw the entry of Muhammad Ali Jinnah (1876-1948), a member of the trading community and a young and energetic lawyer of Bombay, into Congress as a nationalist Muslim. In the 22nd session of the Congress held in Calcutta in 1906 it was Jinnah who had stated that 'The foundation upon which the Indian National Congress is based is that we are all equal, that there should be no reservation for any class or community.' At the time of the establishment of the Muslim league in 1906, its first president, Aga Khan, wrote to Dunlop Smith about Jinnah that he 'came out in bitter hostility toward all that I and my friends had done and were trying to do. He was the only well-known Muslim to take this attitude...He said our principle of separate electorates was dividing the nation against itself.'[1] Jinnah became secretary of Gopal Krishna Gokhle (1866-1915), the moderate and liberal President of Congress in 1905 and founder of the Servants of India Society. Jinnah was regarded as his political heir. During this time the British troubles had not remained limited to the hard-liner Congressmen. Many Muslim leaders, on whose support Britain had depended so heavily, had begun to lose faith in the British sincerity towards self-government. Such disgruntled and disillusioned Muslims were ready to work with Congress and present a joint defiance to the British authority. The two parties seemed to be focusing on the same goal: self-government. The meeting of the Muslim League of 1910, drew attention to the need for a rapprochement between Hindus and Muslims; and the representative of the Congress in these negotiations was Jinnah. He started working to bring together the two rival communities in joint efforts for freedom, so much so that he earned the appellation of the 'Ambassador of Hindu-Muslim Unity'. At this moment the Muslim League invited Muhammad Ali Jinnah to join them, which he did in 1913 without giving up his membership of the Congress and with a 'solemn preliminary covenant that loyalty to the Muslim League and the Muslim interest would in no way and no time imply even the shadow of disloyalty to the larger national cause, to which his life was dedicated.'[2] Joining the Muslim League, his immediate task turned out to be to forge greater unity between the two organizations and, thereby, between the Hindus and the Muslims. In 1916, Jinnah became the president of the Muslim League. In 1915 both the moderate leaders of the Congress, Pherozeshah Mehta and Gokhale died, and the field was left clear for Tilak to emerge as the undisputed leader of the Congress. Strangely, he too came forward to forge an alliance with the Muslim League thus dissipating the old label of his parochialism and fanaticism. At the joint session of Congress and Muslim League, held in Lucknow in 1916, the crowning victory for Jinnah came out in the shape of the famous 'Lucknow Pact'. In *Pilgrimage to Freedom*, K.M. Munshi writes: 'In a sense Jinnah dominated the Congress and the League at the time. He had played the key role in preparing a draft constitution for India and getting it adopted by the sessions both of the Congress and the League.

'The historical Lucknow Pact was an integral part of this constitution. Under it, the Muslims led by the League promised to work with the Hindus to achieve freedom in return for the Congress conceding to the Muslims separate electorates with weightage far in excess of their numerical strength.'[3]

The Pact, which was to become the basis for further cooperation and collaboration was composed of two parts: one presented the British with a demand to raise India's status to that of an equal partner in the empire as a self-governing dominion. The other part spelled out the percentage of seats to be allocated to the Muslims through separate electorates. The Muslims were given greater representation in Muslim-minority provinces than what was warranted by their population and, by the same token, a slightly lesser representation in Muslim-majority provinces. But even here in this pact of unity the poisoned arrow of 'separate electorates' was not discarded. It continued to play its designated role and to serve the British interest in divisiveness. Through this Pact, Congress, which had denounced the politics of communalism, gave official recognition to a communal electorate and agreed to the termination of a truly democratic approach to nationalism. Congress came to be recognized as an organization that represented only the non-Muslims while the Muslim League, as usual, the party of the Muslims looking solely after their own interests in any scheme of independence. But even this price was justified if independence was to come sooner that way.

But independence came much later, after thirty long years, and that too in a mutilated shape.

With the outbreak of the First World War in 1914, and the involvement of Britain in the war, the people of India started nurturing hopes that they would be given more self- government. At this moment, Annie Besant, an English women, who was in favour of India's freedom set up a new organization, the All India Home Rule League on August 1, 1916. In June 1917, Annie Besant and her co-workers were arrested by the British government. But the Home Rule movement spread rapidly throughout the country. The Indians were not deterred by the arrest of Annie Besant. Whereas Motilal Nehru and Sir Tej Bahadur Sapru organized the Allahabad branch of Home Rule League, Muhammad Ali Jinnah did so for Bombay. While the new movement was in mid-stream, Secretary of State Montague came out with a statement on August 20, 1917 declaring that the Raj would henceforth aim at "increasing association of Indians in every branch of the administration and the gradual development of self-governing institutions with a view to the progressive realization of responsible government in India as an integral part of the British Empire." It seemed for a moment that the British had yielded to the demand of Home Rule. It greatly enhanced the prestige of the Home Rule League. Annie Besant was released in September 1917, and in December at the Calcutta session of the Congress she was elected President of the Congress. Home Rule was adopted as the objective of the Congress at that session.

In the meantime another great leader had arisen. This was Mohandas Karamchand Gandhi, who had successfully fought against discrimination and ill treatment of the Indian labour by the Government of South Africa. In 1915 Gandhi had returned to India. He had now to lead the nation against the slavery of the British from the Congress platform. Tilak died in 1920, and it was left to Gandhi to seize the top position in the Congress. He aimed at forging communal harmony, but unfortunately in his life-long struggle his role always appeared somehow controversial to one or the other party. The same year he was appointed president of the Home Rule League in place of Annie Besant who had left the organization because it had become "intertwined with religion". In that role Gandhi, through a simple majority, changed the objective of the Home Rule from self-government to swaraj, i.e. total freedom, and for attainment of freedom the words "by peaceful and legitimate means" were substituted for "by constitutional means". Jinnah objected on matter of principle that the League's constitution could only be changed by a three-fourth majority. He also feared that unconstitutional means would lead to violence. But he was overruled by Gandhi. Unhappy, Jinnah left the League along with 19 members. K.M.Munshi, who had followed Jinnah in walking out of the League, writes in *Pilgrimage to Freedom*:"When Gandhiji forced Jinnah and his followers out of the Home Rule League and later the Congress, we all felt with Jinnah, that a movement of an unconstitutional nature, sponsored by Gandhiji with the tremendous influence he had acquired over the masses, would inevitably result in widespread violence, barring the progressive development of self-governing institutions based on a partnership between the educated Hindus and Muslims. To generate coercive power in the masses would only provoke mass conflict between the two communities, as in fact it did. With his keen sense of realities Jinnah firmly set his face against any dialogue with Gandhiji on this point."[4]

Jinnah resigned from the Congress in 1920. His disagreement with Gandhi again came to the forefront when, the latter started mixing religion in his politics. In the opinion of Gandhi, religion would appeal to Hindu minds, and politics mixed with religion would draw greater force. Tilak had thought in a similar way earlier. The difference between the two, however, was that Tilak's reference to religion was anti-Muslim while Gandhi's was pro-Hindu. For example, Gandhi often referred to ushering in of Ram Rajya, which seemed to establish a Hindu religious government. Some have taken this reference not as the rule of the Hindus but as a good governance. Little did Gandhi realize that any reference to Hindu religion and its legends in a national movement would fall hard on the sensitivities of the Muslims and sound alarm in their ears, specially when the Indian nation was already standing on slippery grounds caused by the arousal of religious differences.

Gandhi strove to create communal harmony by supporting the Muslims in their Khilafat Movement, launched to save caliphate in Turkey, which was threatened with extinction by the Allied peace terms. Gandhi wrote in Young India of October 20, 1921:"I claim that with us both the Khilafat is the central fact, with Maulana Muhammad Ali because it is his religion, with me because, in laying down my life for the Khilafat, I ensure the safety of the cow, that is my religion, from the Mussalman knife."[5]

Jinnah was not happy with this move. He warned Gandhi to desist from arousing fanaticism in Muslims by supporting Khilafat Movement. The Governor of Bengal, Richard Casey, noted in his diary dated December 6, 1945, that during one of his interviews, Gandhi informed Casey that:"Jinnah had told him that he (Gandhi) had ruined politics in India by dragging up a lot of unwholesome elements in Indian life and giving them political prominence, that it was a crime to mix up politics and religion the way he had done."[6]

Jinnah was alienated by the utterances and ideas of Gandhi, whom he described as "the one man responsible for turning congress into an instrument for the revival of Hinduism" and the establishment of "Hindu Raj in the country." Resigning from Congress Jinnah seemed to have concentrated his energy in reorganizing Muslim League and to protect Muslim interests. But still he wished to see some form of cooperation between the two communities so that a united front could be presented to the British. In the meeting of the Muslim League in Lahore in May 1924, Jinnah declared: 'The advent of foreign rule and its continuation in India is primarily due to the fact that the people of India, particularly the Hindus and Muslims, are not united and do not sufficiently trust each other...I am almost inclined to say that India will get Dominion Responsible Government the day the Hindus and Muslims are united.'[7]

In 1925, the Secretary of State for India, Lord Birkenhead, challenged that instead of constantly criticizing the constitutional steps taken by the British, the Indians should demonstrate their unity by themselves framing a constitution 'which carried behind it a fair measure of agreement.' When this challenge was repeated by Brickenhead in 1927, it was accepted by the Indians and in the All Party Conference a committee was established under Motilal Nehru, which initially prepared a report, known as Nehru Report, laying down the principles for framing an All-India Federal Constitution. This Committee rejected the principle of separate electorates. The Muslim League suggested amendments to the Committee in order to include separate electorate for the Muslims, to give weightage in the legislatures in excess of the Muslim population and for residuary powers to be conferred on the Provinces; the last one meaning formation of a federal government. At the All-Party Conference, which discussed Nehru Report and the amendments suggested by the Muslim League, Jinnah pleaded for acceptance of League's amendments if 'revolution and civil war' were to be avoided. When all the amendments were rejected Jinnah is said to have stated: 'This is the parting of the ways". The Hindu-Muslim conciliation on a constitutional framework, which was achieved with Lucknow Pact, was rejected by a Committee, which had been formed specifically to meet the challenge of harmony.

But still Jinnah remained a staunch federalist. In October 1929 the Viceroy, Lord Irwin, announced that the British Government intended to hold a Round Table Conference in England for finding solutions of the Indian problem, and that the goal of India's political development was to grant her Dominion Status in consultation with both Indian princes and political leaders of all shades of opinion. Taking it as another step to weaken Indian nationalism, the Congress at its 1929 session voted against participation in the proposed Conference. Gandhi declared the 26th of January 1930 as Independence day for swaraj. In 1930 Gandhi also started his civil disobedience campaign over the issue of the state salt tax. With the Congress non-cooperating, the British invited to the First Round Table Conference (!930-31) representatives of various Indian interests like Hindu Mahasabhites, Muslims, Sikh, representatives of "depressed classes", Princely States, Indian Christians, and Anglo-Indians. Nationalist Muslims were left out of the invitation list. Jinnah argued that any constitution that could be conceived for India would have to transfer responsibilities of India's central government to a Cabinet "responsible to the legislature".Writing in Transfer of Power, V. P. Menon describes the support of various Indian groups for forming a federal government in India in these words:"Contrary to general expectation, the first Round Table Conference achieved outstanding results, the most important being the unanimous agreement of all parties, including the rulers, on the issue of federation. Upto this time, an all-India federation had been regarded as only a remote possibility. But at the very outset of the Conference Sir Tej Behadur Sapru boldly declared himself for a federal system of government for India and invited the rulers to support his suggestion. The Maharajah of Bikaner and the Nawab of Bhopal stated on behalf of the rulers that they were prepared to come into the proposed federation provided their internal sovereignty was guaranteed. Sir Muhammad Shafi for one wing of the Muslim League and Jinnah for the other, also welcomed the proposal."[8]

Embodying the above principle, the Government of India Act of 1935 gave the princes the right to nominate one-third of the members of the lower house and two-fifths of the upper house. At the same time it was stipulated that accession should be voluntary, and that the federal machinery would not come into operation only after the princes representing half the total princely population had acceded to the federation. This gave the princes who were opposed to the concept of a federal Government an opportunity to avoid its creation. William Francis Hare, The Earl of Listowel, who was the Secretary of State for India at the time of Independence, writes in his Memories about this stipulation as follows: " There can be no doubt that the British alone had the power to transfer their sovereignty to a united India. Gandhi had asked for dominion status at the Round Table Conference in 1931, and he was the voice of the majority. Before 1940 the transition could have undoubtedly been made without providing seperate homelands for the two religious communities. But British statesmanship in the decade of appeasement was at the lowest ebb that I can remember. It is not surprising that the vision was lacking and that the last opportunity was thrown away. The 1935 India act might have been that opportunity, if we had insisted on its implementation instead of allowing the Princes to exercise their veto. Instead of granting the self-government which had been promised since 1917, or insisting on federation, we clung to power under the cloak of respectability lent by protection for the minorities until we were forced to part with it by our own reduced circumstances after five years of war. The transfer of power in 1947 was no more than a mitigation of the failure of British policy to part with power earlier to an united India."[9] When the Government of India Act was introduced in 1935, Jinnah expressed his dissatisfaction over it and declared that the Muslim League stood for "full national government for the people of India."

Jinnah was invited to first two Round Table Conferences. He was not invited to the third. In September 1931, Jinnah went back to England where he set up a flourishing Privy Council practice. He even thought of entering the British Parliament as a Conservative member, but could not get a party ticket to contest the election. In the meanwhile, in July 1933 Liaquat Ali Khan, the future prime Minister of Pakistan, persuaded Jinnah to come back to India and to resume the leadership of Muslim League. As a result, Jinnah returned to India and became the President of the Muslim League.

1. M.J.Akbar, Nehru: The Making of India, Ch. 8
2. Mrs Sarojini Naidu, *Muhammad Ali Jinnah: An Ambassador of Unity,* See H. V. Hodson: *The Great Divide* Ch. 2.
3. K.M.Munshi, Pilgrimage to Freedom, Quoted in *Partition of India: Legend and Reality,* Ch II, H.M. Seervai
4. K.M.Munshi, Pilgrimage to Freedom, Quoted in *Partition of India: Legend and Reality*, Ch II, H.M. Seervai
5. Gandhi, M.K., in *Young India* of October 20, 1921, Quoted in *Partition of India: Legend and Reality*, Ch. II H.M. Seervai. It may be noted that later Jinnah himself fell for mixing religion with politics. In 1939 he concurred with a deputation of the *ulema* led by Ashraf Ali Thanvi that religion could not be divorced from politics in Islam. In 1945 he helped the League to formulate a full-fledged scheme for approaching the *sajjada-nashins* of U.P., for holding *ulema* conference throughout the province. The same year he persuaded Shabbir Ahmad Usmani to mobilize the ulema in support of Pakistan issue. Thereafter *pirs* and *mashaikh* played an important role in Pakistan movement. See *Legacy of a Divided Nation*, Ch. 3, Mushirul Hasan
6. V. P. Menon *The Transfer of Power*
7. Quoted in *The Great Divide,* Ch 4, H. V. Hodson
8. India: A Concise History, Ch. Eight, Francis Watson V. P. Menon, *Transfer of Power*, Quoted in *Partition of India: Legend and Reality* Ch. II, H.M. Seervai
9. William Francis Hare, *Memories of the Earl of Listowel*, Chapter 9

44
POLITICS OF A HINDU SAINT

On his return from South Africa in 1915, Mohandas Karamchand Gandhi was to dominate the Indian political scene leading India to her independence. A few months after independence he fell to the bullet of an assassin in January 1948. He was the member of a respectable Hindu family of Porbandar in Gujerat. Earlier he had fought against white racism in South Africa which was heaping oppression, discrimination and indignities on the poor migrant community of Indian labourers. From 1906 onwards various disabilities were prescribed for them. By assuming the leadership of the Indian community, Gandhi was able to force the government of South Africa to remove most of the disabilities through his weapon of *satyagraha* (the force of truth) and *ahimsa* (non-violence). On his return to India he was hailed by Rabindranath Tagore as Mahatma (great soul). As long as Tilak was alive, Gandhi was unable to come to the forefront in the leadership of Congress. He had proven his acumen of leadership in South Africa and it was now his turn to show his mettle in the politics of India. Gandhi had the quality to shine brilliantly whenever occasion arose to lead the nation against social injustices, but he was not as much a success as when he had to lead them in politics. But he remained as the father, the *bapu*, of the nation till his death.

In February 1919, the government was about to pass the Rowlatt Acts to curb subversive activities. These acts provided for stricter control of the press, and gave the government summary powers of arrest and punishment. The Rowlatt Acts, to which every Indian member of the Imperial Legislative Council had voted against, became effective in March 1919. Jinnah was the first member of the Viceroy's Imperial Council to resign over the passage of this act. Gandhi decided that the time had come for him to assume command of the Congress. An air of restlessness was pervading all over the country and large-scale violence could have erupted any moment. Gandhi anxiously wished such a situation not to happen. Therefore, he made a call for an all-India protest against the Acts in the form of a *hartal* (closing of shops and businesses) on 6th April. Traveling extensively he preached *ahimsa* (non-violence) and satyagrah. His appeal proved very forceful and was followed by a large section of the population. One might be surprised to find a Hindu fanatic leader like Swami Shraddhanand of Arya Samaj, addressing a mammoth gathering of Muslims, Hindus and Sikhs at the Jama Masjid[1] on March 30. Gandhi was arrested on April 8. Both Hindu and Muslim citizens of Amritsar protested this arrest by peacefully parading the streets of the city on 9th April.

A few days later two popular leaders, a Muslim and a Hindu, were arrested in Amritsar for making speeches against the Rowlatt Acts. It resulted in widespread disorder in Punjab in which three Europeans were killed. The governor of the Punjab placed Amritsar under martial law and General Dyre, was appointed martial law administrator. He banned all public gatherings. April 13 was the day of celebration of the festival of Baisakhi. On this day, people from the neighboring villages used to congregate at Amritsar for festivities and camping at the Jallianwalla Bagh, a public garden. It was a large walled area with only one entrance. Most of the illiterate villagers, aloof from the politics, had no idea about the government ban on gathering. They gathered there as usual with their families. All of a sudden, General Dyer appeared on the scene with his soldiers and opened fire at the trapped crowd. The officially announced figure of casualty was 379 killed and 1,208 wounded. Gandhi declared that "cooperation in any shape or form with this satanic government is sinful." A few months later, Muslims had launched the Khilafat movement and Gandhi lent his full support to it. Once again it seemed that Hindu-Muslim unity had gained strength.

But things soon turned sour and Hindu-Muslim unity was shattered. Following the banishment of the Turkish Sultan *cum* Khalifa in 1924 by the new republican leadership under Mustafa Kamal Ataturk, the Khilafat movement in India collapsed. But here it took its own toll. The agitated Moplas of Malabar, in the heat of their anger against the British government, which was punishing Turkey after the War, overthrew the local administration for a brief moment in 1921 and set up a Khilafat regime. Sentiments were so aroused that they killed some Hindu landlords and converted many lower class Hindus to Islam in the process.[2] Arya Samaj, which was ever ready to take up a communal challenge, responded by organizing a re-conversion campaign. The All-India Hindu-Mahasabha (Great Hindu

Assembly), a Hindu communal party launched in 1913 by Madan Mohan Malaviya (1861- 1946) coined the offensive slogan "Hind-Hindi-Hindu." The Muslims thereupon came out with their own conversion campaign. In 1925. The race for communalism was at full steam. The communal Hindus set up yet another party, the Rashtriya Swayam Sewak Sangh (National Self-Reliance Association) at Nagpur. The President of the Hindu Mahasaha declared at the Ajmer session of 1933: 'Hindustan is the land of the Hindus alone, and Musalmans and Christians and other nations living in India are only our guests. They can live here as long as they wish to remain as guests.' As for the language of the Muslims, the Mahasabha resolved: 'Urdu is a foreign language which is a living monument to our slavery. It must be eradicated from the page of existence. Urdu is the language of the Malechas which has done great harm to our national ends by attaining popularity in India.' The result was a marked deterioration in the Hindu-Muslim relations and an eruption of Hindu Muslim riots across North India. The immediate reason for a sudden increase in riots was the assassination of Swami Shraddhanand, the fanatic leader of Arya Samaj and a diehard supporter of the re-conversion movement, by a Muslim extremist. Between 1924 and 1926 communal riots erupted in large numbers in which hundreds were killed. The number of such riots in 1927 alone was thirty-one. Hindu-Muslim riot was becoming an accepted feature of everyday life. But Jawaharlal Nehru, the future Prime Minister of India, was full of optimism who felt that communalism "may be a giant today, but it has feet of clay. It is the outcome largely of anger and passion, and when we regain our tempers it will fade into nothingness. It is a myth with no connection with reality and it cannot endure. It is really the creation of our educated classes in search of office and employment."[3]

When nationalism had fallen into disarray it was roused again ironically by the action of the British Government itself. In November 1927 they announced that a British Royal Commission would visit India in the near future to assess the need for further constitutional reforms. Surprisingly, no Indian was included in this team, and none except the leader, Lord Simon, had a high political stature. Both Congress and Muslim League leaders, including Jinnah, considered it an affront to the self-respect of the Indians. It was with the combined strategy of both the parties that massive hartals were observed, Simon's welcome was observed with black flags and India began resounding with the protest shout of "Simon, Go Back".

At the Second Round Table Conference, Gandhi was the sole representative of the Congress amongst a host of Indian delegates coming from a variety of sectarian and special interests, each clamouring for separate electorates. The minorities demanded of Gandhi that their claims should be settled first, but he was unable to solve the communal problem. He returned with the feeling that the Conference had widened the gap between the Congress and the Muslim League. It was now left to the British Government itself to provide a solution of its own. In August 1932, Prime Minister Ramsay Macdonald announced his Communal Award. Again, it was a scheme of separate electorates to be incorporated in India's new Constitution. Apart from introducing various new communal elements, the most noteworthy step taken in this Award was the creation of a Depressed Class amongst the groups themselves, and to whom separate electorates were allotted. Thus a sizeable chunk was separated from the Hindu community itself. The Award provided for reservation of seats for minorities, and even for Depressed Classes in communities of Hindus and Muslims. A further division in major communities was thus created. Gandhi launched his fast-unto-death protest after a month, arguing that as "a man of religion" he had "no other course left open" to him. This protest was not against the British government but against his own fellowmen in favour of Hindu untouchables. According to him this issue was central to survival of Hinduism itself. "I believe that if untouchability is really rooted out," he said, "it will not only purge Hinduism of a terrible blot but its repercussion will be worldwide. My fight against untouchability is a fight against the impure in humanity."[4] Unfortunately, the Hindu religious concept of untouchability, not only with sudras but also with mlechchas in which category Muslims had fallen, had kept the Hindus and Muslims for centuries from coming closer as a community. This element was one of the many which had helped others to sow discord between them. To save Hinduism Gandhi was now ready to concede more seats to the so-called Depressed Class. All he wanted from them was not to accept this political categorization of Depressed Class and consider themselves belonging to the Hindu community. He, however, could not discard the classification of sudra in religious term. Certainly he had no control on the religion, but he tried to raise the status of sudras by calling them harijans (children of God). Ambedkar, the leader of the untouchables, denounced Hinduism for treating untouchables "as lepers, not fit for ordinary intercourse." Gandhi admitted of the excesses perpetrated on the untouchables in the name of religion, and exhorted his followers and caste Hindus to open their temples to harijans. After frenzied negotiations between Hindu leaders and Ambedkar an agreement was reached in Yeravda jail, called Poona Pact, according to which depressed classes were assured of 147 seats on provincial councils in place of the 71 awarded to them by the Award. Also, as long as they ran for election by the general electorate they would hold 18 percent of the Central Assembly seats. The Poona Pact was given due consideration by the British Government and included as an amendment to the Communal Award. Reservation of seats for the Depressed Classes continued but with joint electorates. This remarkable achievement was celebrated throughout India as Untouchability Abolition Week.

Following the Poona Pact, a Hindu Leaders Conference was called to resolve "that henceforth, amongst Hindus, no one shall be regarded as an untouchable by reason of his birth, and those who have been so regarded hitherto, will have the same right as other Hindus in regard to the use of public wells, public schools, public roads and other public institutions."[5] It was only after gaining independence that India could outlaw this institution. But it is so tenaciously featured in Hindu religion and society that no legal measure has shown the ability to root it out. After fifty years of Independence, the constitutional and legal measures to abolish untouchability have made only a small dent. The refinement in this regard has come more from modern education and institutions of development than due to enforcement by law. Indian population is overwhelmingly illiterate, hence untouchability continues with full force throughout the country.

After this achievement, the focus of Gandhi's activities was directed more towards untouchability and the cause of the harijans rather than to politics. He toured the country extensively to secure entry for harijans into Hindu temples and collect subscription for Harijan Fund. He also edited a weekly dedicated to the promotion of their welfare. But this was not taken kindly by Ambedkar who bitterly criticized him for doing nothing to fight the caste system itself. On the other hand, orthodox Hindus accused him of tampering with Hindu tradition. Disappointed, many Congress leaders called for "a radical reorganization of the Congress on a new principle with a new method, for which a new leadership is essential". Sensing the change in the mood of the Congress leaders, Gandhi nominated Jawaharlal Nehru as his successor whom he considered "the natural wearer of the Congress crown of thorns". He did not only give up the

Congress leadership but also decided to quit politics altogether. He did so temporarily and returned to politics when Congress called upon Gandhi to resume its leadership to face the challenge posed by Jinnah and the British Government around the middle of 1940. In March, the Muslim League had passed the Pakistan Resolution and the Prime Minister Winston Churchill, who regarded India as 'the most truly bright and precious jewel in the crown of the King' authorized Viceroy Linlithgow in mid 1940 to make a declaration promising a post-war Dominion Status constitution designed to ensure that power was not transferred to "any government whose authority is directly denied by large and powerful sections of India's national life."[6] When the Viceroy Linlithgow announced that future efforts at constitution-making would involve "consultation with representatives of several communities" Congress ministries resigned in protest in November. Overjoyed, the Muslim League declared that 22 December would be celebrated as the 'Day of Deliverance'.

1. *A Panormic History of the Indian People*, Ch. Twelve, D.B.Vohra
2. *A Panormic History of the Indian People*, D.B.Vohra
3. The Making of India, Ch 21, M. J. Akbar
4. *A History of India*, Ch 21, Stanley Wolpert
5. *A History of India*, Ch 21, Stanley Wolpert
6. *A Panoramic History of the Indian People*, D. B. Vohra

45
TEST OF ATTITUDES

For planting the philosophy of 'two-nation' into the political soil of India, the British supplied enough fertilization through their policy of divide et impera. Then, they nourished it with diverse measures, most notable among them the introduction of separate electorates. The tree, now matured, was ready to bear fruit. The result was that in the war of succession to the British the heir was not to be the Indian nation but the two communities of Hindus and Muslims. The subsequent struggle for freedom thus became the grand spectacle of the attitudes of the two communities, or in other words it was the real test of tolerance.

In 1937, elections to Provincial legislatures were held under the Government of India Act of 1935 on the basis of separate electorates. Of the eleven provinces, the Congress gained clear majority in Madras, Bihar, Orissa, U.P. and C.P. In Bombay it won nearly half of the seats. Surprisingly, in NWFP and Assam it was the largest single party. In Bengal, Sind and Punjab, the Muslim League was the winner. Two events, one while forming the governments and another after the formation, deserve special mention which describe the level of tolerance with which the country was passing. Unfortunately, intolerance comes in handy with victory. First, as a result of this election, Congress ministries were formed in eight provinces. In U.P., Congress had contested 9 out of 66 Muslim seats but did not win even a single one. So was the case with Bombay where it had contested 2 seats out of 30. The question was how to associate Muslims in the new governments. This could be possible only through a coalition with Muslim League. Before the elections, Congress had not anticipated a clear majority in U.P., and so it had entered into a tacit agreement with the Muslim league to form a coalition government. But with the gaining of a clear majority, the Congress refused coalition. Constitutionally, the decision of the Congress could not be challenged. But expediency had required otherwise. K.M.Munshi writes in *Pilgrimage to Freedom*: "A serious situation arose with regard to the choice of the Muslim member, wherever Congress Ministries were formed. At that time it did not appear to be formidable; but as events were to show ten years later, it was the beginning of the end of united India."[1] This has been described by R.C. Majumdar in *The History of the Freedom Movement in India*, Vol. III, as "The Muslims now fully realised that as a separate community, they had no political prospects in future. The Congress ultimatum was the signal for the parting of the ways, which, by inevitable stages, led to the foundation of Pakistan."[2] Abul Kalam Azad writes in *India Wins Freedom*: "If the U.P. League's offer of cooperation had been accepted, the Muslim League party would for all practical purposes have merged in the Congress. Jawaharlal's action gave the Muslim League in the U.P. a new lease of life....It is from the U.P. that the League was reorganised. Mr. Jinnah took full advantage of the situation and started an offensive which ultimately led to partition."[3] In *Nehru, A Political Biography*, Brecher writes: "The immediate and most far-reaching effect of the Congress victory at the polls was a widening of the breach with the Muslim League. Flushed with success the Congress adopted an imperious attitude to all other political parties, a 'Himalayan blunder', for which it was to pay dearly in the years to come. Nehru himself set the tone with his haughty remark in March 1937: 'There are only two forces in India today, British imperialism, and Indian nationalism as represented by Congress.' Jinnah was quick to retort: 'No, there is a third party, the Mussulmans.' History was to bear him out."[4]

Brecher further says that as late as March 17, 1938 Jinnah had written to Nehru: 'It is the duty of every true nationalist to whichever party or community he may belong' to help achieve a united front..[5] Shiva Rao writes about Jinnah in *Framing of India's Constitution,A Study*: "In a public statement, shortly after the elections in 1937 he declared, 'nobody will welcome an honourable settlement between the Hindus and the Muslims more than I and nobody will be more ready to help it'; and he followed it with a public appeal to Gandhi to tackle this question. The latter's response was somewhat depressing: 'I wish I could do something, but I am utterly helpless. My faith in unity is bright as ever; only I see no daylight but impenetrable darkness and in such distress I cry out to God for light'."[6]

On April 6, 1938, Nehru wrote, on behalf of the Congress, to Jinnah: "Obviously, the Muslim League is an important communal organization and we deal with it as such.....Inevitably, the more important the organization, the more the attention paid to it, but this importance does not come from outside recognition but from inherent strength...." Jinnah replied: "Your tone and language again display the same arrogance and militant spirit, as if the Congress is the sovereign power....I may add that, in my opinion, as I have publicly stated so often, that unless the Congress recognizes the Muslim League on a footing of complete equality and is prepared as such to negotiate for a Hindu-Muslim settlement, we shall have to wait and depend upon our 'inherent strength' which will 'determine the measure of importance or distinction' it possesses..."[7] This measure of importance and distinction was demonstrated later in elections. In the 1945 elections to the Central Legislative Assembly the Muslim League won every seat, 30 out of 30, reserved for Muslims.

Another unhealthy attitude shown by of the Congress governments was to act as the government of the Hindus. The Congress foisted the song of Bande Mataram, which had an undertone of anti-Muslim bias, as the national anthem. Children in schools and legislators in assemblies were forced to sing it. The new governments in the provinces also encouraged Hindi at the expense of Urdu. There was naturally a hue and cry from the Muslim quarters. In the 1937 Lucknow session of the Muslim League the following resolution was passed:

"This meeting of All-India Muslim League strongly condemns the attitude of the Congress in foisting the Bande Mataram as the national anthem upon the country, in callous disregard of the feelings of the Muslims, and considers this song not merely positively anti-Islamic and idolatrous in its inspirations and ideas, but definitely subversive of the growth of genuine nationalism in India. This Meeting further calls upon the Muslim members of the various legislatures and public bodies in the country not to associate themselves in any manner with the highly objectionable song." At the 1938 session of the All-India Muslim League, Jinnah said: "There is not the slightest doubt that the most aggressive attitude was taken up by the Congress Government on the threshold of their assuming office. They endeavoured to impose the *Bande Mataram* song in the legislatures, and it is only after much bitterness and opposition that it has been dropped. They are pursuing a policy of making Hindi compulsory language, which must necessarily, if not completely, destroy—at any rate, virtually undermine—the spread of the development of Urdu; and what is worse still, is that Hindi with its Hindu Sanskrit literature and philosophy and ideals will and must necessarily be forced upon Muslim children and students."

The division among the Hindus and Muslims had become so deep that even the President of Hindu Mahasabha, Savarkar, had to admit in 1937 that "India cannot be assumed today to be a unitarian and homogenous nation, but on the contrary there are two nations in the main, the Hindus and the Muslims.'[8] An assessment of the provincial governments in respect of susceptibilities of the minorities can be found in the words of V.P.Menon in his letter of July 7, 1945 to Evan Jenkins, Personal Secretary to Viceroy, also Governor of Punjab: "Upto 1935, Muslims, generally speaking, were under the impression that their interests would be safeguarded if they could get adequate representation in the legislatures. Thanks to the Congress policy of excluding all the other parties from the Provincial Executive, the minorities learnt that the majority party in the legislature could set at nought the wishes of the minorities and that representation in the legislatures would not alone be a sufficient safeguard. This was the real motive power behind Jinnah's cry of Pakistan. Exclusion from a share in the power was the real foundation on which the present position of the Muslim League was built up. It is therefore not surprising that the cry of Pakistan is more vociferous in the Provinces in which the Muslims are in a minority than in the majority Muslim Provinces."[9] Consequently, Congress came to be regarded as the Hindu counterpart of the League. Subsequently, the Muslim League had to change its strategy: it became more Muslim and less nationalist in its outlook and approach. Jinnah's prestige rose by leaps and bounds among the Muslims. He was hailed as the "Quaid-i-Azam" (Great Leader), and in the 1938 session held at Patna this title was formally conferred on him. At that session he was handed over through Resolution No. 4 the power of 'direct action', which he kept in reserve to be used at a critical moment.

1. K.M.Munshi, *Pilgrimage to Freedom*, Quoted in *Partition of India: Legend and Reality*, Ch. III, H.M. Seervai

2. R.C. Majumdar, *The History of the Freedom Movement in India*, Vol. III, Quoted in *Partition of India: Legend and Reality*, Ch. III, H.M. Seervai

3. Abul Kalam Azad, *India Wins Freedom* Quoted in *Partition of India: Legend and Reality*, Ch. III by H.M. Seervai

4. Brecher, *Nehru, A Political Biography*, Quoted in *Partition of India: Legend and Reality*, Ch. III, H.M. Seervai

5. Brecher, Nehru, A Political Biography, Quoted in *Partition of India: Legend and Reality*, footnote, Ch III, H.M. Seervai

6. Shiva Rao writes about Jinnah in Framing of India's Constitution, A Study, Quoted in *Partition of India: Legend and Reality*, Ch III H.M. Seervai

7. Hector Bolitho, Jinnah, Quoted in *Partition of India: Legend and Reality*, Ch. III, H.M. Seervai

8. Sarvepalli Gopal, *Indian Muslims: A Political History*, Quoted in *The Making of India: A Historical Survey*, Ranbir Vohra

9. V.P.Menon, Transfer of Power, Vol. XII, Appendix I, p. 790, Quoted in *Partition of India: Legend and Reality*, Ch IV, H.M. Seervai

46
WATERSHED

In February 1940, the Viceroy gave a suggestion to the Muslims that the League should formulate its political plans early so that "the Muslim case may not go by default in the U.K."[1] In March 1940, a session of the Muslim League was convened in Lahore in which, Jinnah, who had been the standard bearer of Indian unity, argued that during the last twelve hundred years India always stood divided into Hindu India and Muslim India. On March 22 he spoke as follows:

"As far as our internal position is concerned we have also been examining it and, you know, there are several schemes which have been sent by various well-informed constitutionalists and others who take interest in the problem of India's future constitution, and we have also appointed a sub-committee to examine the details of the schemes that have come in so far. But one thing is quite clear. It has always been taken for granted mistakenly that the Mussulmans are a Minority and of course we have got used to it for such a long time that these settled notions sometimes are very difficult to remove. The Mussulmans are not a Minority. The Mussulmans are a nation by any definition. The British and particularly the Congress proceed on the basis, 'Well, you are a Minority after all, what do you want?' 'What else do the Minorities want?' Just as Babu Rajendra Prasad said. But surely the Mussulmans are not a Minority. We find that even according to the British map of India we occupy large parts of this country, where the Mussulmans are in a majority — such as Bengal, the Punjab, North-West Frontier Province, Sind and Baluchistan.

* * * *

"Now, I should like to put before you my views on the subject as it strikes me taking everything into consideration at the present moment. The British Government and Parliament and more so the British nation, have for many decades past brought up and nurtured with settled notions about India's future, based on developments in their own country which have built up the British Constitution, functioning now through the Houses of Parliament and the system of

Cabinet, their concept of party government functioning on political planes has become the ideal with them as the best form of government for every country, and the one-sided and powerful propaganda, which naturally appeals to the British, has led them into a serious blunder, in producing the Constitution envisaged in the Government of India Act of 1935. We find that most leading statesmen of Great Britain, saturated with these notions, have in their pronouncements seriously asserted and expressed a hope that the passage of time will harmonize the inconsistent elements in India.

"A leading journal like the *London Times*, commenting on the Government of India Act of 1935, wrote, 'Undoubtedly the difference between the Hindus and Muslims is not of religion in the strict sense of the word but also of law and culture, that may be said, indeed, to represent two entirely distinct and separate civilizations. However, in the course of time, the superstition will die out and India will be moulded into a single nation.' So, according to the *London Times* the only difficulties are superstitions. These fundamental and deeprooted differences, spiritual, economic, cultural, social and political have been euphemized as mere 'superstitions'. But surely it is a flagrant disregard of the past history of the Sub-continent of India as well as the fundamental Islamic conception of society vis-a-vis that of Hinduism to characterize them as mere 'superstitions'. Notwithstanding a thousand years of close contact, nationalities which are as divergent today as ever, cannot at any time be expected to transform themselves into one nation merely by means of subjecting them to a democratic constitution and holding them forcibly together by unnatural and artificial methods of British Parliamentary Statutes. What the unitary government of India for 150 years had failed to achieve cannot be realized by the imposition of a central Federal Government. It is inconceivable that the fiat or writ of a Government so constituted can ever command a willing and loyal obedience throughout the sub-continent by various nationalities except by means of armed force behind it.

"The problem in India is not of an inter-communal character but manifestly of an international one, and it must be treated as such. So long as this basic and fundamental truth is not realized, any constitution that may be built will result in disaster and will prove destructive and harmful not only to the Mussulmans but to the British and Hindus also. If the British Government are really in earnest and sincere to secure peace and happiness of the people of this subcontinent, the only course open to us all is to allow the major nations separate homelands by dividing India into 'autonomous national states'. There is no reason why these states should be antagonistic to each other. On the other hand the rivalry and the natural desire and efforts on the part of one to dominate the social order and establish political supremacy over the other in the government of the country will disappear. It will lead more towards natural goodwill by international pacts between them, and they can live in complete harmony with their neighbours. This will lead further to a friendly settlement all the more easily with regard to Minorities by reciprocal arrangements and adjustments between Muslim India and Hindu India, which will far more adequately and effectively safeguard the rights and interests of Muslims and various other Minorities.

"It is extremely difficult to appreciate why our Hindu friends fail to understand the real nature of Islam and Hinduism. They are not religions in the strict sense of the word, but are, in fact, different and distinct social orders, and it is a dream that the Hindus and Muslims can ever evolve a common nationality, and this misconception of one Indian nation has gone far beyond the limits and is the cause of most of your troubles and will lead India to destruction if we fail to revise our notions in time. The Hindus and Muslims belong to two different religious philosophies, social customs, literatures. They neither inter-marry nor inter-dine together and, indeed , they belong to two different civilizations which are based mainly on conflicting ideas and conceptions. Their concepts on life and of life are different. It is quite clear that Hindus and Mussulmans derive their inspiration from different sources of history. They have different epics, different heroes, and different episodes. Very often the hero of one is a foe of the other and, likewise, their victories and defeats overlap. To yoke together two such nations under a single state, one as a numerical minority and the other as a majority, must lead to growing discontent and final destruction of any fabric that may be so built up for the government of such a state. [2] *[Note how the cue was provided thirty-one years earlier by Viscount Morely in his speech of 1909 in the House of Lords. See Chapter 41, Divisive Electorates].*

"History has presented to us many examples, such as the Union of Great Britain and Ireland, Czechoslovakia and Poland. History has also shown to us many geographical tracts, much smaller than the sub-continent of India, which otherwise might have been called one country, but which have been divided into as many states as there are nations inhabiting them. Balkan Peninsula comprises as many as 7 or 8 sovereign states. Likewise the Portuguese and the Spanish stand divided in the Iberian Peninsula. Whereas under the plea of unity of India and one nation, which does not exist, it is sought to pursue here the line of one Central Government when we know that the history of the last 12 hundred years has failed to achieve unity and has witnessed, during the ages, India always divided into Hindu India and Muslim India. The present artificial unity of India dates back only to the British conquest and is maintained by the British bayonet, but the termination of the British regime, which is implicit in the declaration of His Majesty's Government, will be the herald of the entire break-up with worse disaster than has ever taken place during the last one thousand years under Muslims. Surely that is not the legacy which Britain would bequeath to India after 150 years of her rule, nor would Hindu and Muslim India risk such a sure catastrophe.

"Muslim India cannot accept any Constitution which must necessarily result in a Hindu majority Government. Hindus and Muslims brought together under a democratic system forced upon the Minorities can only mean Hindu raj. Democracy of the kind with which the Congress High Command is enamoured would mean the complete destruction of what is most precious in Islam. We have had ample experience of the working of the Provincial Constitutions during the last two and a half years and any repetition of such a Government must lead to civil war and raising of private armies as recommended by Mr. Gandhi to Hindus of Sukkar when he said that they must defend themselves violently or non-violently, blow for blow, and if they could not, they must emigrate.

"Mussulmans are not a Minority as it is commonly known and understood. One has only got to look around. Even today, according to the British map of India, 4 out of 11 Provinces, where the Muslims dominate more or less, are functioning notwithstanding the decision of the Hindu Congress High Command to non-cooperate and prepare for civil disobedience. Mussulmans are a nation according to any definition of a nation, and they must have their homelands, their territory and their state. We wish to live in peace and harmony with our neigbours as a free and independent people. We wish our people to develop to the fullest our spiritual, cultural, economic, social and political life in a way that we think best and in consonance with our own ideals and according to the genius of our people. Honesty demands and the vital interests of millions of our people impose a sacred duty upon us to find an honourable and peaceful solution, which would be just and fair to all. But at the same time we cannot be moved or diverted from our purpose and objective by threats or intimidations. We must be prepared to face all difficulties and consequences, make all the sacrifices that may be required of us to achieve the goal we have set in front of us".[3]

In that Session, the Muslim League passed the historic Resolution on March 23, 1940, popularly known as Pakistan Resolution, for a homeland for Muslims as follows:

"Resolved that it is the considered view of this Session of the All-India Muslim League that no constitutional plan would be workable in this country or acceptable to the Muslims unless it is designed on the following principles, viz., that geographically contiguous units are demarcated into regions which should be so constituted, with such territorial readjustments as may be necessary, that the areas in which the Muslims are numerically in a majority, as in the North-Western and Eastern zones of India, should be grouped to constitute Independent States in which the constituent units shall be autonomous and sovereign.

"That adequate, effective and mandatory safeguards should be specifically provided in the Constitution for Minorities in these units and in the regions for the protection of their religious, cultural, administrative and other rights and interests in consultation with them *and in other parts of India where the Mussulmans are in a minority, adequate, effective and mandatory safeguards shall be specifically provided in the Constitution for them* and other Minorities for the protection of their religious, cultural, economic, political, administrative and other rights and interests in consultation with them."[4]

People had grown intolerant to each other, yet they had not felt themselves really divided and as two nations. In order to keep India united, the subsequent political fight of the Muslim League was directed more on gaining parity in the Legislature than for the division of the country. For this purpose Bhulabhai Desai, leader of the opposition and a member of the Congress Party in the Indian Legislative Assembly and Liaquat Ali Khan, Deputy Leader of the Muslim League Party in the Indian Legislative Assembly, met and reached at an agreement known as Desai-Liaquat pact. According to this pact Congress and League would nominate equal number of members in the Central legislature. But this Pact was repudiated by the Congress. A similar arrangement for parity was arrived at by Sapru Committee which was composed of members unconnected with either Congress or Muslim League. Parity was needed because the Muslims were afraid of a Hindu raj in a democratic and united India. Jinnah argued: "brother Gandhi has three votes; I (brother Jinnah) have one". But, to the Congress, the system of parity was opposed to 'the basic principles of democracy'.

On March 24, 1946 the British Government sent a mission to India under Lord Pethick-Lawrence, the Secretary of State for India, known as the Cabinet Mission. The Mission's talks with Indian leaders at the Second Simla Conference in 1946 miserably failed. The Cabinet Mission then decided to put forward its own Plan for transfer of Power. While unveiling their Plan, the Cabinet mission observed: "We and our Government and countrymen hoped that it would be possible for the Indian people themselves to agree upon the method of framing the new constitution under which they will live.' Since 'this has not been possible' they have devised what they 'trust will enable you to attain your independence in the shortest time and with the least danger of internal disturbance and conflict.' The Statement on the Cabinet Mission Plan was published on May 16, whose main features were:

* There should be a union of India, embracing both British India and the States, which should deal with the following subjects: foreign affairs, defence, and communications; and which should have the power necessary to raise the finances required for the above subjects. All other subjects and all residuary powers should vest in the Provinces;

* Provinces should be free to form Groups with executives and legislatures, and each group could determine the provincial subjects to be taken in common. Group B was to embrace Punjab, Sind, Northwest Frontier Province and Baluchistan; Group C would contain Bengal and Assam, and Group A, everything else;

* The constitution of the Union and the Groups should contain a provision whereby any province could, by majority vote of its Legislative Assembly, call for a reconsideration of the terms of the constitution after the initial period of 10-yearly intervals thereafter.

* As soon as the new constitutional arrangements have come into operation, it shall be open to any province to elect to come out of any group in which it has been placed.

The Cabinet Mission Plan had preserved the unity of India, which was the cherished goal of the Congress. It had allayed the fears of the Muslims, which was behind the demand for Pakistan, because the Muslim majority provinces could form their own groups and have their own governments therein. It may be noted that while discussing the Plan with Muslim League leaders on May 16, Sir Stafford Cripps had assured them of the right of a Province to opt out after the Constitution had been framed, but had not said so to the Congress leaders. It was on December 6, 1946 that the British Government categorically announced that the grouping provision was an essential part of the Plan, and must be accepted by all parties in the Constituent Assembly. Muslim League accepted the Cabinet Mission Plan in the first instance because of the compulsory grouping provisions, and regarded compulsory grouping as a fundamental part of the Cabinet Mission Plan, i.e., the respective provinces would have to join their group first, whether they liked it or not, and if they wished to opt out of it they could do so only at a later stage after the constitution had been formulated. Cabinet Mission looked at it the same way. Gandhi and Nehru considered 'grouping' of provinces optional, and that the provinces were free to opt out of a group to which they did not wish to belong. They hoped to win over the Hindu majority province of Assam and Northwest Frontier Province, which had Congress ministries, at that time, to opt out of Groups B and C in case of grouping provision being optional. There was another point of disagreement: Congress held that once a constituent Assembly was convened, it was a sovereign body not bound by the Cabinet Mission Plan. Jinnah insisted that this scheme once accepted, must be binding on everybody concerned all the times.

In the meeting of the Muslim League Council, Jinnah admitted that there could be no fairer solution of the minority problem than that presented in the Plan. He told the Council that it was the maximum he could secure, and advised them to accept it. On June 6, 1946 the Council passed a Resolution that "It is for these reasons that the Muslim League is accepting the scheme, and will join the Constitution-making Body, and it will keep in view the opportunity and right to secession of Provinces or groups from the Union, which have been provided in the Mission's Plan by implication. The ultimate attitude of the Muslim League will depend on the final outcome of the labours of the Constitution-making Body and on the final shape of the constitutions which may emerge from the deliberation of that Body jointly and separately in three sections. The Muslim league also reserves the right to modify and revise the policy and attitude set forth in this resolution at any time during the progress of the deliberations of the Constitution-making Body, or the Constituent Assembly, or thereafter if the course of events so require, bearing in mind the federal principles and ideals herebefore adumbrated, to which the Muslim League is irrevocably committed."[5] The Congress also accepted the Plan on June 25, but with reservations about interpreting the grouping provisions. Gandhi argued that the Plan only made recommendations, and was thus not binding as an award. Therefore, either party was free to amend or reject any of its provisions, as it thought fit. On 10th July, Jawaharlal Nehru took over the Presidentship of Congress from Abul Kalam Azad, and held a press conference in Bombay. He said to the press that Congress would enter the Constituent Assembly 'completely unfettered by agreement and free to meet all situations as they arose'. On further inquiry he said emphatically that the Congress had agreed only to participate in the Constituent Assembly and regarded itself free to change or modify the Cabinet Mission Plan. According to Abul Kalam Azad (*India Wins Freedom*) this was 'one of those unfortunate events which change the course of history.' To Jinnah, Nehru's statement was 'a complete repudiation of the basic form upon which the long-term scheme rests and all of its fundamentals.' It was, to him, one more example of Congress's treachery and of 'its petty-fogging and higgling attitude.' Distrusting the sincerity of the Congress, Jinnah called a meeting of the Muslim League, which passed a resolution on July 29, 1946 revoking League's acceptance of the Plan. In another resolution the Working Committee was asked to draw up a plan for Direct Action and asked all members of the League to renounce the titles conferred by the Government. According to V.P. Menon in *Transfer of Power*, Jinnah said after that: 'What we have done today is the most historic act in our history. Never have we in the whole history of the League done anything except by constitutional methods and by constitutionalism. But now we are obliged and forced into this position. This day we bid goodbye to constitutional methods.' He recalled that throughout the fateful negotiations with the Cabinet Mission the other two parties, the British and the Congress, each held a pistol in their hand, the one of authority and arms and the other of the mass struggle and non-cooperation. 'Today' he said, 'we have also forged a pistol and are in a position to use it'"[6] Muslim League's withdrawal of the acceptance of the Plan was seen as an opportunity by the Congress to form its own Interim Government, turn it into a Dominion Cabinet, eliminate Viceroy's veto, capture the machinery of the Central Government and armed forces, and then deal with the Muslims on their own terms. The statement of Vallabbhai Patel, which he gave to the press later on March 9, 1947, reflected fully this point of view. According to him the political impasse would be broken at once if power were transferred to the Central Government, and with 'Viceroy standing out...if there were conflicts in the Cabinet on any question, the majority would rule.'

The initial confusion and misunderstanding had led to another chance of a united India being lost. 'We have exhausted all reason', said Jinnah. 'There is no tribunal to which we can go. The only tribunal is the Muslim Nation.' The Direct Action Day, which was set by Muslim League on August 16, 1946, erupted in communal riots in Calcutta, and left about 5000 people dead. The trouble soon spread to Noakhali and Tippera districts of Bengal and thence to all over Bihar. Gandhi told his followers in Bihar when he visited the riot torn area: 'To me the sins of the Noakhali Muslims and the Bihar Hindus are of the same magnitude and are equally condemnable.' The Viceroy, Lord Wavell was convinced that if some sort of agreement between the Congress and the Muslim League was not brought about soon, such recklessness would be repeated all over India. He then brought both parties to some sort of agreement over the Cabinet Mission Plan and made them agree to form the Interim Government. He now hoped that the two parties would iron out their differences while sitting together in the Government and Constituent Assembly, and thus there would be an orderly transfer of power to a united India. The Viceroy proposed a 14-member Executive Council, six of Congress (including one of Scheduled Caste), five of Muslim League, one Sikh, one Indian Christian and one Parsi. Congress accepted the offer but Muslim League rejected it. The Interim Government, led by Nehru was sworn in on September 2, 1946. Later at the personal intervention of the Viceroy with Jinnah, the League agreed to participate in it. Coming to 'the conclusion that in the interest of the Mussalmans and other communities it will be fatal to leave the entire field of administration of the Central Government in the hands of the Congress', Jinnah nominated five members on behalf of the League.[7]

The Interim Government was born in the midst of mistrust, which unfortunately was never resolved, despite the Lord Chancellor's interpretation on the Statement of the Cabinet Mission Plan: "That the recommendation involves that it is for the majority of the representatives in each section taken as a whole to decide how Provincial constitutions shall be framed and to what extent, if any, they shall be grouped."[8] Anyway, it was now the turn of the Constituent Assembly, which was convened in December 9, 1946, where disagreement again arose. Elected members of the Muslim League were absent. Muslim League had not agreed to the convening of the Constituent Assembly till the Congress had categorically accepted the Mission's interpretation of the grouping provisions of the Plan. Later, Muslim League demanded parity among provincial Groups at the Centre so as to avoid a situation making the Muslims live perpetually under domination of a Hindu raj. Gandhi and other Congress leaders objected to the unrealistic situation of equating two groups of provinces. In a letter to Cripps Gandhi said: "As to merits the difficulty about parity between six Hindu majority Provinces and five Muslim majority Provinces is insurmountable. The Muslim majority Provinces represent over 9 crores of the population as against 19 crores of the Hindu majority Provinces. This is really worse than Pakistan. What is suggested in its place is that the Central Legislature should be formed on the population basis. And so too the Executive." Abul Kalam Azad too objected: 'This is unfair and will lead to trouble. Such a provision contains in itself the seed of inflict and the destruction of free growth.'[9] According to Vallabhai Patel "that is the one thing we have been fighting against and will never agree." The intransigence of Congress and Muslim League led unfortunately to the failure of the Cabinet Mission Plan.

The India Committee of the Cabinet was reconstituted by Attlee after the Labour Election victory in 1945. The Committee in its recommendations had remembered what had been offered to India in 1942 during the war: it was to be completely an independent Indian Union as soon as hostilities were over. The Earl of Listowel, Secretary of State for India, writes:

"The recommendations of the India Committee had of course to be endorsed by the Cabinet, and it was in the Cabinet Room that Attlee took the lead. He, not Cripps, put the case for the Committee, and it was inevitably agreed by the whole Cabinet. The only colleague whose opposition he may have feared, because at heart he deplored the dissolution of the British Empire, was that of the Foreign Secretary, Ernest Bevin. But there seemed to be a tacit agreement between the two men that, if Attlee gave Bevin a free hand over foreign policy, Bevin would give Attlee a free hand over India. The most important consequence of Bevin's "freehand" was his determination to get "our lads" (British troops) out of Palestine. He did not care in the least about our legal obligations, which probably went back to the Mandate we accepted from the League of Nations after the First World War that deliberately left Arabs and Jews to fight it out, and hence the creation of Israel as a sovereign state. So it was that the recommendations of the India Committee sailed through the Cabinet with little discussion and no substantial alterations. The absence of argument was not due to indifference, but a general agreement between Ministers about the direction of policy, which had indeed been laid down in our Election Manifesto in 1945, and dates far back to pre-war Labour policy".[10]

On February 20, 1947, Prime Minister Clement Atlee announced His Majesty's Government's intention to quit India and to transfer its power 'to responsible Indian hands' by June 1948. Lord Wavell was recalled and in his place Lord Louis Mountbatten was appointed Viceroy on March 24, 1947. He was given plenipotentiary powers. There had been no precedent for any Viceroy to have this power. The letter of March 1947 of the Prime Minister to the new Viceroy, Lord Mountbatten, sets out the terms and dates of the transfer of power, as well as the date when he had to report back on the non-prospect of a settlement. It says:

"It is the definite objective of His Majesty's Government to obtain a unitary Government for British India and the Indian States, if possible, within the British Commonwealth, through the medium of a Constituent Assembly, set up and run in accordance with the Cabinet Mission's plan, and you should do your utmost in your power to persuade all Parties to work together to this end., and advise His Majesty's Government, in the light of developments, as to the steps that will have to be taken.

"Since, however, this plan can only become operative in respect of British India by agreement between the major Parties, there can be no question of compelling either major Party to accept it.

"If by 1st October you consider that there is no prospect of reaching a settlement on the basis of a unitary Government for British India, either with or without the cooperation of the Indian States, you should report to His Majesty's Government on the steps which you consider should be taken for the handing over of power on the due date.

"The date fixed for the transfer of power is a flexible one to within one month; but you should aim at 1st June, 1948, as the effective date for the transfer of power." [11]

Only within a few days of his assuming office Mountbatten came to the conclusion that Jinnah would not accept anything less than Pakistan. He then proceeded to evolve his own plan of partition of India. The Prime Minister's directive with all its emphasis on the deadline of transfer of power by June 1948 had suddenly lost its importance. There was even no need of reporting back by October 1947. The Earl of Listowel writes:

"Mountbatten set out on his task in characteristic fashion. For the first week in New Delhi he spent his time making friends with Jinnah and renewing friendship with Nehru, the leaders of the League and Congress respectively, and their families, without even breathing a word about politics. He then put his plan for a united India to the two party leaders. He reported to us with deep regret that Jinnah was adamant about the establishment of Pakistan as a separate nation, and would accept nothing less. They could only agree to disagree. He was therefore in the process of drawing up his own plan for the division of India. Such a plan, we of course realised, was the only safeguard against an even greater evil than partition. For if the British left India within a year, without any agreement between Muslims and Hindus to set up a separate Government for the predominantly Hindu and Muslim areas, the two communities would fight for mastery, and the sub-continent would break up, like the Mogul Empire of the 17th century, into a welter of warring fragments. This was the situation as I found it when I arrived at the India Office at the end of April 1947. We were still waiting for the promised partition plan.

"We did not have long to wait before it reached us in London, brought by Lord Ismay, personal adviser to Mountbatten, to explain the contents. It was considered by the India Committee at three long meetings in the first week of May, and approved with only minor alterations on May 8th. Attlee was asked to report to the Cabinet on May 13th. In the meantime we heard, to our dismay, that Mountbatten had changed his mind about the plan. In his own words "he had a hunch" that he should show it to Nehru, in spite of the contrary advice of his staff. Nehru, he said, was aghast when he had studied it. But our feelings in Whitehall can well be imagined. We were being asked to reverse a decision that had just been taken at Cabinet level.

"I took the view that the Viceroy must be allowed to change his mind, but that he would be unlikely to convert the Cabinet unless he came home to put his case in person. I consulted Lord Ismay, as I knew Attlee would consult him, but he disagreed, probably wishing to protect his master from an unwelcome recall to London. It would also put him in the shade. I always turned to Cripps for advice in an emergency, and this seemed just such an occasion. I found, to my relief, that he, Cripps, agreed with me, and said he would tell Attlee he was in favour of Mountbatten's recall to London. The Viceroy's account of this episode is slightly different; he has said that the alternative to his return was to send a Cabinet Minister to New Delhi. This may have been suggested privately by Attlee, but I was unaware of it. If the suggestion was made I am delighted Mountbatten turned it down.

"So it was that Attlee, instead of reporting to the Cabinet about the partition plan on May 18th, simply informed his colleagues that Mountbatten had been asked to return for talks with the India Committee. On the following day Mountbatten appeared before the Committee to explain the reasons for his change of mind, and to submit a revised plan which he said met Nehru's agonising doubts about its predecessor. We were told that Nehru's main objection to the original plan was that it would allow the Provinces to choose independence, either alone or in groups. He thought the Princely States would follow suit, and that this would result in the "balkanisation" of India.

"The revised plan closed this loophole by confining the Provinces to a straight choice between India and Pakistan, and in this form it was acceptable to both Congress and the League. Mountbatten went on to inform us that both new nations now wanted to stay in the Commonwealth, while reserving the right to secede, but only if their independence could be expedited to a much earlier date than we had anticipated. We were particularly surprised and delighted by the change in the attitude of the Congress leaders, who had so recently declared for an "Independent Sovereign Republic". Mountbatten pointed out that Jinnah had always wanted Pakistan to become a Dominion in the Commonwealth, with the same status as the old Dominions. Congress realised that this would place them at a serious disadvantage, and had therefore asked for a similar constitutional status provided only that the transfer could be effected much earlier than June 1948".[12]

There was no better way of making both Congress and League agree on partition than the threatened free-for-all and the consequent balkanisation of India. Thus, after seeking the final approval of the British Government of the partition plan, Mountbatten returned from England on June 2, 1947. The next day on June 3, he announced the scheme of India's division from All India Radio. His broadcast was followed by those of Nehru, Jinnah and Baldev Singh accepting the Partition Plan. Insisting the Congress for the last time not to accept the partition of India, Abul Kalam Azad observed: 'The verdict would then be that India was divided as much by the Muslim League as by the Congress'. The damage had been done. Relations of the communities had been poisoned. The cleavage had put at stake the most valuable asset of the country. It was the entity of India, the solidarity of the nation. Its value was of Himalayan proportion. But it was unfortunate that none of the parties thought of damage control and repair. They became too stiff to bend, even to the point of breaking down. Or, did they take it too lightly, not anticipating that the quarrel would actually result in the catastrophe of Partition, till they found themselves confronted with Mountbatten's plan ? Was nothing left for face saving? Was it for them a point of no return? Rigidity is the nemesis of politics. History is witness that acts of diplomacy, compromise and concession have saved countries from destruction. The Indians failed to save their country. One week before the actual date of Partition Gandhi observed: 'The rot began with the alien government. We, the inheritors, have not taken the trouble to rectify the errors of the past.'[13] Nehru's 'tryst with destiny' was, in fact, a tragedy of history. The Bill for Indian Independence, was introduced in the House of Commons on July 4, 1947, and was passed on July 15. The House of Lords passed it the next day, and on July 18, 1947, the Bill received the Royal assent by a Royal Commission sitting in the House of Lords.

Indian Independence Act, 1947 of July 18, 1947 stipulated:

Be it enacted by the King's Most Excellent Majesty, by and with the advice and consent of the Lords Spiritual and Temporal, and Commons, in this present Parliament assembled, and by the authority of the same, as follows:

1. The New Dominions

(1) As from the fifteenth day of August, nineteen hundred and forty-seven, two independent Dominions shall be set up in India, to be known respectively as India and Pakistan.

(2) The said Dominions are hereafter in this Act referred to as "the new Dominions", and the said fifteenth day of August is hereafter in this Act referred to as " the appointed day".

With this Act, the suzerainty of His Majesty over the Indian States and tribal areas also lapsed, and with it, all treaties and agreements in force between His Majesty and the rulers of Indian States and tribal authorities. Such Princely states, numbering about five hundred and sixty, had the option of joining either of the two dominions or to sustain their precarious independence without the buttress of British power.

When a question was put to Mountbatten on fixing the date of Independence his reply was:

"The date I chose came out of the blue. I chose it in reply to a question. I was determined to show I was master of the whole event. When they asked: had we set a date, I knew it had to be soon. I hadn't worked it out exactly then—I thought it had to be about August or September and I then went to the 15th of August. Why? Because it was the second anniversary of Japan's surrender.'[14]

The nonchalance of Mountbatten about fixing the date of such an important event appears somewhat out of place. It is specially so when this haste did not give his administration sufficient time for adequate preparation to avert or cope with the subsequent large scale massacre in Punjab, despite the repeated warnings given by the Governor. The deadline of June 1948 was about a year from the date when the partition plan was being formulated. It was advanced not by a month or two, but almost immediately, in August 1947. Why? Would the hands of the British Government have been too full in June 1948 which was reflected in the concern of foreign Secretary Ernest Bevin to get 'our lads' out of Palestine in order to facilitate the unilateral declaration of independence by Israel. in May 1948? Or was it that by June 1948 Jinnah would probably have died (actually in September 1948) of acute tuberculosis, without whom the idea of Pakistan would have fizzled out? ' If Nehru had realised how precarious the health of his arch adversary was, he might well have waited, instead of agreeing to Lord Mountbatten's proposed partition plan,[15] Or, it may be that the British Parliament really respected the sentiments of the Viceroy for the date of 15th August, and agreed to free India on that date!

1. *A Panoramic History of the Indian People*, D. B. Vohra
2. See Viscount Morley' speech at the second reading of the Indian Councils Bill in the House of Lords on February 23, 1909, in Ch. 41 'Divisive Electorate' above
3. India's Struggle for Freedom Vol. II ch. XVII by Jagdish Saran Sharma
4. India's Struggle for Freedom Vol. II ch. XVII by Jagdish Saran Sharma
5. Quoted in Partition of India, Legend and Reality, by H.M. Seervai, Ch. VI
6. Wolpert, *Jinnah Of Pakistan* (1984), pp. 282-283; *Transfer of Power*, V.P.Menon as Quoted in *Partition Of India, Legend And Reality*, Ch VI, H.M. Seervai;
7. *A New History of India* (Fifth Edition) Ch. Twenty-Two, Stanley Wolpert; H.M. Seervai , *Partition Of India, Legend And Reality*, Ch. VI
8. *Transfer of Power*, V. P. Menon, Quoted in Partition Of India, Legend And Reality, Ch VI, H.M. Seervai
9.Transfer of Power, V. P. Menon, Quoted in Partition Of India, Legend And Reality, by H.M. Seervai, V
10. William Francis Hare, Memoirs of the Earl of Listowel, Chapter 9
11. *The Great Divide*, Appendix I, H. V. Hodson
12. William Francis Hare, Memoirs of the Earl of Listowel, Chapter 9
13. *A New History of India* (Fifth Edition) Ch. Twenty-Two, Stanley Wolpert
14. Larry Collins & Dominique Lapierre, *Mountbatten and the Partition of India, March 22-August 15, 1947*, (Tarang paperbacks, 1985), p. 72, Quoted in *Partition of India: Legend and Reality*, Ch. VIII, H. M. Seervai
15. Stanley Wolpert, *Zulfi Bhutto of Pakistan*, ch. 2

47
OVERVIEW

The history of India has not told us stories only of tolerance, open hearts and cooperation. In accordance with human nature it has also brought forth accounts of competition, of discrimination, of bigotry and of exclusiveness. Such phenomena, of course, have provided some dark spots, though not much prominent. Anyway, they did impart a color of their own among the many on the bigger canvas. At the highest level, efforts have been made by rulers to maintain balance between the communities, and barring a few cases the tradition of harmony has, in fact, prevailed. Setting aside the episodes of struggle for political power and even the ensuing brutalities at high level, strife and agitation at ground level have been generally absent. Good features of life like love, sympathy, understanding, support, and sharing appear to have been all-pervading, brightening the bigger canvas.

Undoubtedly, the syncretic nature of Hinduism has made it one of the most tolerant of religions. It advocates that there are many paths to reach the Ultimate Reality, God, and every body is free to pursue his own. It is, therefore, for this reason that after the Aryans completely settled down in India, there was a spectacle of interesting developments on almost all major planes of life: society, politics, religion, foreign invasion, etc., beginning from the middle of the first millennium B.C. It was the time of springing up of kingdoms and republics; political unification of the country; philosophical speculations; evolution of the Vedic religion into present day Hinduism; birth of two great religions, Buddhism and Jainism; elimination of Aryan and non-Aryan distinctions, kings and rulers patronizing and even accepting religions other than their own; peaceful co-existence of followers of different faiths and racial origins; and foreign hordes marching into the land from time to time and being totally assimilated in the Brahmanical social and religious set up .

Scanning the history of this period, however, one encounters a very intriguing situation starting at the very outset of history. It is understandable that in the primitive ages, the conquering nation of the Aryans, being too proud of their physical features and fair colour of the skin, treated the vanquished indigenous people with utter contempt. But the whole process of this treatment seems paradoxical in two ways. First, it has been done by a religion and a society which has been pluralistic, liberal, and absorptive in nature. Secondly, despite the liberal nature of Hindu religion, the institution of apartheid and the ghettoization of society, which were built in the beginning with some purpose, were never dismantled so much so that the caste system continues to be one of the chief distinguishing features of the Hindu society even to this day. The broad distinction between conquerors and conquered is no doubt natural and universal. With the change of time such man-made social barriers have been either weakened or done away with in other societies, but they have remained firmly ingrained in India, which means that human institutions have received the sanction of a religion which has been concerned more with the preservation of social order than with the advancement of mankind.[1]

An orthodox follower of this religion holds that caste system is of divine appointment and that it has existed for all time. But this religious sanction which was meant for a strict maintenance of the four divisions of caste may be dating back not to the Rig Vedic period but to a later time when mixed marriages among the Aryans and non-Aryans had gone so far as to threaten the whole system. The invocation laying one important task upon the mighty Indra: 'O Indra, find out who is an Aryan, and who is a Dasa, and separate them!' is indicative of a desperation.

Hindu religion maintains that all living beings have immortal soul. The quality of actions (*karma*) of a person during his life time determines the status in which he would be born in his next life with this eternal soul. Thus it has to pass through a succession of lives and deaths, until it achieves liberation (*muksha*). The underlined fatalism that one's own karma of the previous life is responsible for his present state or caste into which he is born forces him to accept unquestionably his status in the society. This religious sanction was so sacred that even with later political developments no government could dare or consider it desirable to enforce equality among citizens. On the contrary, it subordinated policies to the exigencies of society.

Hinduism is not a revealed religion. It has no set doctrines, and is such a composite of varied beliefs that it belies easy definition.

It has no church or hierarchy of priests, nor congregational set up of any sort. Two factors have been detrimental in effecting reforms from within. First, the lack of an authoritative body which could assess the needs of the society from time to time and make pronouncements. For instance, a measure of reform like abolition of *sati* (widow burning on the funeral pyre of dead husband) could only come from outside and not from within the Hindu society. Second, the basic character of Hinduism, which is 'all things to all people all the time', gives freedom to every individual to establish a personal relationship with God and even seek salvation by discarding the tenets of society. The caste system is not a small component of the faith; rather it encompasses the entire structure of Hinduism within its fold. Necessarily, very gigantic and revolutionary steps were needed if reforms were to be made. Also, the measures to reform this institution might not be thought out in short run; they had to be evolved and the society to be conditioned for it over a long period of time. Unfortunately, initiative did not come forth as it suited those who alone could bring change, the higher castes. The inequality of the caste system was thus perpetuated.

The next phase of India's life when Muslim conquerors settled down in this country and became native rulers for another thousand years gave a new cultural tinge to the Indian society. There is a famous axiom: Hinduism has a wonderful power of assimilation; it has always conquered its conquerors. When the Aryans, Greeks, Kushans, Huns and other invaders came here they were absorbed and assimilated fully in the local culture and were completely Hinduized. But this maxim is also partially untrue. Hinduism has conquered only those communities which did not have their own strong religious codes or beliefs. It was unable to bring in its fold even those small communities of early Jews, Christians and Zoroastrians that had settled here two thousand years ago, or even earlier. Similarly it was the case with the Muslims. They found no ground to merge in Hinduism. The ways of life and whole philosophy of the two communities differed too radically with each other. For instance, idolatry and caste were anathema to the unequivocally monotheist Muslims, and so were such doctrines as *karma* or the law of consequences and reincarnation, fundamental to Hindu thought.

Muslim rule in India is also not devoid of instances of intolerance. Undoubtedly, in the haughtiness of victory and overwhelming power, some Muslim rulers and their marching armies have acted in contravention to such Qur'anic commandments as *Let there be no coercion in religion* (Surah 2:256) and Say! *O Unbelievers!...To you be your religion and to me mine* (Surah 109:1,6). They resorted sometimes to iconoclasm and proselytizing. But such measures do not seem to have been carried out as a matter of state policy. No records testify to it, except some boasts of over-zealous court chroniclers. The over-all picture, therefore, this episode of history presents is again that India did not digress from its tradition of tolerance. Here we should not, however, be concerned with the behaviors of raiders like Mahmud Ghaznavi, Taimur and Nadir Shah. They entered India, sacked cities, looted wealth, slaughtered local population indiscriminately, and went away. The real issue to be considered is whether the ruling kings or the people, who were part of this society, were intolerant to their subjects or to their fellow citizens.

In *Mankind And Mother Earth*, Arnold Toyanbee writes:

> ' The Arab conquests were also facilitated by the directive, in the Koran, that 'People of the Book' were to be tolerated and protected if they submitted to the Islamic Government and agreed to pay a surtax. The benefit of this directive was extended from Jews and Christians to Zoroastrians, and eventually to Hindus as well....In Arabia, Islam was obligatory, but in the subject territories conversion, so far from being imposed, was positively discouraged.'[2]

Similarly, Jizya in India was neither constantly nor universally applied. But whenever it was levied, this tax was intensely hated for it smacked of discrimination between the Muslims and non-Muslims.

The Muslim population which we find in the sub-continent today is, to begin with, the result of immigration in early Muslim period into India from places like, Afghanistan, Persia, or Central Asia, being attracted by opportunities of service. The second factor was the *sufi* cult which had a great impact on local population. Their noble character, simple life and preaching inspired the people. Perhaps the most significant factor was the discrimination of the Hinduism itself against its own lower castes which induced them to voluntarily accept other religions (Buddhism, Jainism, Islam, Sikhism, Christianity, etc.) so that they could elevate their social status to the level of caste Hindus. The twice-born dvijas had not realized that that this blatant discrimination would, in due course, have the paradoxical effect of assisting in the supercession of the Vedic faith by less exclusive religions. The fact that the Muslims have always been a minority community in India would suggest that the vast majority of Hindus were not in so desperate a plight as to seek conversion.[3] Further, any pressure, specially in proselytizing, would have generated bitter animosity between the Muslims and the Hindus and massive riots and revolts. History has not recorded such riots.

The next phase of history relates to the period when the Europeans came to this land as colonizers in the guise of merchants. One of them, the British rulers, undoubtedly gave the country a good governance, much better than other colonial masters elsewhere on the globe. When the British left in 1947, India, though was not an industrialized country, had its rural economy amply strengthened by its own machine industries. If not well fed and clothed, an average Indian had more amenities in the shape of general security, transport, public health, and freedom from total famine. But two other features of their rule are very prominent. First, the western conquerors, notably the Portuguese, considered their rule as divinely ordained with a view to show to the heathens the godly path. Fortunately, the British did not take this as a matter of state policy. The task was assigned to private missionaries, who very wisely realized that the most effective medium to preach gospel to an impoverished people was the provision of food and clothing to them! Second, being free from this task, the British rulers concentrated on the more important affairs of state. It is in this sphere that we experience a unique type of intolerance. It was not their own intolerance; rather it was a calculated act of breeding of intolerance within the indigenous society with the political objective of ruling by division. The result was the appearance of a wedge causing a grave fissure in the harmonious Indian society. Differences and divisiveness, based mainly on religion, were flared up among the people, which bred so much intolerance that one major Indian community started to consider itself a nation by itself, separate from the other. This group was of the Muslims, who were encouraged to ask for the division of the country and to have a separate corner of their own.

In this regard it would not be out of place to quote William Jaferson Clinton, President of the United States, who stated in a conference of Federalism held in Canada in October 1999: "It seems to me that the suggestion that a people or tribal group or religious group can only have a meaningful political existence if they are an independent nation...is a questionable assertion in a global economy where cooperation pays greater benefits in every area of life than destructive competition." He further said: "our major threat is the most primitive human feeling—the fear of 'the other', and the sense that we can only breathe and function and matter if we are somehow free of the necessity to associate and deal with, and may be even under certain circumstances, subordinate our own opinions to, the feelings of 'them' "

He asked several pertinent questions as to why people support separation:

Is there an abuse of human rights?
Is there a way that people can get along if they come from different heritages?
Are minority rights as well as majority rights respected?
What is in the long term economic and security interests of the people?
How are they going to cooperate with their neighbours?
Will it be better or worse if the people are independent or when they have a federalist system?[4]

The demand of the Indian Muslims for a separate state appeared absolutely without the seriousness of purpose or a sense of direction. It was rooted in a perception clouded with fear and negativism, with a preconceived notion not to share their lives with the 'other'. Anyway, Pakistan was created and a sizeable population of the Muslims remained in India. But, even with their continued presence the Muslims have given India a good thing: they did not deprive India of its distinctive flavor of communities; the clan continues.

The great country, India, was thus torn apart because the people were made to grow intolerant of each other. The antagonism which filled the hearts of the people is still so fierce that the two divided nations, their saner elements excepting, have come to conceive that they are really two peoples. There is no myth greater than the concept of 'two nations' of Hindus and Muslims on the basis of religious beliefs. Religion alone does not make a nation. Throughout the times it has not happened so. In the present day reality too, the followers of a single religion living in different countries do not constitute one nation, nor the followers of many faiths living in one country make many nations. A nation is made of many components beside religion, such as values, culture, customs, traditions, language, geography, degree of social assimilation, and simply living together for a very long period, which in case of Indian Hindus and Muslims involves about half of the country's historical period. Together they have made a significant and positive history.

The most unfortunate part of the two-nation theory has been that the exogenous sense of differences has been misleading many people even today to believe that over many centuries the Hindus and Muslims lived only as two separate communities. For instance, even a scholar like R.C. Majumdar writes in the *History And Culture of the Indian People*, Vol. V, Ch. XVI :

"For the first time in the history of India, the country was permanently divided, from a religious and social point of view, into two distinct entities, the gulf between which even seven centuries of *peaceful existence side by side* has not been able to bridge. (Emphasis added). This religious and social aloofness places the Muslim invasions of India on an entirely different footing from similar invasion elsewhere. Analogy has been drawn, for example, between Saxon and Norman invasions of England and the Turkish invasion of India in order to prove that since the invaders became the children of the soil, they can hardly be regarded as foreigners, and the 'foreign conquest' of India is misnomer so far as the pre-British period is concerned. This analogy is however fallacious. For while within a century or two of the conquest of England by William, the Duke of Normandy, nobody could possibly distinguish the Saxon, Norman or other elements of which the English people were composed, it does not require a moment's thought today to draw a clear line between the Hindu and Muslim population, even though more than seven hundred years (in the case of Sindh, twelve hundred years) have elapsed since the Muslims first settled in the country. Nor can we reasonably visualise a period when this difference will cease to exist."

In Chapter XVII he writes: "The advent of Islam constituted the first great rift in the solidarity of the Indian community since the incorporation of the aboriginal peoples into the Aryan society. Henceforth there were two communities in India-Hindus and Muslims-who formed two entirely separate entities, so far at least as religious and social ideas and political and civil rights were concerned."

Not commenting on the above, but writing about a period as early as the Sultanate, Romila Thapar, another eminent historian, states:

"In the last fifty years many attempts have been made to prove that the Hindu and Islamic cultures at no time approached any kind of fusion, and that over the many centuries when they lived side by side Hindus and Muslims existed as two separate communities. This is a clear example of a case of historical 'back projection', where sanction is sought from the past to justify contemporary attitudes. The concept that there was a separate community or 'nationality' of Hindus and Muslim did not exist during this [Sultanate] period. Had the Turks and Afghans preserved their foreign identity and had they, as foreigners, constituted the majority of Muslims, the persistence of such a separate nationality might have been possible: but in fact the vast majority of Muslims were Hindu converts.

"The argument for the reality of a separate nationality is drawn from the writings of the theologians and court chroniclers, who consciously emphasized the distinctions between Hindus and Muslims because it was in their interests to do so. Sources such as these cannot be accepted uncritically, since their own prejudices are writ large in their attitudes. The fusion of cultures in any case cannot be judged by the writings of a prejudiced minority determined to hold aloof: it can only be judged by the cultural pattern of the society as a whole. From the pattern of society in the Sultanate period it is evident that a synthesis of the two cultures took place, although this synthesis did not occur at every level and with the same intensity. Furthermore, the pattern which emerged was to mature in the period subsequent to that of the Sultanate..."[5]

It is true that the Muslims, though were largely converts from the Hinduism, felt more closeness to their Arab and Persian co-religionists in their spiritual and philosophical make-up, but they never felt a physical bondage with them. The soil where they were born and the people with whom they had been living created more magnetism in their social life. The local society was the one they claimed as their own and always felt themselves strangers to that society with which they never had come into contact. "India beyond all doubt possesses a deep underlying fundamental unity, far more profound than that produced either by geographical isolation or by political suzerainty. That unity transcends the innumerable diversities of blood, colour, language, dress, manners and sect."[6]

It is in the nature of things that no two units are exactly the same. So is the case with human beings. Even two members of the same family find differences in the ways of their lives, make-up of their minds and feelings of their hearts. Differences persist even between two real brothers and a happily married couple. It is not humanly possible for any two units of life having their own separate natures, habits, sensitivities and susceptibilities to be merged completely into one another. But they continue living their lives together harmoniously. So was the case with the Hindus and the Muslims. Lytton, Bengal's governor in the 1920s, had noticed how well the rank and file of the communities got on with each other in all the daily business of life.[7] The interaction of the ways of life of the two major communities, Hindus and Muslims, was so strong that sometimes they seemed to be merging with each other even in matters of religion, which was the single most powerful factor in creating distinction between them. Both communities participated and mingled with each other in the cultural fairs and religious festivals like Dipavali, Holi, Ram Lila, Basant, Eid, Muharram, and Urs of Muslim saints. Bindi make-up was not restricted to the foreheads of Hindu women, as the veil of Muslim women covered also the former. Muslims have been found in remote countryside sometimes revering Hindu deities, for instance, the smallpox goddess Sitla, speaking 'Ram Ram' as salutation, and wearing a purely Hindu dress *dhoti*. For Muslim women, sari became their staple dress in many of the provinces of India. As Hindu's worshipped idols, an ordinary Muslim's veneration of pious men verged on worshipping their graves. Hindus too started venerating Muslim saints and offered *chadder* and sweets on occasion of their death anniversary. Like the Hindu community's practice of taking out their idols in procession in the streets with music and festivities, Muslims began the practice of holding festivals (*Urs*) on occasion of death anniversary of pious men, and taking out *tazia* processions on occasion of *Muharram*, in which, strangely, sometimes both communities participated. Caste system, which is not sanctioned in Islam, was adopted by the Muslims of India. Today the Muslims of the subcontinent belong to various castes, higher or lower, by descent or by profession. A Muslim started craving for the birth of a male child, as their Hindu brethren did although because of a different reason: it was deemed holy by the latter to have the funeral pyre lit by a male progeny. Another glaring instance of mutual adoption of cultural values related to the widows. According to old Hindu tradition, a widow is supposed to burn herself on the funeral pyre of her husband, and if remained alive she was not to re-marry. In Islam a widow's re-marriage is permitted, rather encouraged. Indian Muslims started to take the re-marriage of a widow as an unpleasant and sometime dishonorable act, although they did not totally forsake it. Hindus, on the other hand, started to look towards a widow's re-marriage not as a taboo.

The relations between the Hindus and Muslim fell in the same category as the relations between Hindus belonging to different castes: they also did not socialize with each other but were interacting with each other in all matters of life. The majority of the population in the undivided India were Hindus, but if some one wanted to find the Hindu community divided into many he could easily find so. The Hindus were fragmented not only by spoken and written languages but also by basic religious beliefs and hundreds of religious cults and mutually exclusive castes. It was not surprising to find that the Hindus themselves were not one nation. It was a similar situation with the Muslims: a Muslim of Bengal or Madras was not as much socially akin to a Muslim of the North West Frontier Province as he was to a Hindu of his own locality. It is, therefore, clear that the differences between the Hindus and the Muslims were exploited to tear the society apart, and similarities were suppressed to achieve a particular objective. If not so, why the myth of two-nation exploded as soon as Pakistan was created? First, almost the total Muslim population, and a very sizeable population for that, inhabiting within the boundaries of the new India did not belong to its so-claimed new nation-state but continued living in India with the separate nation of Hindus. Second, just after twenty-five years of its existence the new nation could not hold on to its identity on the basis of religion and split itself into two, a new country calling itself Bangladesh and another new country retaining the old name of Pakistan. The Pakistan of 1947 was no more!

1. E.J. Rapson, *The New Cambridge History of India*, Vol. I, Chapter II.
2. Arnold Toyanbee, *Mankind and Mother Earth*, Ch. 50
3. Romila Thapar, *A History of India,* Vol. One:
4. Clinton, William Jaferson , news item in *Toronto Star*, October, 1999
5. Romila Thapar, A History of India, Vol. One, Ch 13
6. *The Oxford History of India*, Introduction, Fourth Edition, Vincent A. Smith, edited by Percival Spear
7. *Echoes of British India*, Ameer Ali, See *Legacy of a Divided Nation* by Mushirul Hasan

48
EPILOGUE

Since the dawn of history in India in the middle of the first millennium before Christ, the country did not experience intolerance and turmoil on political, social and religious planes on an extensive scale. However, starting from the nineteenth century the curse of communal tension between the two largest communities of Hindus and Muslims erupted over the length and breadth of the country with such force and fanfare that it climaxed in the twentieth century in the break-up of the country itself. But what a beautiful picture even then it had presented! During the periods of high tension an atmosphere of love-hate relationship prevailed and the two communities lived their times together in cities and in villages, on streets and in market places, peacefully sharing each other's sorrows and joys, values and sensitivities, festivities and celebrations. Occasional killings were, of course, there but the name of the game was politics. And that too occurred in pockets and neither frequently nor for long periods of time. After the mayhem the atmosphere was calm, the two communities continued in the struggle for life together. Only a fear persisted: it might happen again any moment.

Before leaving India for Pakistan to assume the Governor-Generalship of the new country, Jinnah was asked by Indian Muslims what he would advise them to do then. Discarding that forceful ideology of 'two-nation' which had created a new country for them he told those Muslims to be loyal citizens of India. On the other hand, in his address to the first Constituent Assembly of Pakistan on August 11, 1947 Muhammad Ali Jinnah prescribed how the two nations of Hindus and Muslims would become 'one-nation' very easily inside Pakistan, a situation that had not be attained, according to him, despite their living together in India for a thousand years:

"Now, if we want to make this great State of Pakistan happy and prosperous we should wholly and solely concentrate on the well-being of the people, and specially of the masses and the poor. If you will work in co-operation, forgetting the past, burying the hatchet, you are bound to succeed. If you change your past and work together in a spirit of that every one of you, no matter to what community he belongs, no matter what relations he had with you in the past, no matter what is his colour, caste or creed, is first, second and last a citizen of this state with equal rights, privileges and obligations, there will be no end to the progress you will make.

"I cannot emphasize it too much. We should begin to work in that spirit and in course of time all these angularities of the majority and minority communities, the Hindu community and the Muslim community, because even as regards Muslims you have Pathans, Punjabis, Shias, Sunnis and so on and among the Hindus you have Brahmins, Vashnavas, Khatris, also Bengalis, Madrasis and so on, will vanish. *Indeed if you ask me this has been the biggest hindrance in the way of India to attain its freedom and independence and but for this we would have been free peoples long long ago.* No power can hold another nation, and specially a nation of 400 million souls in subjection; nobody could have continued its hold on you for any length of time but for this.

"Therefore, we must learn a lesson from this. You are free; you are free to go to your temples. You are free to go to your mosques or to any other places of worship in this State of Pakistan. *You may belong to any religion or caste or creed that has nothing to do with the business of the state.*

"As you know, history shows that in England conditions some time ago were much worse than those prevailing in India today. The Roman Catholics and the Protestants persecuted each other. Even now there are some States in existence where there are discriminations made, and bars imposed, against a particular class. Thank God we are not starting in those days. We are starting in the days when there is no discrimination, no distinction between one community and another, no discrimination between one caste or creed and another. We are starting with this fundamental principle that we are all citizens and equal citizens of one State. The people of England, in course of time, had to face the realities of the situation and had to discharge the responsibilities and burdens placed upon them by the Government of their country and they went through that fire, step by step. Today you might say with justice that Roman Catholics and Protestants do not exist: What exists now is that every man is a citizen of Great Britain and they are all members of the nation.

"Now, I think we should keep that in front of us as our ideal and you will find that *in course of time Hindus would cease to be Hindus and Muslims would cease to be Muslims*, not in religious sense, because that is the personal faith of each individual, but in the political sense as citizens of the State."[1]

In his early political life Jinnah had protested strongly on the introduction of religion in politics. Later, he became a strong votary of religion for achieving political ends and for creation of a separate nationhood for the Muslims on that basis. In Pakistan, he once again discarded religion as 'the business of the state'. He admitted that the existence of various communities in India and their differences provided as an effective leverage to the alien rulers to deprive India of its freedom. A fighter for the Indian nationhood, he turned into an advocate of two-nation theory in the later years not perceiving that the differences amongst the people and their divisiveness was created deliberately by others to deprive India of its freedom for as long as possible. Wary of this danger, therefore, he prescribed for both Hindus and Muslims living in the new country to cease to be what they were religiously, and to become only Pakistanis.

Why then this catastrophe, as it happened? Francis Watson argues thus in *India: A Concise History*, "The theory that Indian divisiveness in general, and the Muslim problem in particular, were creations of the ruling power of its own perpetuation, was understandable in the circumstances. But the Congress's consequent failure to take the Muslim question seriously while conciliation was still feasible approached a fateful point with the return as president of the Muslim League of the gifted Bombay lawyer M. A. Jinnah, who had been hailed as 'ambassador of Hindu-Muslim unity', before he withdrew in disillusion from the politics of the 1920s."[2] In the atmosphere of an all-pervading religious differences, which had amply been exploited, a new psyche both of Hindus and Muslims had emerged. This factor had a deep impact on the whole process. During the struggle for freedom, the attitude of Hindus, even of as liberal and enlightened a person as Jawaharlal Nehru, seemed to be under exhilaration of conquerors who had before them the sight of wresting their land after centuries of subjugation, and now it was their turn to have full freedom of action as the new rulers. For the Muslims the intoxication of being the ex-rulers had not dissipated. They believed: 'If we do not get India back, nobody gets it.'

Muslim League seemed to have little patience to realize that the democratic traditions of the time would not let a very big community like the Muslims to be mistreated by another major community. Scared, rightly or imagined, of the impending religio-majority rule, the ambassador of unity thus had to turn into an architect of division. So the big question remains to be answered by the Indian nation: should the solution for this induced perception of 'two-nation' have been so drastic as for one party to demand for, and for the other party to consent to, the partition of the country itself, while the two-nation syndrome was to continue to plague both the countries?

The demand for the division of the country appears to be a strange sort of demand, unique in the annals of political struggle. First, it was a demand not solely by the inhabitants of a specific area to grant them a separate homeland, rather more by a very sizeable portion, more than one third of the Muslim population, who never intended to live in the new country. Second, the history has shown that break-up of a country is an extreme measure and the people who wanted it, and those who did not, both had to plunge into blood-baths before achieving their respective objectives. In this case all the concerned parties agreed to the division of the country without going through the necessary trauma.[3] Third, a demand for separation is made when the minority community is oppressed by the majority. In this case, the majority had no yet been in power and they never had the occasion to brutalize the minority. Fourth, in 1947, the power structure of the country was like this: Muslim population of India was less than 25 per cent, hence numerically very weak; Hindus constituted about 70 percent, hence numerically very strong; the British owned 100 per cent of armed and administrative power, hence the owner of absolute authority. Surprisingly, the smallest 'pistol' had won the war despite the common belief that the real powers of India, the Hindus and the British, were against partition.

Had the ensuing events brought peace and prosperity, the break-up of the country was to be considered a worthwhile occurrence. But the case was just the opposite. In the wake of Partition, there was a carnage of unimaginable proportion, specially in Punjab. Then happened a massive two-way migration of refugees, estimated at ten million; one million of them never made it and were massacred on the way to their new places of refuge. 'The stream became a flood, the flood a holocaust of pain, looting, rape and murder.' But it did not stop there. Periodic communal riots continue to this day. In the post-partition India and Pakistan the hatred of communities has turned inward. It has almost consumed both of them by wars, political bickering, massive defence spending, neglect of the economy, occasional engagement in communal and religious riots, sacrilege of mosques, temples and churches, and erecting walls of caste, creed, race and ethnicity around them. Encouraged by the Partition, every disgruntled community or sectarian group in the two countries is now ever ready to foster the politics of separate nationalism and to break up from the main body.

The partition of the country did not impart any additional gain to any party. On the balance it was a net loss to all. A united country would have been much better off than what the two are today, like a power to be reckoned with at international level and a model of economic prosperity internally. Many Asian tigers of today were just economic pygmies in 1947 as compared to India but now the roles have been reversed. Who would have kept the country from gaining a permanent seat in the United Nations Security Council? Who would have held Hindustani from being accepted as one of the United Nations' official languages like Spanish, Arabic and Chinese? Who would have denied Indian Muslims the position of the largest Muslim bloc and their voices to be heard by the world? Who would have stopped those Muslims, who wanted a country to have power or recognition, from playing the role of king-makers in the future democratic elections of a united India? Who would have destroyed their cultural hallmark, the Urdu language, for which the Muslims were crying earlier?

The Mughals regarded India as one and indivisible. Their concept of empire was an all India one. Therefore, they did not consider their extension of power to the geographical limits of India and annexation of Rajput, Maratha and Muslim kingdoms as an act of aggression but an expression of the country's indivisibility. They deemed such regional independence only as an infraction and a temporary state of affairs, hence the corrective action taken by them as an expression of natural law.[4] Theirs' was the 'concept of an India potentially greater than the sum of its parts'. How ironical it appears that the children and grand-children of the same Mughals were seen appealing to the alien rulers in the twentieth century to render this country in parts!

When viewed in totality, the fact would emerge that the Muslim population of India was not in such a desperate situation as to actually want to break up the country. Still, it is also true that the overwhelming majority of them were raising loud slogans to achieve Pakistan.Religion was definitely not the cause of desperation as they did not apprehend any restriction or, in that respect, coercion. They did not voice their concern to this effect. They wanted economic and political power, more as a balancing act in a united India. It was obviously the main plank of the fight by them. Muslim League always talked of separate electorates, parity, privileges, quotas and seats (in the interest of the elite class), seemingly unfair in view of a very unequal proportion of the two communities of Hindus and Muslims. Not only that such a demand was against the democratic spirit of the twentieth century, but also that the Muslim League never expressed concern at social, educational and economic backwardness of Muslims and solution of their day to day problems like land revenue, debt, water rates or employment. In short, it was the bogey of more than due share in politics and economics. If they really wanted power and economic opportunities through a new country, they must have realized that these were, anyhow, to come their way more in a democratic India: in the Muslim majority provinces (forming Pakistan) as well as through the federal government. Also, such a serious demand for partitioning the country and getting a *'homeland for the Muslims of India'* was devoid of any solid plan for the Muslims of the minority provinces. They had simply to be left in the lurch. Thus, the theory that the Muslim League and Jinnah, the undisputed leader of the Muslims, seriously wanted Pakistan seems to contain not much substance. Despite the Pakistan Resolution of 1940, Muslim League's negotiations for securing more privileges during this period, their acceptance of the Cabinet Mission Plan in as late as June 1946 and their subsequent joining of the Interim Government in September 1946 clearly demonstrate that they had no conviction for Pakistan, and wished India to remain united. Perhaps it materialized only when they did not expect it to actually happen. The struggle for Independence of India or, in other words, Pakistan Movement appears to be simply a political game so arranged that in which the Hindus and Muslims were made to contest, and contest ferociously, with each other. In the end both had to be losers.

1. Quoted in *The Indus Saga and the Making of Pakistan*, Aitzaz Ahsan
2. Francis Watson , *India: A Concise History*, Ch. Eight
3. Before partition the animosity between Hindus and Muslims had resulted, of course, in some communal riots and killings in Northern India but they were not aimed directly to achieve Pakistan; they happened because the social and religious feelings had been so poisoned that the two communities had sometime to lose tolerance for each other. After the Hindu-Muslim riots of Noakhali and Bihar, some Muslim young men of Noakhali put a question to Gandhi as to what was his objection to the setting up of a seperate Muslim State "after the events in Bihar". He replied that he had no objection to the setting up of such a state (See *India's struggle for Freedom*) Vol.II, Ch. XVII, by Jagdish Sharma
4. *A History of India*, Vol. Two, Percival Spear

INDEX